'Through a remarkable blend of psychoanalytic insight and phenomenological observation, Eitan-Persico offers a nuanced portrait of queer kinship that is neither utopian nor dystopian. As a result, we are given the opportunity to appreciate both the vulnerability and vigor that compose queer families, along with the innovation they bring to our shopworn ideas about kinship.'

Ken Corbett, *Clinical Assistant Professor at the NYU Postdoctoral Program in Psychotherapy and Psychoanalysis; author of* Boyhoods: Rethinking Masculinities, *and* A Murder Over a Girl: Justice, Gender, Junior High

'*Oedipal Experiences in Same-Sex Families* is a brilliant book that presents an original and innovative psychoanalytic perspective on same-sex families. Eitan-Persico offers outstanding insights on both children and parents' internal worlds, challenges heteronormative notions of genetics and kinship, birth and procreation. Her research integrates psychoanalytic thinking with LGBTQ family research and presents rigorous rethinking of the Oedipal model in light of contemporary social changes. This is an important and fascinating book.'

Galit Atlas, PhD, *faculty member at NYU Postdoctoral Program in Psychotherapy & Psychoanalysis; author of* Emotional Inheritance: A Therapist, Her Patients and the Legacy of Trauma

'An innovative and profound book, resting on incisive thinking, comprehensive knowledge and sophisticated critical analysis. In addition to its important contribution for the crucial updating of theory, the book deepens our clinical sensitivity and understanding of same-sex families, and illuminates the changing reality of child-rearing in the 21st century.'

Emanuel Berman, *Haifa University and the Israel Psychoanalytic Society; Recipient of the Sigourney Award, 2011*

Oedipal Experiences in Same-Sex Families

This book updates the Oedipus complex for a contemporary audience in the light of social and cultural changes and explores its implications for psychoanalytic treatment and our understanding of queer families.

Growing evidence over the past few decades indicates that children who grow up in same-sex families adapt well. These findings, which do not conform to the predictions of Oedipal theory, expose the theory's biases, and call for reexamination of its premises. This book is based on ground-breaking research and pursues a methodical investigation of the characteristics of same-sex families that defy the expectations of Oedipal theory. Furnished with vivid illustrations, it invites the reader to engage actively in the interpretive effort and presents a diverse and complex story about kinship, opening a window onto a rich world of infantile phantasies and parents' psychological conflicts, at the fascinating intersection of the personal and the social.

Oedipal Experiences in Same-Sex Families will appeal to psychoanalysts, psychotherapists, educators and policymakers, same-sex parents, and parents who were assisted by gamete donation.

Dr. Yifat Eitan-Persico is a practicing clinical psychologist and a candidate in the Israel Psychoanalytic Society. She is a translator and editor of psychoanalytic writings, and a lecturer in post-graduate psychoanalytic programs. The Hebrew edition of this book was awarded the prestigious Bahat Prize for the best academic book, 2021.

Relational Perspectives Book Series
ADRIENNE HARRIS & EYAL ROZMARIN Series Editors
STEPHEN MITCHELL Founding Editor
LEWIS ARON Editor Emeritus

The Relational Perspectives Book Series (RPBS) publishes books that grow out of or contribute to the relational tradition in contemporary psychoanalysis. The term *relational psychoanalysis* was first used by Greenberg and Mitchell[1] to bridge the traditions of interpersonal relations, as developed within interpersonal psychoanalysis and object relations, as developed within contemporary British theory. But, under the seminal work of the late Stephen A. Mitchell, the term *relational psychoanalysis* grew and began to accrue to itself many other influences and developments. Various tributaries – interpersonal psychoanalysis, object relations theory, self psychology, empirical infancy research, feminism, queer theory, socio-cultural studies, and elements of contemporary Freudian and Kleinian thought – flow into this tradition, which understands relational configurations between self and others, both real and fantasied, as the primary subject of psychoanalytic investigation.

We refer to the relational tradition, rather than to a relational school, to highlight that we are identifying a trend, a tendency within contemporary psychoanalysis, not a more formally organized or coherent school or system of beliefs. Our use of the term *relational* signifies a dimension of theory and practice that has become salient across the wide spectrum of contemporary psychoanalysis. Now under the editorial supervision of Adrienne Harris and Eyal Rozmarin, the Relational Perspectives Book Series originated in 1990 under the editorial eye of the late Stephen A. Mitchell. Mitchell was the most prolific and influential of the originators of the relational

---

1 Greenberg, J., & Mitchell, S. (1983). *Object relations in psychoanalytic theory*. Cambridge, MA: Harvard University Press.

tradition. Committed to dialogue among psychoanalysts, he abhorred the authoritarianism that dictated adherence to a rigid set of beliefs or technical restrictions. He championed open discussion, comparative and integrative approaches, and promoted new voices across the generations. Mitchell was later joined by the late Lewis Aron, also a visionary and influential writer, teacher, and leading thinker in relational psychoanalysis.

Included in the Relational Perspectives Book Series are authors and works that come from within the relational tradition, those that extend and develop that tradition, and works that critique relational approaches or compare and contrast them with alternative points of view. The series includes our most distinguished senior psychoanalysts, along with younger contributors who bring fresh vision. Our aim is to enable a deepening of relational thinking while reaching across disciplinary and social boundaries in order to foster an inclusive and international literature.

A full list of titles in this series is available at www.routledge.com/Relational-Perspectives-Book-Series/book-series/LEARPBS.

Oedipal Experiences in Same-Sex Families

Yifat Eitan-Persico

LONDON AND NEW YORK

Designed cover image: © Getty Images

First English edition published 2024
by Routledge
4 Park Square, Milton Park, Abingdon, Oxon OX14 4RN

and by Routledge
605 Third Avenue, New York, NY 10158

Routledge is an imprint of the Taylor & Francis Group, an informa business

© 2024 Yifat Eitan-Persico

The right of Yifat Eitan-Persico to be identified as author of this work has been asserted in accordance with sections 77 and 78 of the Copyright, Designs and Patents Act 1988.

All rights reserved. No part of this book may be reprinted or reproduced or utilised in any form or by any electronic, mechanical, or other means, now known or hereafter invented, including photocopying and recording, or in any information storage or retrieval system, without permission in writing from the publishers.

Trademark notice: Product or corporate names may be trademarks or registered trademarks, and are used only for identification and explanation without intent to infringe.

First Hebrew edition published by the University of Haifa Press and Pardes Publishing, 2023

British Library Cataloguing-in-Publication Data
A catalogue record for this book is available from the British Library

ISBN: 978-1-032-66331-9 (hbk)
ISBN: 978-1-032-66329-6 (pbk)
ISBN: 978-1-032-66333-3 (ebk)

DOI: 10.4324/9781032663333

Typeset in Times New Roman
by Apex CoVantage, LLC

Dedicated to the anonymous "birth others" and the wonderful families they created, and to my sisters, who taught me the power of triangulation.

Contents

Acknowledgments		*xiii*
Foreword		*xv*
Introduction. A bridge between two islands: psychoanalytic thinking and the research field		1

PART I
What does Oedipal development have to do with the parents' sex, anyway? — 37

One	"I want to marry you, Mommy": on Oedipal configurations in same-sex families	39
Two	Oedipal configurations: mutual illumination of theory and research findings	75

PART II
What does genetics have to do with kinship, anyway? — 105

Three	On biological affiliation and kinship	107
Four	A new hierarchy: asymmetry between the birth mother and social mother in lesbian couples	118
Five	Back to the closet: the issue of the child's genetic origin among gay fathers	145
Six	The dual role of the extended family	159
Seven	The power of interpellation: kinship conceptualization among same-sex parents and their children	166

xii Contents

PART III
What does procreation have to do with parental coitus, anyway? 179

Eight   Between longing and dread: representations of gamete
         donors and surrogates in the children's inner-worlds   181

Nine   Gamete donation in light of the primal scene: the
         parental challenge of integrating the donor's imago   226

PART IV
Afterword 259

Ten   Oedipus for everyone? Biases in the Oedipal model:
         their roots and how to overcome them   261

Eleven   How to work with same-sex families   266

         Coda. *The Kids Are All Right*: a psychoanalytic reading
         in Lisa Cholodenko's film   275

         Appendix A   286
         Appendix B   287
         Index   289

Acknowledgments

The English translation of this book was made possible thanks to the generous support of the Bahat Prize. I wish to extend my sincere thanks to the members of the award committee and to the Bahat family for selecting my manuscript as the recipient of the Bahat Prize for the best original work of nonfiction.

I am deeply grateful to Ken Corbett, Galit Atlas, and Emanuel Berman for their warm endorsement of the book and to Eyal Rosmarin, Georgina Clutterbuck, and Kate Hawes at Routledge for their helpful guidance along the way. I was blessed to have had on board the gifted and well-read translator Ilana Goldberg. Her thoughtful, creative, and nuanced work was indispensable, and I truly couldn't have done it without her.

Thank you to Kerin Adams for granting permission to reproduce images of two cards from the CAT-A test, and to Inbar Heller Algazi for the series of illustrations she created for the book, with a deep sensitivity to the language of the child's psyche and her remarkable ability to tap into the depths of the unconscious.

I am grateful to Prof. Dana Amir for her generous reading of the manuscript and for actively encouraging its publication; to Marganit Ofer for being the whetting stone against which I sharpened my arguments, a companion, and a chaperone; to the relentless Dafna Grinner, for her enthusiastic and continuous assistance, and to Esther Rapoport for her helpful comments and unreserved support of the book project.

Special thanks go to Attorney Daphna Cohen-Stow for sharing with me her vast knowledge of the legal aspects of reproduction and same-sex parenting in Israel, to Avi Saroff for his guidance on diagnostic issues, and to Maya Lavie-Ajayi for her expertise in qualitative methodologies. To Geva Shenkman, Offer Maurer, Ron Nasim, Ofer Salman-Sagi, Sharon Zack, and

xiv Acknowledgments

again to Marganit Ofer – for sharing their unpublished work, and providing valuable insights. To my friends: Omer Rotem, Noga Ariel, "The Culture Club," "The Return of the Girls' Clique," and "The Saharu Girls," and especially to my close friend Shir Bar Emet, for serving as a hotline for obsessive consultations.

My heartfelt gratitude is given to Nitza Yanai, and Amal Ziv, who supervised the PhD dissertation on which this book is based. Their immense contribution to articulating the ideas in the book, their flashes of brilliance combined with precisely hewn turns of phrase, were paralleled only by their abundant sharing of knowledge, and their generous embrace of my ideas. I am also thankful to Emanuel Berman, whose inexhaustible reservoir of psychoanalytic learning enabled him to envisage the eventual fruition of still unripe ideas, and to nurse them into maturity with curiosity and devotion. I am similarly indebted to Anat Palgi-Hacker, a guiding light and force of nature, whose pioneering work paved the way for this book; to the late Lew Aron, whose legacy as a relational theoretician, a wizard of comparative thinking, and a storyteller, can be found woven between the lines of this book; to Yael Khenin, for her insightful comments, and for being both a haven and a breath of fresh air; to Avner Bergstein, for his ongoing contribution to the development of my own thinking. Thank you all for your inspiration and for the license to think anew. It is a great privilege to have been incubated professionally under your caring mentorship.

Thank you to the research participants who opened their homes and their hearts to me.

To my beloved family members, whose destinies are bound to each other by the ties of blood, law, or choice.

To Oren, for plucking our smile from among the chariots.

To Amal, my labor of love.

Foreword

The release in 2010 of *The Kids Are All Right*, filmmaker Lisa Cholodenko's star-studded feature, was a landmark moment announcing the acceptance of the same-sex family[1] into the cultural mainstream. A commercial and critical success, a recipient of two Golden Globe Awards, and nominated for several others including four Academy awards, it was the first film in Hollywood's history to place at the center of its narrative a lesbian couple raising children conceived through donor insemination.

The message was clear: not only are the kids all right, the family unit *in toto* is not all that different from any other middle-class family, with its characteristic conflicts and crises. This is not a film about lesbians, the reviewers and filmmakers alike declared, but rather about the importance of the institutions of marriage and family (Heffernan & Wilgus, 2018; Ebert, 2010; Austerlitz, 2010; Sharkey, 2010).

"The kids are all right" has become a catchphrase most frequently identified with the cumulative research findings from studies of same-sex families, which have repeatedly demonstrated that the children of lesbian women and gay men develop well, or at least as well as children raised in heterosexual families: they do not suffer from developmental or emotional difficulties any more than others do, they are well-adjusted socially and academically, and they do not exhibit higher rates of homosexuality or gender dysphoria than the general population.

This overwhelming message – "The kids are all right" – has been of crucial importance for the recognition of the legal status of same-sex families

---

1 The term "same-sex family" will be used throughout the book as shorthand, instead of "same-sex parented family," to describe families in which the parents are of the same sex, even if the children are of another sex.

and for creating a climate of social acceptance in the Western world. But there is also a fly in the ointment when this message serves to intensify the pressure felt by same-sex parents to produce "poster children," and even more so when it contributes to the oppressive identification of good parenting with the production of children who conform to heteronormative expectations in terms of sexuality and gender expression (Levi-Hazan, 2020; Hartman & Peleg, 2019). Since the end of the first decade of the current century, the preceding critical argument has precipitated a shift in the research field to a focus on the unique conflicts and experiences of same-sex parents and their children, one based on close encounters that do not seek to measure the children's achievements or compare them to those of children raised in heterosexual families. Similar critical arguments have been voiced in respect to the representation of the family in Cholodenko's film (see, e.g., Eaklor, 2012; Brooks, 2014; Walters, 2012) – arguments to which we will return in the coda of this book.

The kids are all right, but what about Oedipal theory?

Freud's legacy in psychoanalysis has two sides to it: on one hand, psychoanalytic thinking is notable for its flexibility and capacity for constant renewal. Just as the work of interpretation deals with the interminable processes of deconstruction and reconstruction, psychoanalytic ideas themselves are subject to renewed scrutiny within each school of thought and from one generation to the next. On the other hand, conservative forces stemming from the hierarchical nature of the psychoanalytic establishment and from the authority of the founding fathers and mothers have a dilatory effect on the processes of theoretical transformation, and therefore, for the most part, the theory tends to assimilate critical ideas and influences of the current moment at some delay and does not hurry to cultivate them.

Like many of the core constructions that make up the psychoanalytic canon, the Oedipal model continues to accord priority to the nuclear family, which was the typical family arrangement among the middle classes in turn-of-the-century Europe, the cradle of psychoanalysis (Rich, 1976). This traditional model – of a married man and woman who raise their biological offspring together – today counts for less than half of the children in Israel and in the Western world generally, but nevertheless continues to enjoy hegemonic status and serve as a cultural ideal (Corbett, 2009).

During the past decades, numerous alternative family configurations have emerged: single parenthood, blended families, parenting partnership among people who join together in order to fulfill their desire for a child, as well as same-sex parenting assisted by gamete donation. The current book focuses on this latter configuration.

Each of the aforementioned alternatives in some way violates the conditions that were considered desirable and necessary for the child's normal development. Couples who choose an alternative family configuration, therefore, find themselves navigating uncharted territory, without the ability to rely on existing cultural knowledge, and are even obliged to contend with suspicious attitudes from representatives of the cultural hegemony (Shenkman, 2016). These "new families" provoke fundamental questions: what is a family? What is parenthood? Is there a difference between fatherhood and motherhood? What is the role of family relations in the child's development (Corbett, 2009)? The processes of conceptualization can hardly keep up with the pace of social and technological changes that redefine parenthood and family. This is evidenced in the lack of an appropriate vocabulary to describe the variety of new relations and family roles.

With the destabilizing of the heteronormative nuclear family's hegemonic status, the need to revise the Oedipal model is deemed, at the time of the writing of this book, to be one of the most urgently attended endeavors in the psychoanalytic world. Since the 1990s, inspired by postmodern ideas and feminist thought, different proposals for revising the psychoanalytic canon and even alternative psychoanalytic models (Aron, 1996) have appeared, but very little progress has been made in understanding the crucial issues concerning child development within alternative familial constellations generally, and within the same-sex family in particular. To some extent, this limited progress might be attributed to the fact that most of the proposals are not empirically informed, or, in other cases, are based on a handful of clinical cases, which, by definition, present some sort of pathology, and frequently include divorce, intense fighting between the parents, or overt symptoms in the child. Against this impasse, *Oedipal Experiences in Same-Sex Families* proposes that the changing reality not only mandates a fundamental revision of the theory, but also provides the opportunity to empirically explore crucial issues regarding parenthood, gender, sexuality, and human development processes – issues which, until recently, could only be addressed hypothetically (Patterson, 2006).

How the same-sex family challenges the Oedipal model

Since the accumulated empirical findings showing that children of same-sex parents develop normally are at odds with the predictions based on Oedipal theory, I will propose viewing the same-sex family as a test case that provides an opportunity to reconsider the fundamental premises of the Oedipal model. An effective way of doing so will be to single out those characteristics of the same-sex family that violate the heteronormative assumptions embedded in the Oedipal model and to interrogate them systematically.

Thus, each part of this book will revolve around one of the challenges that the same-sex family presents to the Oedipal model and will examine it both empirically and analytically, based on the evidence collected during meetings with same-sex parents and their children.

Which characteristics of the same-sex family pose a challenge to the heteronormative assumptions embedded in the Oedipal model? First, it is necessary to clearly define the same-sex family configuration as follows: parents of the same sex in a couple relationship, living in a shared household, and raising their children, who were created with the assistance of sperm donation or egg donation and surrogacy, such that each child is biologically affiliated with only one of their parents.

The aforementioned definition emphasizes the similarity between the same-sex family configuration and the traditional family model – in which parents in a couple relationship raise offspring in a joint household – and thus exposes three characteristics that violate the heteronormative assumptions of the Oedipal model.

The first characteristic is the fact that both parents are of the same sex. Oedipal theory famously assumes that normal development requires parent figures of two different sexes, based on the reasoning that the recognition of the difference between the sexes underpins the organization of the child's configuration of desire and identification with her or his parents (Laplanche & Pontalis, 1973). Furthermore, it is this recognition that provides the first impetus for the Oedipal process, by means of castration anxiety. The question then arises whether the development of children in same-sex families includes an Oedipal stage, and if so, how do these children organize their configurations of desire and identification with their parents if these processes are not grounded in their parents' sex? These questions are the focus of the book's first part: "What does Oedipal development have to do with the parents' sex, anyway?"

The second characteristic is the inherent biological asymmetry in same-sex family relations; in other words, the fact that in same-sex families the child is biologically affiliated with only one of her or his parents. This characteristic undermines the assumption contained in the idea of the primal scene, where the child is always the product of sexual intercourse between the child's two parents. Embedded within this psychoanalytic axiom are heteronormative perceptions that associate biological affiliation with kinship. What part then does biology play in the creation of kinship relations? Does biological affiliation or the lack thereof play a role in attachment processes and in the child's object choices, or in the parents' bonding processes? How does the asymmetrical structure affect the division of parental roles, the couple relationship, and relations with the extended family? These questions are the focus of the book's second part "What does genetics have to do with kinship, anyway?"

The third characteristic relates to the inevitable involvement of birth others – a sperm donor or an egg donor and a surrogate – in the process of procreation. This characteristic also upends the assumption embedded in the idea of the primal scene. According to the latter notion, parental coitus, as a symbol, connects the child's phantasy about how she or he came into the world with the threat represented by the creation of sibling rivals, as well as with the child's experience of exclusion from the parents' couple relationship. However, toward the end of the second decade of the 21st century, fewer and fewer children are born as a result of spontaneous intercourse between parents, and therefore the inseparable link between parental sexuality and childbirth is losing its integrity and validity. Within families that have been assisted by gamete donation, some of the questions at stake are: what meanings are attributed to the fact that the parent's sexuality is not a procreative one? What is the status of the birth others, who play a part in the creation of the child, in his or her inner world and in the parents' psyche? And what part does the family reverie play in shaping the child's inner experience? Will the child's deep Oedipal structure relate to both partners in his or her creation – the biological parent and the birth other – or perhaps to both her or his parents? These questions form the center of discussion in Part III of this book: "What does procreation have to do with parental coitus, anyway?"

As can be seen, the structure of the book reflects its purpose: to systematically address the central challenges that the same-sex family presents to the Oedipal model. This undertaking is motivated by the belief that we

A few notes on the research: scope, sample, and methods

This book is the product of psychoanalytic qualitative research. The material presented in it was collected during meetings with the families of 33 children in the age range of four to six – a range recognized in developmental terms as the Oedipal phase.

Initially, my goal had been to include in my research as diverse a population as possible, representing the various identities comprising the LGBTQ community (parents who identify as gay, lesbian, bisexual, transgender, and queer), as well as the variety of existing family configurations (two parents raising a child born with the assistance of gamete donation, adoption, single parenting, and different kinds of parenting partnerships). This goal was informed by the assumption that each family configuration presents specific complexities that need to be studied and mediated (cf. Corbett, 2009), as well as by an ethical position that accords importance to the inclusion of marginalized groups. However, my preliminary attempts at processing the research materials during the first recruitment phase led me to the conclusion that the diversity of the sample impedes the formulation of clear insights; therefore, despite the ethical justifications for selecting a diverse population, this choice was less suited for a qualitative study that aims to produce generalizations in the context of a small sample. For this reason, I decided to narrow down the inclusion criterion for the study and to focus on families in which same-sex parents in a shared household are raising at least one child who was born with the assistance of gamete donation.

The chosen configuration most closely resembles the traditional family model, and, perhaps not coincidentally, it is also one of the preferred configurations currently among same-sex parents in Israel. Be that as it may, since this configuration preserves the Oedipal structure in its most typical form, it is eminently suited for the stated task: to isolate and reexamine questions pertaining to gender, sex, and sexuality that are embedded in Oedipal theory.

Following the narrowing of the inclusion criterion, I excluded from the study six families that had been recruited in the first round: a family of a lesbian couple who had adopted a daughter, a family with one parent who had come out as transgender, a family based on a parenting partnership between a lesbian mother and a gay father, and three other families based on a parenting partnership between a gay father and a heterosexual mother. The material collected in the encounters with these families was used in the current study for the sake of expanding the research perspective, but does not form part of the actual body of research. I hope to use this gathered material as a point of departure for future studies that will focus on other family configurations.

As far as demographic variables are concerned, I made a concerted effort to include as diverse a population as possible. Nonetheless, it should be acknowledged that the family configuration that I studied is thriving mostly among the upper-middle-class Jewish, secular, urban population[2] (Salman-Sagi, 2019; Shechner et al., 2010). Despite my efforts, all the participants in my study are Jewish, and same-sex families from a lower socio-economic bracket represent a minority of the study sample. In regard to the sex of the participants – one of the important variables in the study – I was able to achieve a balanced sample, despite the relatively lower incidence of gay men who have had children with the assistance of egg donation and surrogacy compared to that of lesbian women who have had children with the assistance of a sperm donation.

The population of gay fathers who participated in this study belongs to a higher socio-economic bracket and is more homogeneous in terms of demographic characteristics compared to the lesbian participants. This discrepancy is due in some measure to the earning capacity of men and women, which in the case of same-sex couples tends to double the effect, but even more so is a reflection of the high cost of the surrogacy process, which requires a level of strong financial support. Furthermore, with the exception of a few cases, the surrogacy process was enabled by the financial support of one or both the fathers' parents. As Salman-Sagi (2019) notes, in line with the findings of the current study, this financial support represents the parents' blessing for the process and is usually accompanied by emotional support and significant involvement in the grandchildren's lives.

---

2 The cultural context will be elaborated more broadly in the next subchapter: "The local context: the same-sex family in Israel."

Among the lesbian mothers, there was more discernible variety in the levels of closeness and acceptance among the families of origin, as well as in the levels of involvement with the grandchildren's lives. In accordance with the preceding point, most of the gay fathers in the study live in Tel Aviv, which is considered the most progressive city in Israel, the country's gay capital, or in cities, suburban villages, and kibbutzim in the center of the country; whereas most of the lesbian mothers live in the satellite cities of Tel Aviv's metropolitan area, and the rest are dispersed among cities representing all socioeconomic strata.

The research sessions took place within the families' natural setting. The hours that I spent in the families' homes provided an opportunity to gather observational data on the interactional patterns among the family members: what designations does the child use to address each parent? What circumstances, or what needs motivate the child to address each of them? What is the distribution of roles between the parents, and how does each of the parents position themselves vis-à-vis the child? How do the family members deal with triangular interactions and with the intimate moments between two members from which a third is excluded? To what degree is there physical contact between the parents and between each of the parents and the child?

The observational information was confronted with data that was collected during interviews with the parents and the children. In-depth couple interviews were conducted with the parents – 12 couples of lesbian mothers and 11 couples of gay fathers – without the presence of their children. The questions addressed their choice to have a child through gamete donation, the effects of this choice on the parental role distribution and on the child's pattern of preferences since infancy, their play habits, and the phantasies they express or enact. In addition to the data obtained directly from the parents' reports, supplementary contents, and unconscious behavioral patterns were elicited through listening to the parents' choice of words (including elisions, repetitions, contradictions, and logical fallacies), symbols, as well as nonverbal layers of communication. Special attention was paid to parapraxes, dreams, and associative chains of thought, which, according to psychoanalytic thinking, offer a window onto the unconscious.

A separate interview was held with each of the children – without the parents' presence, to the extent possible. These interviews dealt with the concept of family generally and with each of the children's personal family experiences, attachment patterns, and libidinal object choices, as well as with the question of how they came into this world. With the goal of uncovering their internal representations and unconscious phantasies – and working with the assumption that verbal communication in these age groups is not adequately developed to convey the emotional complexities surrounding the issues at stake – two projective tasks were integrated into the interviews.

The first task was a unique apperception test that was formulated for the purpose of this research, based on the standard apperception test used in diagnosing children (Children Apperception Test – A). The CAT-A consists of ten cards illustrated with personified animals. The child is asked to make up a story about them as a way of giving expression to their phantasy life: representing the significant figures in their life and their relationship with them, their feelings, wishes, conflicts, and defenses (Bellak & Bellak, 1949; Byrd & Witherspoon, 1954). Since the original cards address a wide range of developmental issues, some of which are not relevant to the research purposes, two cards that deal with the Oedipus complex and the primary scene were selected for inclusion, whereas the others were replaced with pictures that were found suitable for eliciting the relevant unconscious contents. Since the study was not designed with the intention of evaluating the children's answers in accordance with developmental indicators, or to compare them empirically with typical responses by children raised in heteronormative families, there was no methodological impediment to substituting new cards for the original ones, about which a great deal of research knowledge has been amassed. Based on the photos presented to the children in the study, the illustrator Inbar Heller Algazi created a new series of cards, which will be presented in the book alongside two of the original CAT-A cards (for the complete list of cards, including the contents they were intended to elicit, see Appendix B).

The second task was the Kinetic Family Drawing (KFD) – a projective technique that enables reflection of internalized family representations, including the effects of culture and the subcultures to which the family belongs (Handler, 1996; Burns & Kaufman, 1972). The original instruction in this task directs the child to draw their family, but in order to explore the child's family concept, and to assess the weight given within this representation to his or her own family experience, cultural schemata, and the inner negotiation between the two, I chose to use one of the alternative formulations proposed in the literature, and asked the children to draw *any* family that comes to mind, as long as the family members are engaged in some kind of activity

(Handler, 1996). As customary, I asked the children to clarify aspects of their drawings and to compose a story about the family they depicted.

Between the ages of four to six, Oedipal contents are expected to take center stage; children at this stage repeatedly ask to hear the story of their birth and tend to enjoy make-believe games and drawing activities, all of which provide them a space for emotional working through (Freud, 1905; Klein, 1926; Aron, 2014; Corbett, 2009). Hence, the tasks aspired to provide the children an opportunity for meaningful working through of contents with which they are preoccupied anyway, in the language that they are accustomed to, with the hope that the family would benefit from the shared processing of these contents. Indeed, in most cases, the children exhibited great enjoyment during the activity. In a few cases, during the apperception task, signs appeared indicating the child's distress, such as wild laughter, aggression, or difficulty concentrating on the task. In these cases, I offered the child another card, showing more positive or neutral content to enable them to finish the task with a sense of satisfaction, and I then suggested we rejoin their parents. After being soothed by their parents, I invited the children to play together with one of their favorite games, relinquishing the goal of completing the tasks. In order to protect the identity of the children, the participants in the book – adults as well as children – are referred to by pseudonyms. Special care was taken to obscure any identifying features that might expose the identity of the families.

The triangulation of information obtained from the observations, interviews, and projective instruments, and its placement within diverse theoretical and empirical contexts produced rich and fascinating material that will be presented throughout the book. At the beginning of my research journey, I would often return from my meetings with the families with a Tolstoyan sense that "Happy families are all alike; every unhappy family is unhappy in its own way," concerned that I would not be able to say anything about these families apart from the fact that they resemble every other family I know. However, increasingly, as I delved into the material and processed it, significant themes began to show through, and finally, through an iterative process of deconstruction and reconstruction, a systematic explanatory framework emerged.

The local context: the same-sex family in Israel

The gayby boom – the sharp increase in the rate of planned parenthood among same-sex couples – burst onto the Israeli stage first among the lesbian community in the mid-1990s. Since the second decade of the 21st century, the scale of the phenomenon has been continuously growing within the male gay community too. No official data is available, but according to existing estimates, the number of same-sex families in Israel is in the thousands and is constantly increasing, especially within the Jewish, secular, and urban middle class (Salman-Sagi, 2019; Shechner et al., 2010). Although the favorable turn in Israeli public opinion toward support of same-sex families can be described as a revolution, among both Jewish and Muslim conservative groups within the population, same-sex families are not an acceptable option.[3]

According to an interview I conducted with a Palestinian therapist[4] who is active in the association for LGBT rights of Palestinians living in Israel and in the Palestinian Authority, although it is not yet possible to lead an uncloseted same-sex family life within Palestinian society, there is growing acceptance of the choice of a same-sex partner within a person's intimate circles. Thus, for example, gay and lesbian Palestinians may have children within a parenting partnership with a member of the other sex, so that they can "pass" within the traditional community as a heteronormative family while raising the children with their partner in one of the progressive urban centers (Haifa or Ramallah, for example), locations that allow them greater liberty. In many of these cases, it is possible to come out of the closet to one's nuclear family, so that the couple's parents, who are mostly happy to welcome grandchildren to the family, support the choice.

This is a good example of the fact that the choice of this or that family configuration is not a completely free choice in the full sense of the word. The contours of the choice are shaped by a range of possibilities and constraints of a biological, technological, legal, social, and economic nature. Lesbian women, for example, find it easier to become parents compared to gay men, owing to their biological capacity to become pregnant. For many years, that biological advantage was enhanced by a social policy that provided lesbians with access to publicly funded fertility treatments, but denied the rights of gay men to have children by means of surrogacy within Israel. The prohibitive costs of surrogacy abroad made this route to creating

---

3 Shortly before the book's publication, Israel's governing coalition created an alliance, for the first time, with an extremist Jewish religious party that carries the banner of anti-LGBT ideology, thus placing the achievements of Israel's LGBT revolution in jeopardy.

4 The interviewee's identity remains confidential at their request.

a family accessible only to people of considerable means (Ziv, 2020b). This state of affairs, which accurately reflects the possibilities and limitations faced by the participants in the study, has been altered by the decision of Israel's High Court in July 2021 to expand Israel's surrogacy law to apply also to gay couples and single men. The implications of this decision for the reality of the lives of gay couples seeking the path of surrogacy are as of yet not fully known.

At the time of the writing of this foreword, Israeli law does not recognize the existence of more than two parents. This means that a lesbian woman or gay man who chooses to have a child through a parenting partnership are aware that their spouse will not be legally recognized as the child's parent, even if they function as de facto parents. Those who choose to create three-parented or four-parented families in Israel do so with the knowledge that there will be no possibility of legally defining all of the parents as such, and therefore the number of such families is very low.

As for adoption as the route for creating a family, at the time of writing, Israeli law does not permit same-sex couples to adopt domestically (except in the case of cross-adoption of the biological children of one of the members of the couple),[5] apart from a few rare exceptions. International adoption is permitted in countries that have signed an adoption treaty with Israel, but these countries prohibit adoption by same-sex couples, and only a few of them permit single-parent adoption. Same-sex parenting via the adoption route is therefore not very common.

Familism and pronatalism among Israeli Jews

Although the gayby boom in Israel is part of a general trend also taking place in North America and most of Northern- and Western Europe, it is also unique in terms of its magnitude and characteristics. This is the product of a cultural clash between technological progress and neo-liberal values on one hand and the central role of religion in the country as well as dominant conservative family values on the other. The same-sex family in Israel thus emerges as a fascinating case study.

---

5 Due to the progressive legislation of recent years, cross-adoption by the non-biological mother has come to be an expected and a fairly habitual choice among lesbian couples, anticipated in the family planning stage.

Israeli society is characterized by familism: the family plays a central role in the life of the individual and the collective (Fogiel Bijaoui, 2002). The centrality of conservative family values in Israeli society, is reflected, among other things, in high marriage rates, low divorce rates, and a very low rate of children born out of wedlock. According to Israel's Central Bureau of Statistics, in 2020, only 7.8% of the children born to Jewish women were born out of wedlock, compared to 73% in Chile, 60% in France, and 52% in the Netherlands.

The familial cultural climate is accompanied by a pronatalist ethos – a complex of beliefs, convictions, and practices that encourage childbirth, glorify the role of parenting, and emphasize the advantages of having and raising children. In Israel, this ethos reflects the predominant social attitudes as well as official policy. The best evidence of the pronatalist ideology is the birth rate itself, which is the highest among developed nations (Ziv, 2020b).

The centrality of the family institution and of the pronatalist ethos within the Jewish population in Israel is the product of several factors: the centrality of family in Jewish religion, the collective trauma of the Holocaust, as well as the Zionist's movement "demographic contest," as pronatalism has been intimately connected to Zionist ideology from the very outset. Jewish women's maternal role is accorded national significance and is therefore culturally constitutedas an entry ticket to participation in the collective, similar to the role of military service for men (Berkovitch, 1997; Hashiloni-Dolev, 2013). As a result, LGBT subjects have been defined as shirking their duty to the collective and as failing to participate in the national effort (Ziv, 2020b). According to this logic, homosexuality was perceived as a threat – not only to the familial order, but first and foremost to the continuity of the Jewish people.[6]

In light of this, it is not surprising that the striking success of the gay rights struggle in Israel, which I described earlier in terms of a revolution,

---

6 This identification between the institution of family and the national struggle should also be understood as a broader characteristic of ethnic minorities. In her study of San Francisco's gay and lesbian community in the 1980s, for example, Weston (1991) reported that African-American or Latino gay and lesbian men and women described an inherent conflict between their sexual identity and their ethnic identity, stemming from the great importance that their culture accords to the institution of family and to blood ties as part of the struggle to preserve their ethnic heritage. In light of this importance, homosexuality is interpreted as a threat to ethnic or racial identity.

relied to a large degree on the strivings of gays and lesbians to participate in the roles that Zionism had carved out for men and women, i.e., the right to serve in the army and the right to create offspring and live a family life (Kadish, 2005). This idea brings to mind the notions of homonormativity and homonationalism, which are frequently mentioned in contemporary discourse about the rights of the LGBT community and its politics.

Homonormativity, homonationalism, and the right to parenthood

The term "homonormativity" was coined by queer theoretician and researcher Lisa Duggan in reference to the neo-liberal sexual politics that does not challenge the dominant heteronormative assumptions and institutions, but rather champions a privatized LGBT culture that has been depoliticized and is anchored in domesticity and consumerism. Jasbir Fuar, another contemporary queer theoretician, has taken Duggan's conceptualization one step further, coining the term "homonationalism," which she defines as "national homonormativity." It is in the context of "homonationalism" that domesticated homosexual bodies provide ammunition for the reinforcement of the national project (Duggan, 2004; Puar, 2007 in: Gross, 2015).

Homonationality is a process in which the homosexual is transformed from someone perceived as a threat to the state to someone who is integrated into the state, and who even distinguishes it from rival states by its degree of liberalism. Homonormativity and homonationality are preconditions for the activity known as "pinkwashing," i.e., using the rights of the LGBT community, and of gay men in particular, as a tool of propaganda by the state, as well as for the complementary striving of gays and lesbians for recognition and inclusion, while disengaging the politics of LGBT rights from the broader agenda of human rights (Gross, 2015; Ziv, 2020b). These trends have brought about the emergence of a discourse about the "right to parenthood" within the LGBT community in Israel, in the context of which parenthood has been constructed as one of the fundamental human rights, and even as a civil right, to which any citizen who fulfills his duties is entitled (Ziv, 2020b).

Within the social climate described, genetic kinship is accorded crucial importance. This is manifested in the highest rates of consumption of assisted reproductive technologies in the world, and in a highly permissive policy regarding their accessibility and public funding: Israel is the only country in the world that pays for an unlimited number of IVF treatments to any woman before the age of 45, even when medical indicators show that the chances of achieving a pregnancy are slim (Gooldin, 2013). Medical policy in Israel includes a much higher willingness than accepted, according to recommendations of the International Federation of Fertility Societies (IFSS), to risk the health of the woman and of the newborn. This policy, which privileges IVF treatments over other alternative routes to parenthood, such as egg donation or adoption, does not merely reflect the separate locations of genetic parenthood and social parenthood within the social hierarchy, but also perpetuates this separation (Hashiloni-Dolev, 2013; Birenbaum-Carmeli, 2009). Genetic affiliation is perceived as integral to the goal of strengthening the Jewish collective, and subsequently as a justification for the political and territorial claims of the Zionist state. Blood ties are perceived, accordingly, as strong enough to sustain any family structure, including alternative ones, whereas non-genetic parenthood is marked as a threat, or as inferior (Hashiloni-Dolev, 2013).

The Israeli gayby boom phenomenon is therefore impacted by the local familial and pronatalist climate in several ways: this climate increases the desire of same-sex couples to raise children since a family life represents the ultimate "good," and any other lifestyle is perceived as less valuable; it normalizes the use of reproductive technologies and increases public acceptance and recognition of same-sex families (Ziv, 2020a). As a result, in Israel, lesbian mothers and gay fathers report an increased experience of social belonging after becoming parents (Ben-Ari & Livni, 2006; Salman-Sagi, 2019). However, the question of the status of the social (non-biological) parent continues to be a source of distress.

Since the emergence of the same-sex family in Israel is closely linked to homonormative and homonational trends, most of the parents that I met displayed clear assimilative aspirations: the adoption of various normalization practices and the hope of raising children who are heteronormative in respect to gender and sexuality; internalization of the heteronormative kinship discourse, and alongside it, attribution of considerable weight to relations with extended family. Similarly, with only a few exceptions, all of the participants identified as cisgender.

xxx Foreword

It is my hope that these aforementioned characteristics of the Jewish-Israeli cultural and social climate would pave the way to a nuanced understanding of the families' experiences, even as the book is proposing a model of broader relevance.

References

Aron, L. (2014). "With you I'm born again": Themes and fantasies of birth and the family circumstances surrounding birth as these are mutually evoked in patient and analyst. *Psychoanalytic Dialogues, 24*, 341–357.

Aron, L. (1996). *A meeting of minds: Mutuality in psychoanalysis*. Analytic Press, Inc.

Austerlitz, S. (2010, July 11). Same-sex, with the same family issues. *The Boston Globe*.

Bellak, L., & Bellak, S. S. (1949). *Children's apperception test*. C.P.S. Co.

Ben-Ari, A., & Livni, T. (2006). Motherhood is not a given thing: Experiences and constructed meanings of biological and nonbiological lesbian mothers. *Sex Roles, 54*, 521–531.

Berkovitch, N. (1997). Motherhood as a national mission: The construction of womanhood in the legal discourse in Israel. *Women's Studies International Forum, 20*(5–6), 605–619.

Birenbaum-Carmeli, D. (2009). The politics of 'The natural family' in Israel: State policy and kinship ideologies [Hebrew]. *Social Science and Medicine, 69*, 1018–1024.

Brooks, J. (2014). The kids are all right, the pursuits of happiness, and the spaces between. *Camera Obscura, 29*(1), 111–135.

Burns, R. C., & Kaufman, S. H. (1972). *Actions, styles and symbols in kinetic family drawings (K-F-D)*. Routledge.

Byrd, E., & Witherspoon, R. L. (1954). Responses of preschool children to the Children's Apperception Test. *Child Development, 25*, 35–44.

Corbett, K. (2009). Nontraditional family reverie: Masculinity unfolds. In *Boyhoods: Rethinking masculinities*. Yale University Press.

Eaklor, V. L. (2012). The kids are all right but the lesbians aren't. *Historical Reflections/Réflexions Historiques, 38*(3), 153–170.

Ebert, R. (2010, July 7). The kids are all right. *Chicago Sun-Times*.

Fogiel Bijaoui, S. (2002). Familism, postmodernity and the state: The case of Israel. *Journal of Israeli History, 21*(1–2), 38–62.

Freud, S. (1905). Three essays on the theory of sexuality. *The Standard Edition of the Complete Psychological Works of Sigmund Freud, 7*, 123–246.

Gooldin, S. (2013). "Emotional rights", moral reasoning, and Jewish–Arab alliances in the regulation of in-vitro-fertilization in Israel: Theorizing the unexpected consequences of assisted reproductive technologies. *Social Science & Medicine, 83*, 90–98.

Gross, A. (2015). The politics of LGBT rights in Israel and beyond: Nationality, normativity and queer politics. *Columbia Human Rights Law Review*, (46), 81–152.

Handler, L. (1996). The clinical use of drawings. In C. S. Newmark (Ed.), *Major psychological assessment instruments* (pp. 206–293). Allyn and Bacon.

Hartman, T., & Peleg, A. (2019). Minority stress in an improved social environment: Lesbian mothers and the burden of proof. *Journal of GLBT Family Studies*, *15*(5), 442–460.

Hashiloni-Dolev, Y. (2013). *The Fertility Revolution [Hebrew]*. Modan.

Heffernan, V., & Wilgus, G. (2018). Introduction: Imagining motherhood in the twenty-first century – images, representations, constructions. *Women: A Cultural Review*, *29*(1), 1–18.

Kadish, R. (2005). Israeli lesbians, national identity, and motherhood. In C. Frankfort-Nachmias & E. Shadmi (Eds.), *Sappho in the holy land: Lesbian existence and dilemmas in contemporary Israel* (pp. 223–250). State University of New York Press.

Klein, M. (1926). The psychological principles of early analysis. In *Love, guilt and reparation and other works 1921–1945 (The Writings of Melanie Klein, Volume 1)*. Hogarth Press.

Laplanche, J., & Pontalis, J. B. (1973). *The language of psycho-analysis* (D. Nicholson-Smith, Trans.). W. W. Norton.

Levi-Hazan, Y. (2020). "Not confusing the kids": Queer parenthood and the double demand for heteronormativity [Hebrew]. *Mafte'akh*, *15*, 35–44.

Patterson, C. J. (2006). Children of lesbian and gay parents. *Current Directions in Psychological Science*, *15*(5), 241–244.

Rich, A. C. (1976). *Of woman born: Motherhood as experience and institution*. Norton.

Salman-Sagi, O. (2019, July). *"Daddy is not mommy": Israeli gay fathers cope with a society which sanctifies motherhood* [PhD dissertation, Tel-Aviv University].

Sharkey, B. (2010, July 8). The kids are all right. *Los Angeles Times*.

Shechner, T., Slone, M., Meir, Y., & Kalish, Y. (2010). Relations between social support and psychological and parental distress for lesbian, single heterosexual by choice, and two-parent heterosexual mothers. *American Journal of Orthopsychiatry*, *80*(3), 283–292.

Shenkman, G. (2016). Classic psychoanalysis and male same-sex parents: A reexamination of basic concepts. *Psychoanalytic Psychology*, *33*(4), 585–598.

Walters, S. D. (2012). The kids are all right but the lesbians aren't: Queer kinship in US culture. *Sexualities*, *15*(8), 917–933.

Weston, K. (1991). *Families we choose: Lesbians, gays, kinship*. Columbia University Press.

Ziv, A. (2020a). Querying lesbian fatherhood. In H. W. Henriksson & K. Goedecke (Eds.), *Close relations: Critical studies of family and kinship* (pp. 21–36). Springer.

Ziv, A. (2020b). Queer kinship [Hebrew]. *Mafte'akh*, *15*, 135–154.

Introduction

A bridge between two islands: psychoanalytic thinking and the research field

The Oedipus complex

During one of the most intense moments of his self-analysis, Freud realized that he was in love with his mother and jealous of his father. He shared this astonishing discovery with his friend Wilhelm Fliess in a letter dated October 15, 1897, in which he attempts to persuade him, evoking the timeless power of tragedies such as *Oedipus Rex* and Shakespeare's *Hamlet*, that the child's infantile wish to see his father dead and realize his love for his mother is a universal one (Ginsburg, 2007). These intimate musings eventually came together in a fluent and persuasive text published as part of his ambitious oeuvre – *The Interpretation of Dreams*, where he states:

> His destiny moves us only because it might have been ours – because the oracle laid the same curse upon us before our birth as upon him. It is the fate of all of us, perhaps, to direct our first sexual impulse towards our mother and our first hatred and our first murderous wish against our father.
>
> (Freud, 1900, p. 262)

Due to the monumental influence that the Oedipal theory has had on Western culture, Freud has solidified his status as a modern oracle – no less than that of his Delphic predecessor. Freud's words in the previous quote thus take on the quality of a prophecy that is delivered to every parent with the birth of their child.

In his paper "The Ego and the Id" (1923a), Freud achieved a comprehensive and audacious description of the Oedipus complex, including the intricate system of identifications and desires that it produces toward both of the child's parents. The Oedipal process, Freud argues, is

DOI: 10.4324/9781032663333-1

affected by the constitutional bisexuality of each individual in two ways: first, the relative strength of primary male and female dispositions determines whether the Oedipal situation will result in identification with the father or the mother, and thus to the formation of a feminine or masculine identity. More importantly, upon deeper investigation, it appears that the Oedipus complex is in fact two-fold, having both a positive and negative aspect. The positive complex relates to the child's sexual desire toward his mother and to his wish to be rid of his father in order to take his place alongside the mother, whereas the negative complex indicates the son's feminine affectionate attitude toward the father, which is accompanied by feelings of jealousy and hostility toward the mother. The degree to which positive and negative Oedipal tendencies are manifested reflects the relative strength of each person's heterosexual and homosexual orientations.

However, alongside Freud's audacity, the text also attests to his ambivalence toward the notion of homosexual desire stemming from the complete Oedipal model. This is sometimes evident in statements that construct a value-laden hierarchy between the positive and negative complex, or, at other times, through his choice, perhaps an unconscious one, to focus the discussion of the negative complex on the female in particular and to minimize its importance for the male.

These expressions of ambivalence can be understood as Freud's attempts to overcome his own homosexual desire as well as feminine aspects of his identification arrays, in light of historical forces that included the pathologization of homosexuality and the racialization of the Jew, in the context of which the Jew was perceived as feminized (Boyarin, 1995; Aron & Starr, 2013).

Whatever the reason, this notion of a two-fold Oedipal model was eventually marginalized in Freudian theory and even more so in the psychoanalytic canon, which for many decades reduced the Oedipus complex to its positive dimension only and accorded the negative complex the status of an undesired development (Chodorow, 1978, Boyarin, 1995; Friedman, 2013). During the 1950s and 60s, a time in which American psychoanalysis was dominated by ego psychology, the pathologization of homosexuality – which was then characterized as an early failure of separation from the mother – took a turn for the worse and gave rise to conversion therapy, a therapeutic approach to which Freud himself had objected (Finkelman, 2012; Freud, 1935 in Grotjahn, 1951).

In the past several decades, writings criticizing and revising the Oedipal model have emerged out of feminist and constructivist approaches. A number of these critiques offer fertile ground for considering the Oedipal situation within same-sex families.

Feminist and Queer critiques of the Oedipal model

Critical feminist theory understands the Oedipal model as a conceptualization that describes a specific, context-dependent family reality, while perpetuating it as possessed of universal and objective validity (Rich, 1976). Nancy Chodorow (1978) argues that the Oedipal structure is reproduced from one generation to the next because it is women who act as primary caretakers of their children, and the differences in the way they relate to boys and girls produces girls with maternal aspirations and abilities and boys whose capacity and need for maternal functioning is systematically oppressed. Following Chodorow, Jessica Benjamin (1988) claims that the Oedipal model constructs a polarity between a regressive mother and a liberating father. The Oedipal resolution is meant to solidify the differentiation between the self and the other, but does so without recognizing the mother's subjectivity. Benjamin does not accept Freud's dichotomous distinction between identification and desire and proposes a model by which the pre-Oedipal identification stage is not supplanted by the Oedipal constellation, but is rather integrated into it, such that identification becomes an important basis for the love of the other (Benjamin, 1991, 1996). Chodorow and Benjamin both assume that a reality in which men function as "mothers," or women function as "fathers" – a reality that could arguably be observed in the same-sex family configuration – is likely to result in an inner transformation of the child. Benjamin (1988) suggests that the child internally negotiates between his or her specific parental figures (which need not be biological mothers and fathers, or even men and women) and the symbolic parental representations familiar to the child's cultural context.

In their radical version, which relies on Judith Butler's performative theory (1990), these ideas lead to the Queer aspiration to deconstruct and dissociate the parental role from his or her biological sex, and thus to discuss the possibilities embodied in maternal or paternal performativity (see: Laur, 2011; Corem, 2015; Shenkman, 2016; Rosenblum et al., 2010; Rosenblum, 2012). Contemporary studies also suggest that hormonal processes and neural pathways develop in accordance with parental roles and in direct proportion to the number of hours that the parent invests in caring for the child, whereas in the homosexual father, one can observe the development of brain functions that connect "female" and "male" parental functions (Abraham et al., 2014). Research of this kind validates Chodorow's argument (1978) that studies that "demonstrated" women's unique adaptation to the role of motherhood did so without considering the possibility that similar physiological phenomena may occur among male caregivers or among caregivers who are not biological mothers.

However, Butler themselves (1995) recognized the partial nature of the idea of gender performativity and set out to seek answers in psychoanalytic thought. Within the Oedipal model, says Butler, it is not just the incest taboo that is submerged, but also a taboo on homosexuality. Gender is thus acquired, at least partly, by the rejection of homosexual attachment and the incorporation of the prohibited object as part of the ego through melancholic identification. The culturally dominant Oedipal model, according to this logic, perpetuates not only the prohibition of homosexuality but also the misrecognition of this inherent loss.

Within the heterosexual family, the son is expected to relinquish the desire for his mother through a process of seduction, rivalry with the father, and reconciliation. As opposed to this, his relinquishing of his desire for the father usually occurs without there having been an opportunity to recognize the desire and work through the loss. The question arises: does the same-sex family allow for the circumvention of the gender melancholy that Butler describes? In other words, does the parent's homosexuality ease the recognition of the child's homosexual desire?

Back to the complete Oedipus complex

Joyce McDougall (1995) celebrates the polymorphism of our love life as derived from Freud's complete Oedipus complex. According to her, "Since most infants have two parents, it is to be expected that children will feel libidinally attracted to both parents, giving rise to the wish to obtain the exclusive love of each parent for themselves" (pp. xi). Although McDougall, influenced by the French psychoanalytic tradition, places a great emphasis on the importance of coming to terms with or accepting the inability "to be and to have both sexes" (p. xii) – an emphasis that she struggles not to reduce to an essentialist point of view, albeit not always successfully – this assumption of hers, that every child is libidinally attracted to both parents, can be validly applied to same-sex families. Desire, therefore, is part and parcel of the emotional attachment, and is not dependent on the parent's sex.

Judy Davies (2015), a prominent relational theorist, openly opposes developmental theorists who assume that attachment and desire are two separate developmental lines. She too returns to Freud's complete Oedipus complex and suggests that, for a child who will develop a mainly homosexual orientation, the initial or main Oedipal attraction will be toward significant others of the same sex, whereas the Oedipal attraction to the opposite sex will serve as a secondary formation; however, for someone who will develop a mainly heterosexual orientation the picture is inverse. The secondary Oedipal formation, whether of homoerotic or heteroerotic nature, is likely to be affected by more powerful conflicts and to be more susceptible to repression and evacuation by means of projection, and therefore it is less available to the erotic imagination and sexual phantasy.[1] Her model takes into account Butler's notion of gender melancholy and offers an exploration of these split erotic dimensions which have been denied a proper working through of loss.

The Oedipus complex and Kleinian theory

In Melanie Klein's thought, too, the Oedipus complex appears in its complete form, comprising its positive and negative aspects. However, unlike the Freudian model – which constructs a split between the mother and the father and posits the recognition of sexual difference, with its derivative castration anxiety, as a driving force of the Oedipal complex – in the context of Kleinian thought, the splitting mechanism is perceived as a fundamental mode of coping with the emotional ambivalence of the early relations with the same object, that is, the mother (Klein, 1945). The Oedipus complex, according to this view, is driven primarily by the search for new objects, out of a need to quell anxieties that arise in the context of dyadic relations (Palgi-Hecker, 2005). The resolution of the complex is

---

1 Although Davies herself spells the term with an "f," following the Object Relations school, I have decided to spell phantasy with "ph," in keeping with the choice made by the translators of Freud's works into English. This choice aims to preserve the particular psychoanalytic meanings carried by the term and to distinguish it from the popular concept of "fantasy," which is associated with fully conscious daydreaming (see Isaacs, 1948).

motivated, according to Klein (1945), not only by fear of castration, but to a large degree by feelings of love and reparation wishes toward the father. On the face of it, Klein's emphases would seem to facilitate comprehension of the Oedipal situation in the same-sex family; however, a Kleinian approach assumes innate knowledge of sexual difference and produces a symbolic order premised on a dichotomous distinction between the sexes and complementary relations between them (Klein, 1945; Bronstein, 2001). Therefore, in some respects, her approach is even less suited than Freud's for representing homosexuality and for understanding the role of culture in the processes of the individual's gender interpellation.[2] One assumption that could be derived from the Kleinian theoretical framework is that in the unconscious phantasy of the child raised in a same-sex family, the Oedipal formation will relate not to its two parents, but rather to its two progenitors: their genetic father or mother, and their "birth other," i.e., their sperm donor or egg donor and surrogate combined (Ofer, 2014).

Contemporary elaborations of Kleinian thought, such as that of Ronald Britton, allow one to draw on the richness of Kleinian theory without committing oneself to her essentialist ideas.[3] According to Britton (1998), the primal family triangle equips the child with two links connecting them separately with each parent and confronts them with the exclusive link connecting between the parents.

The child's increasing ability to tolerate the exclusive relationship between the parents introduces a third position from which object relations can be observed. This, according to Britton, provides the foundation for empathy and introspection. Absent this function, which Britton calls "triangular space," the child cannot tolerate the bond between the object and a third object – a bond that is then interpreted as catastrophic. The concept of "triangular space," therefore, redefines the center of the drama entailed in the Oedipal situation. The developmental achievement implied by it is no longer concerned with organizing the familial relations according to gendered patterns and by distinguishing between desire and identification, but

---

2 The term "interpellation" was coined by Louis Althusser (1971) to signify the way in which ideology constitutes (and is itself constituted by) the subject. Ideology subjects individuals to its authority if it obtains recognition from them that they are indeed occupying the space that it points to as their place in the world.

3 Additional thinkers whose elaborations enable this are Steiner (1996, 1999) or Ogden (1989, 2009).

rather with the shift from a dyadic structure of relations to a triadic one, and therefore this concept can be easily applied to same-sex families.

Primal phantasies

The Oedipus complex is one of three imaginary scenarios recognized and designated by Freud, in the analyses he performed, as primal phantasies. These are infantile theoretical constructions "whereby the neurotic – and perhaps 'all human beings' – seek an answer to the central enigmas of their existence" (Laplanche & Pontalis, 1973, p. 332). The fact that these phantasies reappeared in independent analyses, unrelated to external circumstances, led Freud (1917) to assume that these were phylogenetic inheritances, in other words, contents reflecting the reality of humankind's primordial history, such that the phantasizing child is simply filling the gaps of his personal truth with a prehistoric truth. Despite this claim, Freud remained preoccupied over the years with an attempt to characterize the relationship between primal phantasies and actual sensory experience. He frequently plays the sleuth, seeking clues that might permit the detailed reconstruction of the original realistic scenario, which he distills from the formulaic phantasy. The picture that emerges is a rich weave that cannot be unraveled, such that "Wherever experiences fail to fit in with the hereditary schema . . . the contradictions between experience and the schema seem to supply the conflicts of childhood with an abundance of material" and these are worked through in phantasy through "a process which might very profitably be followed out in detail" (Freud, 1918, p. 119).

Indeed, examining infantile phantasies of children in same-sex families proved to be of great value. Throughout this book, infantile phantasies will be considered as a rich site of conflictual contents, where vital working through is carried out in the attempt to reconcile contradictions between personal experiences and organizing psychological structures. However, in the spirit of constructivism, I prefer to identify the source of these organizing mental structures not in a phylogenetic inheritance, but rather in social constructions that furnish the individual's preconceptions.

The three scenarios that Freud identified as primal phantasies are the seduction phantasy (the *Oedipal phantasy*), the *castration phantasy*, and the phantasy of witnessing parental coitus (the *primal scene*). An examination of these scenarios reveals that all three of them share the child's preoccupation with the question of origins: "In the primal scene, it is the origin of the subject that is represented; in seduction phantasies [the Oedipal phantasy], it is the origin or emergence of sexuality; in castration phantasies, the origin of the distinction between the sexes" (Laplanche & Pontalis, 1973, p. 332).

While these three themes are interrelated and interwoven, each of them also represents a developmental milestone in its own right.

Castration phantasy: the castration complex and penis envy

Freud (1905 addendum from 1915, 1923b, 1924) believed that children initially assume that everyone else has a sexual organ similar to the one they have and that the discovery of anatomical sex differences, and all that this implies, is a constitutive experience for the construction of what today is commonly designated as the child's gender identity. The discovery of anatomical differences, according to Freud, affects boys and girls differently. Whereas the boy struggles profoundly with the observed facts and ultimately reaches the terrifying conclusion that his mother once had a penis that was eliminated by castration – a conclusion that often results in an aversion from or disdain toward women (Freud, 1925, 1908) – the daughter does not respond with the same aversion to the sight of the male organ. She is willing to recognize it immediately and is overcome by penis envy and by the wish to become a boy (Freud, 1905). The girl, according to Freud, also assumes that her sexual organ is the outcome of castration, and consequently develops an inferiority complex. The castration phantasy drives the girl to turn away from the mother, thus accelerating her entry into the Oedipal stage, through which she is destined to supplant her desire for the penis with a wish to receive a child from her father. For the boy, the fear of castration actually signifies the closure of the Oedipal stage, with the process of identification with the father (Freud, 1924). The son's fear of castration is proof of the fact that he is not castrated. The fear therefore represents the subject's anxiety about losing himself and regressing to a state of inseparability from the mother (Friedman, 2013). Freud's attempts to distinguish between the divergent implications of the castration complex for boys and girls led him to formulate a theory that at once constructs and simultaneously glorifies the development of the male superego and produces a deficient female superego.

The critique of the castration concept

The feminist critique of the idea of castration focuses on its phallocentric dimension, which constructs sexual inequality while attempting to explain it. The theoretical models ensuing from this argument plot a developmental trajectory that begins with the experience of gender overinclusiveness and continues with both sexes' inevitable and constitutive recognition of their anatomic "partialness" (which afflicts most of us), the cultural meanings thereof, and the prohibitions it entails. Such writers argued that vaginal sensations play a role in the development of female identity and vis-à-vis penis envy, they have posited "womb envy," an unconscious envy harbored by men and boys of women's ability to conceive, breast-feed, and mother (Horney, 1926; Klein, 1957; cf. Palgi-Hecker, 2005; Rich, 1976).

While proposals in this vein do indeed correct the built-in inequality of Freudian theory, they paradoxically err on the side of essentialism (Chodorow; Mitchell, cited by Palgi-Hecker, 2005), which Freud insisted on avoiding by formulating an asymmetrical model in which motherhood was constructed as a social role more than a biological instinct. Today it is commonly assumed that the recognition of anatomic partiality does not lead to the working through and full acceptance of the loss, but rather results in the splitting of gender-contradicting parts of the self, which continue to exist unconsciously through psychological defense mechanisms (Dimen, 2002; Goldner, 2002; May 1986; Limentani, 2003). Lew Aron (1995) suggested viewing the grandiose phantasy of embodying both sexes as a constructive and positively valued human motivation, which is conducive to psychic multiplicity and creativity. This notion signals a shift from essentialist thinking to the integration of the main tenets of Queer criticism – a shift characteristic of American relational thought of which Aron was one of the most eloquent representatives.

Queer theory points toward more radical questions, whether in respect to the incontrovertibility of the link between anatomy and gender, the stability and coherence of gender, or its naturalness (Harris, 2002). Revisions in this vein speak of processes of gender interpellation by means of which each individual is classified as one of two and only two genders, in keeping with dichotomous social constructions (Dimen, 2002; Goldner, 2002). These interpellation processes are responsible for the child's increasing sense of gender affiliation (Fast, 1999), or if we wish to go even further, following

10 Introduction

Butler (1990), perhaps even produce them as having a gender affiliation, thereby creating a universal "false self" system[4] (Goldner, 2002).

The question of castration and the Oedipal question are bound up together in the same way that the issue of gender and sexuality are. The meanings attributed to sex and the degree of freedom in expressing gender-contradicting parts of the self are closely tied to the question of the child's identification with their parents. This question brings us back to the Oedipal scenario.

The primal scene

The primal scene is an infantile construction of an actual memory or phantasy involving the witnessing of parental intercourse (Freud, 1918). References to its impact on the child's psyche and development are strewn throughout Freud's writings since the moment he shared his thoughts on the matter with Fliess (Freud, 1896, Letter 46, 1897, Letter 61, 1900, 1905, 1908, 1917). According to Freud, every aspect of sexual contact to which the child is exposed – whether the sexual position or the noises the parents make – is seen as "something that the stronger participant is forcibly inflicting on the weaker" (Freud, 1908, p. 220), where Freud assumes that the stronger side is identified with the father and the weaker side with the mother. Freud (1908) believed that "the sadistic view of coition" is at least partially an appropriate characterization of the reality of many couples' married lives. The role distribution that Freud describes, which identifies aggression and sexual drive with the father and helplessness and lack of desire with the mother, reflects a split that was prevalent in Western society during Freud's time, and perpetuates it.

Some of Freud's other formulations (1905, with an addendum from 1915; 1908) suggest that the child interprets the accidently witnessed scenes of their parents' intercourse in accordance with their own drives. Yet, since Freud's thought concentrates on the ages of three to five, he mostly relates to anal and phallic drives. According to his argument, children's sexual exploration is instigated by the tantalizing conundrum "Where do babies come from?" – recognizable in an inverted form in the riddle of the Sphinx

4 For Winnicott's concept of the false self, see Winnicott (1960), Berman (2009).

in *Oedipus Rex* – (1905a, with an addendum from 1915); however, at this stage, they do not understand that the answer lies in parental coitus. Instead, they interpret intercourse as a violent act, while the mystery of birth is answered through anal phantasies of fecal offspring.

Freud never included the primal scene as part of the Oedipus complex itself. It was Klein who connected these two notions and gave a central place to the primal scene in what she and her followers would call "the Oedipal situation" (Klein, 1945; Britton, 1998). Kleinian theory assumes an a-priori, innate knowledge of parental coitus and its potential to result in fertilization; this is interpreted in oral, anal, and genital terms, corresponding to the child's developmental stage, arousing a fierce yearning for sexual union with the parent alongside jealousy and tremendous anxiety (Durban, 2002). As in Freudian theory, Kleinian theory assumes that parental coitus is likely to be interpreted through the prism of childish sadistic phantasies and to be imagined as a frightening and dangerous event, in which one of the parents appears as the victim of a cruel act; however, it does not a-priori identify the role of the aggressor with the man and the role of victim with the woman, but rather assumes that both formations exist, as reflections of both the positive and negative Oedipal situation (Klein, 1945).

The earliest version of the primal scene, according to Klein, is a phantasy about a combined parental figure. It is an image of the parents engaged in violent intercourse, with their sexual organs entangled inseparably. Klein relates this image to the recognition of separateness and the frustration and jealousy entailed in the exclusion from the parental relationship, while the intensity of the aggression attributed to the intercourse reflects the intensity of the child's jealousy. In normal development, this image will eventually be supplanted by a more realistic perception of the parents as separate and whole figures who maintain a positive relationship. However, when jealousy is overwhelming, the child's feelings of ignorance in the face of the mysteries of the parents' sexuality may result in inhibition of the epistemophilic drive; in other words, to a damaging of curiosity (Klein, 1952, 1923, 1929). This idea was developed by Klein's disciples into a theory that describes thinking and creativity as developmental achievements that are based on the internalization of parental coitus (Bion, 1962; Segal, 2001; Birksted-Breen, 1996; Meltzer, 1973).

Kleinian theory provides rich insight into the interrelationship between sexual phantasies, the feelings of envy and jealousy they entail, and the development of thinking and creativity. Nevertheless, two aspects of the theory present a substantial challenge to understanding the reality of same-sex families. The first aspect relates to the theory's assumption of the existence of innate preconceptions concerning the complementary relations between sexes. The second aspect stems from the subsuming of the primal scene phantasy within the Oedipus complex, which, as explained, were understood in the context of Freudian thought as two separate phantasmatic configurations – albeit interrelated ones. These two aspects together encourage the assumption that the Oedipal situation is concerned with the two partners in the act of fertilization. Such an assumption – in the context of the same-sex family, or any other family situation in which children were conceived by gamete donation – necessarily entails the identification of the genetic parent and the sperm or egg donor as participants in the child's Oedipal phantasy.

Corbett (2009) critiques psychoanalytic approaches to the primal scene in which the representation of heterosexual parental coition is accorded the status of reality testing in regard to sexual reproduction. He correctly argues that the contemporary reality is open to diversity, since the creation of a child no longer requires heterosexual intercourse between a man and a woman; he consequently proposes a distinction between phantasies of parental sexual union and conception phantasies.

The family romance

Another infantile construction that Freud identified, although not included in the cluster of primal phantasies, is "the family romance."[5] Because of its close association with the Oedipus complex and its importance for children born via gamete donation, it will serve as an important theoretical layer throughout the chapters of this book.

At the center of the family romance, which Freud first mentioned in a letter to Fliess (Freud, June 20, 1898) and later elaborated into a comprehensive treatise (Freud, 1909), is the child's belief that he was not born to his

---

5 In a note that Freud added in 1920 to his paper "Three essays on the theory of sexualitym," he includes the family romance alongside the primal scene, the seduction phantasy, and the threat of castration, as one of the most prominent phantasies in the psychic life of the individual which are not dependent on personal experience. In this context, Freud also mentions phantasies related to incubation in the womb.

Introduction   13

actual parents. This idea is rooted in the child's need to invent an alternative family for themselves. Freud associates this need with the developmental task of freeing oneself from the shackles of parental authority – a desired development, albeit not a painless one, since from the perspective of a small child:

> his parents are at first the only authority and the source of all belief. The child's most intense and most momentous wish during these early years is to be like his parents (that is, the parent of his own sex) and to be big like his father and mother. But as intellectual growth increases, the child cannot help discovering by degrees the category to which his parents belong. He gets to know other parents and compares them with his own, and so acquires the right to doubt the incomparable and unique quality which he had attributed to them. Small events in the child's life which make him feel dissatisfied afford him provocation for beginning to criticize his parents, and for using, in order to support his critical attitude, the knowledge which he has acquired that other parents are in some respects preferable to them.
>
> (1909, p. 237)

The child's strongest wish during his early years is to be similar to his parents (to the parent of the same sex, Freud adds) and to be as "big" as they are. Over the years, the child starts to gain familiarity with the social categories to which his parents belong, to compare them to other parents, and to cast doubt on the uniqueness that he had attributed to them. Minor events in the child's life, which are a cause of dissatisfaction, prompt him to begin criticizing his parents. Thus, for instance, a child's acquaintance with a person of a higher social status may instigate envy that will receive expression in a phantasy of one's parents being replaced by upper-class substitutes. Children of gay and lesbian parents become aware at an early age of the social category that is applied to their family as a minority group that deviates from the hegemonic model, because of its greater visibility compared to other social categorizations, such as education level or socioeconomic class – this issue is likely therefore to feed into their family romance phantasies.

According to Freud, this emotional ferment begins at a stage where the child does not yet have an understanding of sexual reproduction. When the child becomes aware of the differences between his parents' sexual functions, and the fact that fatherhood is always uncertain whereas mother-hood is relatively certain, the family romance focuses on the father alone, while the maternal origin ceases to be a source of doubt. The revenge motif, which receded into the background at an earlier phase, now moves to the front of the stage.

The study of neurotics, Freud argued, shows that the intense sexual rivalry, i.e., the Oedipal situation, is among the factors that contribute to the consolidation of the family romance. It is a psychological experience of feeling slighted by the fact that the child does not enjoy the parent's exclusive love but is obliged to share it with a sexual rival, as well as with his siblings. These feelings find an outlet in the infantile idea – which can be consciously reconstructed at a later age – of being either a stepchild or an adopted child. Usually, Freud remarks, one finds evidence of the impact of the biological sex: the boy tends to develop more hostile feelings toward the father than toward his mother, and a more intense passion to free him-self of the father's emotional hold. Any other issue that arises and requires the child to contend with it, Freud stresses, will influence the formation of the family romance constructed by the child, because it is a broad and suf-ficiently flexible phantasmatic system. Thus, for example, the child might "get rid" of one of his sisters, if he experiences a threatening sexual attrac-tion toward her.

Freud entreats us not to be alarmed by these phantasies, and by their manifest hostility. The child's ingratitude and faithlessness are only at face level; in fact, under a thin veil, these phantasies preserve the child's original affection toward his parents. If we examine these phantasies in-depth, we will see that the substitute parents are equipped with attributes that the child has derived from his relationship with his actual parents. The psychological effort to replace his actual parents with "grander" parents is no more than an expression of the child's longing and yearning for the times in which his father appeared to him as the strongest and most decent of men, and his mother seemed the dearest and most enchanting of women.

Since the appearance of Freud's work, the family romance has been widely studied and today is considered one of the normative psychological processes of childhood. It is recognized as a process that helps the child maintain narcissistic equilibrium and cope with an entire spectrum of con-flictual feelings toward their parents.

The contemporary analytic literature focuses on the way in which adopted children, or children conceived through gamete donation, use the family romance in order to work through questions of identity and belonging (Corbett, 2009; Ehrensaft, 2007, 2008). Among these children, the representation of the unknown genetic origin merges with the phantasmatic representation of the alternative parent who becomes the object of the child's innermost wishes. In this way, the family romance not only serves as a release from parental authority, as previously mentioned, but also plays a central role in working through a real experience of loss, or of curiosity about origins and genetic heritage.

In an article dealing with the family romance that underlies adopted children's search for their biological parents, Lyle Warner (1993) offers a reading of George Eliot's novel *Daniel Deronda* (1876), which follows the journey of a young man adopted by an English nobleman in search of his identity, who discovers his Jewish roots as he approaches adulthood. Warner's reading of Eliot's novel emphasizes the adopted child's need for integration between his real and phantasized relationships in relation to both sets of parents. Warner argues that the actual presence of alternative parents may impede the willingness to relinquish the grandiose element that characterizes the childish family romance and delay the resolution of conflict regarding the adoptive parents, which under normal circumstances is expected to take place during adolescence. The encounter with the biological parent, according to Warner, provides an opportunity for disillusionment and reconciliation with the adoptive parents. In Chapter Eight, I will describe the grandiosity that informs the representation of "birth others" (i.e., the gamete donor and the surrogate) when the opportunity for disillusionment by means of actual acquaintance is absent. Thus, the child in a family that has been assisted by a gamete donation is likely to develop a phantasy about the fabulous donor who will appear one day to claim their parental rights and endow the child with wealth or fame (Ehrensaft, 2007).

Noelle Oxenhandler (2001) points to the motif of children who are not raised by their own parents as reflected in numerous myths and fairy tales (Joseph, Moses, and Oedipus, who occupied Freud's thinking, were such children). She suggests that the family romance has an additional role, enabling the working through of realistic phenomena such as kidnappings or putting children up for adoption. From here, Oxenhandler shifts into a discussion of parents' universal anxiety that their child might be kidnapped. She relates this anxiety to the parents' intense bonding with their child, which is accompanied by guilt over their inevitable parental failures and by the awareness that one day the child will grow up and leave home. These

16 Introduction

inherent feelings of guilt and anxiety are projected onto an "other," to whom the malicious intent of kidnapping a child is imputed.

Ehrensaft (2007) argues, following Oxenhandler, that for parents who were assisted by a sperm or egg donation, the donor easily becomes the "other" onto whom such feelings are projected. The fact that this same other shares genetic material with the child only exacerbates the anxiety. It is immeasurably intensified, according to Ehrensaft, when the birth other is an individual known to the child, who has a close relationship with him or her – i.e., in the case of a non-anonymous donation.

Ehrensaft stresses that the family romance phantasy, despite all its unsettling potential, is based on a safe attachment to the parents. She adds that without this anchor, the space permitting emotional exploration outside the boundaries of the family and thus also for the construction of a family romance, is likely to collapse.

Same-sex families – research trends

Beginning in the 1970s, a growing corpus of meaningful empirical knowledge about same-sex parenting and its implications has been amassed. The first of three central research waves began in the 1970s and increased in momentum in the 1980s. These studies examined lesbian women whose children were born in the context of heterosexual relationships, a fact that made it difficult to isolate and distinguish the unique circumstances of same-sex parenting from the influences of the heterosexual family of origin, on one hand, and from the impacts of dismantling the original family unit, the parents' separation, and their coming out at a later stage in life, on the other.

The gayby boom phenomenon – a sharp increase in the number of planned births by same-sex parents – which has emerged in the 21st century following legislative processes related to LGBT rights, has led to the consolidation of the second wave. This wave did not just examine planned same-sex parenting but was characterized by an effort to include more diverse populations: participants were recruited from across the entire LGBT spectrum[6]

---

6 The 21st century has ushered in the first pregnancies of transgender men. Transgender parenting has been receiving increasing research recognition, but transgender people are still the smallest and most discriminated against group within the LGBT community, a fact also reflected in their representation in the research.

Introduction   17

and from a broad socio-economic spectrum as well[7] – as part of a more rigorous approach to ensuring empirical validity of research designs (Patterson, 2006; Biblarz & Stacey, 2010).

The first two research waves focused on examining the level of parental functioning and child development, using heterosexual families as a comparison group (Clarke, 2002; Johnson, 2012). It seems that the timely need, with the acceptance of new families as part of the social landscape, was to prove that "the kids are all right" and that same-sex families are not essentially different from heterosexual ones, among other things because of a realistic fear of compromising parental rights regarding custody, access to reproductive technology, and adoption (Clarke, 2002; Stacey & Biblarz, 2001). Gradually, critiques started to be voiced against this defensive research position, which aims to obscure differences as much as possible, especially in regard to findings relating to the gender and sexual development of children. It was argued that not only was there no satisfactory theoretical explanation for the similar rates of homosexuality among the children of same-sex parents and those of heterosexuals, but that the very need to prove that same-sex parenting does not influence the formation of identity and sexual orientation of the child is based on implicit heterosexist assumptions (Patterson, 2009; Stacey & Biblarz, 2001), the perpetuation of which may be damaging to same-sex parents and their children.

As of the writing of this chapter, the greater the increase in the social acceptance of same-sex families, the more we are able to witness a movement toward a third wave of research – which focuses on the unique challenges faced by these families and which strives to understand and accept the differences from an internal point of view, instead of through comparison with heteronormative families (Johnson, 2012). The difference is not merely methodological, but rather a shift toward a research approach that emphasizes a pluralistic gaze toward diversity rather than hierarchical judgment.

---

7 It should be noted that, due to social and institutional discrimination, access to various paths toward parenthood is still easier for middle- to upper-class urban, educated same-sex families, certainly when it comes to male couples who turn to surrogacy – a very costly process. This state of affairs is also well reflected in the representation of various research populations today, despite efforts to increase diversity.

Findings

There is a broad research consensus demonstrating that children of lesbian mothers develop at least as well as children in heterosexual families (Field, 2002; Bos et al., 2004; Stacey & Biblarz, 2001; Patterson, 2009). These findings, based mostly on a white and educated population, have also been replicated in studies in which parents did not have a college education, and in a study in which around a third of the children were defined as "non-white" (Potter, 2012; Bos et al., 2016; Wainright et al., 2004).

Lesbian parenting was found to be more advantageous than heterosexual parenting in respect to the following indicators: availability, problem-solving, respect for the child's autonomy, the quality of parent-child interaction, joint activities, and expressions of warmth and affection (Bos et al., 2007; Brewaeys et al., 1997; Flaks et al., 1995; Golombok et al., 1997; MacCallum & Golombok, 2004). Respectively, children of lesbian mothers received higher scores in the following areas: secure attachment (Golombok et al., 1997; Golombok et al., 2003), perception of the parents as available and reliable (MacCallum & Golombok, 2004), and the ability to discuss emotional issues, including issues related to sexual development (Vanfraussen et al., 2003). Nonetheless, in a study of children's coping with the fact of having been born through donor insemination, most children reported that they never shared with their mothers their thoughts about the sperm donor who was involved in their conception (Vanfraussen et al., 2001). This gap points to the way in which quantitative studies that present isolated findings may miss the larger picture and its complexities.

Few studies isolated planned parenting by gay fathers who were assisted by egg donation and surrogate pregnancy. The existing findings show that children of gay fathers develop favorably and exhibit emotional wellbeing similar to that of children of lesbian and heterosexual parents (Baiocco et al., 2015; Wainright et al., 2004; Rosenfeld, 2010). Similarly, it was found that children who were adopted by gay couples exhibit the same adjustment capacity as that of children adopted by lesbian or heterosexual parents, and that gay adoptive parents tend toward more cooperation, higher levels of expressions of warmth toward the child, lower levels of disciplinary aggression, and higher degrees of responsiveness than those found among heterosexual adoptive parents (Golombok et al., 2014; Goldberg & Smith, 2013; Erich et al., 2005).

Parenting and gender: challenging the heteronormative order

Studies of same-sex families refute the essentialist assumptions regarding the "naturalness" of feminine motherhood and the division of labor between men and women. A meta-analysis of first wave and second-wave studies does indeed reveal a certain advantage to women in indicators of parenting ability, but also proves that parenting abilities are neither dichotomous nor exclusive. One needs to take into account that ours is the first generation of male "mothering" and that social processes are likely to continue to reduce the gaps between men and women. Either way, the gender of the parent has been found to have a negligible impact on the child's social and psychological adjustment.

Since the role of the main caregiver has been traditionally allocated to the woman, the phenomenon of a male couple raising a child together is perceived as a more severe undermining of gender practices, compared to lesbian parenting, in which women, at least ostensibly, perform according to societal gender expectations (Stacey, 2006). Studies that have examined prejudices about same-sex parenting have found that more negative perceptions are expressed in relation to gay men's parenting than in relation to lesbian parenting (Ioverno et al., 2018).

A qualitative study from Israel suggests that, at the stage of planning a pregnancy, the future social mothers (i.e., the non-genetic mothers) reveal a great deal of gender flexibility and will play with the idea of their being the "father," but this flexibility diminishes after the birth of the child (Corem, 2015). The few studies focusing on gay men's parenting reveal that these parents tend to adopt "feminine" parenting practices when compared to heterosexual fathers (Biblarz & Stacey, 2010). It appears that the hormonal processes and neural pathways in the brain develop in accordance with the parenting role and in correlation to the number of hours invested in childcare, with gay men developing patterns of brain functionality that connect "feminine" and "masculine" parenting roles (Abraham et al., 2014).

Genetic asymmetry and its implications

The same-sex family is characterized by a built-in genetic asymmetry, whereby each child is genetically related to only one of the parents. Among lesbian couples there exists the possibility of raising a child that is biologically related to both mothers, by using the ovum of one of the partners for a pregnancy that will be carried by the other. This possibility requires an invasive medical procedure (IVF) and as of the writing of this chapter is not legally authorized in Israel, unless indicated by reproductive problems. In cases where this situation does occur, the law requires that it be framed in terms of an egg donation or surrogacy, instead of recognizing both partner's maternal status.

A US study that compared lesbian couples with adopted children, couples who were assisted by donor insemination, and couples whose children were biologically related to both mothers, found that the asymmetric model, i.e., the one based on donor insemination, was correlated with increased expressions of envy and power struggles between the mothers (Pelka, 2009).

Studies that focus on the asymmetrical lesbian model show that the birth mother tends to take on greater parental responsibility than her partner (Brewaeys et al., 1997), and to enjoy a greater degree of intimacy with the children (Bos et al., 2007; Wainright et al., 2004). The social mother was indeed found to be more invested and possessed better parenting skills compared to a father in a heterosexual relationship (Brewaeys et al., 1997; Flaks et al., 1995), but at the same time was found to have a greater need to prove her parenting skills in comparison with the biological mother or heterosexual parents (Bos et al., 2004).

Similar findings relating to the feelings of inferiority of the social mother, self-doubts regarding her parental status, jealousy of the relationship between the biological mother and the child, and dependence on the delegation of the parenting role by the biological mother, were also raised by qualitative and auto-ethnographic studies (Livni, 2004; Hartman & Peleg, 2019; A. Ziv, 2020; Corem, 2015; Wojnar & Katzenmeyer, 2014; Paldron, 2014).

How is the stage of early infancy experienced by the social (non-genetic) parent in gay male couples, in which neither of the parents has a bodily "advantage" conferred by carrying a pregnancy? Gay fathers describe the child's genetic affiliation as only having a marginal significance for their parenting experience (Smietana et al., 2014). Similarly, no difference was found in the degree of social and familial support awarded to genetic and non-genetic fathers after the birth (Blake et al., 2017). Nevertheless, many of the gay fathers chose to conceal the identity of the genetic father (Blake et al., 2016) – a finding that suggests the existence of conflict around the child's genetic affiliation.

How do children respond to asymmetrical genetic relations? As Patterson (2017) notes, very little is known to date about the role of genetics in shaping family relationships – this is a topic deserving of broad inquiry.

Issues related to gamete donation

The current state of research does not provide sufficiently reliable information about the long-term emotional impact of the use of gamete donation or surrogacy. Early studies failed to distinguish between children who were told a false story about their origins, children who were informed about their origins at an older age, and children who grew up with trustworthy and complete information about their origins (Agigian, 2004). Since more research has been amassed about heterosexual couples who were assisted by gamete donation, I will present the main findings revealed by these studies.

Studies of heterosexual families assisted by gamete donation

Before the 2000s, most heterosexual couples who were assisted by anonymous gamete donation chose to hide this fact from their environment and from their child. Thus, for example, a European study found that out of 111 heterosexual couples assisted by gamete donation, less than 10% revealed this fact to their child before the age of 18. This rate of concealment stood in stark contrast to the practice of adoptive parents, all of whom, without exception, shared the fact of adoption with their children before the age of seven (Golombok et al., 1996; Golombok et al., 2002; Owen & Golombok, 2009; MacCallum & Keeley, 2012; Gottlieb et al., 2000).

Since 2000, there has been a sharp increase in the proportion of heterosexual parents who choose to disclose to their children that their conception was aided by gamete donation, but they still represent a minority (Blake et al., 2010). Notably, among heterosexual parents who were assisted by an open donation (which allows the child to contact the gamete donor upon reaching adulthood), there was a much higher proportion of disclosure to the child and to the social environment (e.g., in California and in the Netherlands) (Scheib & Rubin, 2003; Brewaeys et al., 2005).

The research literature attests that only between the ages of seven to ten does the child's cognitive understanding mature sufficiently to grasp the full meaning of sperm or egg donation (Blake et al., 2010). Nevertheless, most heterosexual parents who choose to disclose to their child, plant the narrative seeds before the child is four or five, in order to avoid the prospect of having to make a dramatic disclosure at an older age. These narrative seeds consist of age-appropriate stories that usually build on images reflecting the child's world – such as an Easter egg, tadpoles, a "special ingredient," etc. – all of which help spark an initial conversation that will later evolve into more realistic representations (Gottlieb et al., 2000; Hargreaves & Daniels, 2007; Hunter et al., 2000; Lycett et al., 2005; MacDougall et al., 2007; Rumball & Adair, 1999). Some parents wait before introducing the topic until the age of seven or eight when the child's cognitive maturity will presumably allow the child to comprehend the meaning of the donation (MacDougall et al., 2007). Most parents produce some version or another of a "replacement parts" narrative – in which the child is given an explanation about which of the parent's body parts was defunct and required help from a sperm or egg donor, or a doctor. In the procreation narratives, many parents emphasize the child's uniqueness or the experience of their birth as a "miracle."

Disclosing to the child the circumstances of their conception via anonymous gamete donation is described by parents as a sometimes difficult and painful process. Many parents articulate the fear that disclosure will have a negative impact on their child's wellbeing, will lead to the child's rejection of them, or will incite questions to which they may not have suitable answers (Hunter et al., 2000; MacDougall et al., 2007). Despite these reservations, most of the parents report a sense of relief and joy about their choice to disclose to their child (Rumball & Adair, 1999; Lycett et al., 2005; MacDougall et al., 2007).

Adolescents' negative feelings about their conception via gamete donation usually arise in cases of prolonged concealment. Whereas children to whom the news is disclosed only in adolescence frequently report feeling shock and experiencing an identity crisis (Turner & Coyle, 2000), the research shows that disclosure at an early age is associated with adolescents' sense of comfort concerning the circumstances of their birth (Blake et al., 2010; Scheib et al., 2005). Studies that compared disclosure versus concealment reveal that in disclosing families the relations between parents and children tended to be more positive (Lycett et al., 2005) and that, according to school reports, those children tended to have less emotional problems (Casey et al., 2008). These cumulative findings indicate that disclosing to the child the circumstances of their conception via gamete donation as well as the child's age at the time of disclosure are crucial variables determining the degree to which this information will be assimilated as an integral part of their identity and experienced benignly (Rumball & Adair, 1999; Jadva et al., 2009).

Curiosity about the birth other

Research has shown that children in heterosexual families exhibit less of a desire to meet the sperm donor compared to children of lesbian and single mothers (Jadva et al., 2010; Freeman et al., 2009). Another study indicates that the presence of two parents reduces the probability that a child will want to meet the donor; in other words, children of single mothers are more likely to search for the donor than are children of lesbian or heterosexual parents (Scheib et al., 2005). Do these differences indeed reflect a descending scale of intensity of the child's need, suggesting that children of single mothers experience the most significant lack of a second parent figure, children of lesbian mothers are more likely to exhibit curiosity about a male parent figure, whereas for children in heterosexual families, the lack is nothing more than barred access to one's genealogical heritage? Or do these differences rather reflect varying degrees of parents' vulnerability in relation to wishes expressed by the child?

Research reveals a gap between the degree of curiosity that children of lesbians evince about the anonymous sperm donor and the degree of curiosity that the mothers themselves feel. This gap may reflect defensive patterns in parents' attitudes toward the donation, as I shall suggest in Chapter Nine. The mothers' minimizing of curiosity may explain the difficulty that most children have sharing phantasies and thoughts about the sperm donor with them.

In addition, it was found that many more sons of lesbian mothers expressed a longing to meet the donor compared to daughters of lesbian mothers (Bos & Gartrell, 2010; Vanfraussen et al., 2003). In Chapter Eight, I inquire whether the daughters of gay fathers are more preoccupied than their brothers with the question of female biological origin – in other words, does this finding reflect a wish for gender identification?

A US longitudinal study (NLLFS) did not find differences between the psychological adjustment of offspring of anonymous sperm donation versus

24 Introduction

those of known sperm donors, in which the donor fulfills some role in the child's life (Bos & Gartrell, 2010). The implication is that even when the offspring of an anonymous gamete donation express curiosity or longing to meet the donor, this does not reflect a developmental deficit, but rather a heartfelt wish. In other words, it is not so much a need for an actual parent figure of the opposite sex in their lives, as much as it is a need for empathetic acceptance on the part of the parents of the child's wishful desires and longings.

Surrogacy

As opposed to heterosexual parents' high proportion of concealment of the involvement of a gamete donor in their child's conception, nearly all heterosexual parents assisted by surrogacy chose to share this fact with their children from a very young age (Jadva et al., 2012; Blake et al., 2014). This openness toward surrogacy is not surprising when one considers the necessity of explaining to one's social surroundings the arrival of a child in the absence of a pregnancy. This explanation is validated by the findings of a British study of heterosexual parents who used traditional surrogacy (a process in which the surrogate is also the egg donor). The study found that by the time children were ten years old, 58% of the parents had disclosed to their children that they had been carried by a surrogate, yet did not mention the fact that it was the surrogate's egg used in the fertilization process (Jadva et al., 2012).

Gay fathers' attitudes to the surrogate and donor

The aforementioned reasoning also explains why gay fathers exhibit remarkable openness in regard to every aspect of surrogacy, but not in regard to egg donation. Whereas most fathers disclosed to their children at an early age that their birth was assisted by surrogacy, very few fathers created a seed narrative that referred to the egg donor or the identity of the genetic father (Blake et al., 2016). This is markedly different from the behavior of lesbian mothers who tended to incorporate the identity of the biological mother and the use of donor insemination in the narrative presented to the child from a young age (Freeman et al., 2009).

Studies from Spain, Italy, and the US that examined the relationship between gay fathers and the surrogates who helped them have children, found that, in most cases, they kept up a positive, long-lasting connection, consisting mainly of the exchange of emails and photos of holidays and birthdays. The only cases in which the connection came to a complete end after the birth were documented for surrogates of Asian origin, where barriers of language, culture, and socio-economic class, as well as the policies of the intervening agency, created obstacles to staying in touch. On the other hand, studies found that most fathers do not stay in touch with egg donors (Ziv & Freund-Eschar, 2014; Blake et al., 2016).

A comparison between the rates of concealment of genetic affiliation among heterosexual, gay, and lesbian couples who were assisted by gamete donation suggests that the more the circumstances permit concealment, the greater the probability that concealment will occur. Thus, the various formations do not differ in the degree to which parents experience difficulty around their need for gamete donation, or around the fact that one of the parents is not genetically related to the child, as much as they differ in the degree to which these factors can be concealed or obscured in practice.

Impact of the social climate

The pluralization that characterized the third wave of research led to an increased interest in environmental factors, such as the social climate of the neighborhood, and the degree of social support awarded to the family. Thus, for example, studies found that gays and lesbians who described their residential environment as "gay friendly" exhibited better emotional adjustment in the transition to parenthood (Goldberg & Smith, 2011; Oswald & Holman, 2013; Lick et al., 2012). Likewise, children of lesbians in the Netherlands, known for its liberal social policies, were more likely to share their mothers' sexual orientation with their peers and reported encountering fewer expressions of discrimination or prejudice toward their families than did children of lesbians in the US (Bos et al., 2008). These findings point to a close correlation between social climate and the emotional wellbeing of same-sex parents and their children, and thus underscore even more powerfully the importance of affirmative research on same-sex families. But no less so, following the lead of Corbett (2009), they highlight the need for parental mediation around issues of familial difference, as well as a need for a space in which family members can share with each other the phantasies and feelings related to these issues.

We are thus presented with two isolated fields of discourse that can benefit significantly from a cross-fertilization of ideas. Psychoanalytic thinking opens a window to an essential understanding of the role of unconscious phantasies in human experience and in family relations, but it is not responsive enough to the pace of social change. Among other reasons, this is because proposals for theoretical revision are not sufficiently anchored in contemporary family realities. On the other hand, the psychological research literature presents statistical data that lack theoretical anchoring or meaningful interpretative schemes. It would seem that the first and second waves of research focused on comparing same-sex families to heterosexual ones, tracing major differences in a wide variety of developmental and functional indicators, and mostly succeeded in showing that no meaningful differences could be found. However important their aspiration of stressing the similarities between same-sex and heterosexual parenting was to facilitating a climate of social acceptance, such studies proved to be a double-edged sword in contributing to the oppressive identification of good parenting with the production of children who conform to heteronormative sex and gender expectations (Levi-Hazan, 2020), as well as in adding to the pressure placed on same-sex parents to exhibit exemplary families (Hartman & Peleg, 2019; Salman-Sagi, 2019; Welsh, 2011). The third research wave, which has been emerging since the 2010s, signals a shift toward the study of conflicts and of the unique experiences of same-sex parents and their children, stemming from close encounters that do not seek to measure the children's achievements or compare them to those of children raised in heterosexual families. This shifting of research goals has led to a blossoming of qualitative studies.

The current book aims, therefore, to build a bridge between two discursive fields – the psychoanalytic and the empirical – and use this bridge to parse the nuances in the subjective experience of children and their same-sex parents, to map conflicts and developmental challenges, and to learn from the families themselves about their coping strategies. It strives to do so from a position of openness to the diversity of human experience, rather than by holding up a single ideal model. Finally, it aims to delve into the dimension of unconscious phantasy, and especially of the internal negotiation in which children engage in their attempt to reconcile their family experience with cultural schemata, as well as explore the role of parental mediation in this process.

Thus, the book offers a body of integrated knowledge of significance to members of same-sex families, mental-health and education professionals, and to anyone who is curious about the elusive ways in which social discourse operates on the individual psyche, or about the interrelations of social forces and unconscious psychological forces in the making of human experience.

References

Abraham, E., Hendler, T., Shapira-Lichter, I., Kanat-Maymon, Y., Zagoory-Sharon, O., & Feldman, R. (2014). Father's brain is sensitive to childcare experiences. *Proceedings of the National Academy of Sciences*, *111*(27), 9792–9797.

Agigian, A. (2004). *Baby steps: How lesbian alternative insemination is changing the world*. Wesleyan University Press.

Aron, L. (1995). The internalized primal scene. *Psychoanalytic Dialogues*, *5*, 195–237.

Aron, L., & Starr, K. (2013). *A psychotherapy for the people: Toward a progressive psychoanalysis*. Routledge.

Baiocco, R., Santamaria, F., Ioverno, S., Fontanesi, L., Baumgartner, B., Laghi, F., & Lingiardi, V. (2015). Lesbian mother families and gay father families in Italy: Family functioning, dyadic satisfaction, and child wellbeing. *Sexuality Research and Social Policy*, *12*(3), 202–212.

Benjamin, J. (1988). *The bonds of love: Psychoanalysis, feminism, and the problem of domination*. Pantheon Books.

Benjamin, J. (1991). Father and daughter: Identification with difference – A contribution to gender heterodoxy. *Psychoanalytic Dialogues*, *1*(3), 277–299.

Benjamin, J. (1996). In defence of gender ambiguity. *Gender and Psychoanalysis*, *1*(1), 27–43.

Berman, E. (2009). Introduction [Hebrew]. In D. W. Winnicott (Ed.), *True self, false self: Essays, 1935–1963* (pp. 199–201). Am-Oved.

Biblarz, T. J., & Stacey, J. (2010). How does the gender of parents matter? *Journal of Marriage and Family*, *72*(1), 3–22.

Bion, W. R. (1962). *Learning from experience*. Karnac Books.

Birksted-Breen, D. (1996). Phallus, penis and mental space. *International Journal of Psychoanalysis*, *77*, 649 657.

Blake, L., Carone, N., Raffanello, E., Slutsky, J., Ehrhardt, A., & Golombok, S. (2017). Gay fathers' motivations for and feelings about surrogacy as a path to parenthood. *Human Reproduction*, *32*(4), 860–867.

Blake, L., Carone, N., Slutsky, J., Raffanello, E., Ehrhardt, A. A., & Golombok, S. (2016). Gay father surrogacy families: Relationships with surrogates and egg donors and parental disclosure of children's origins. *Fertility and Sterility*, *106*(6), 1503–1509.

Blake, L., Casey, P., Readings, J., Jadva, V., & Golombok, S. (2010). "Daddy ran out of tadpoles": How parents tell their children that they are donor conceived, and what their 7-year-olds understand. *Human Reproduction*, *25*(10), 2527–2534.

28 Introduction

Blake, L., Zadeh, S., Statham, H., & Freeman, T. (2014). Families created by assisted reproduction: Children's perspectives. In T. Freeman, S. Graham, F. Ebtehaj, & M. Richards (Eds.), *Relatedness in assisted reproduction: Families, origins and identities* (pp. 251–269). Cambridge University Press.

Bos, H. M. W., & Gartrell, N. K. (2010). Adolescents of the US national longitudinal lesbian family study: The impact of having a known or an unknown donor on the stability of psychological adjustment. *Human Reproduction, 26*(3), 630–637.

Bos, H. M. W., Gartrell, N. K., van Balen, F., Peyser, H., & Sandfort, T. G. M. (2008). Children in planned lesbian families: A cross-cultural comparison between the United States and the Netherlands. *American Journal of Orthopsychiatry, 78*(2), 211–219.

Bos, H. M. W., Knox, J. R., van Rijn-van Gelderen, L., & Gartrell, N. K. (2016). Same-sex and different-sex parent households and child health outcomes: Findings from the national survey of children's health. *Journal of Developmental and Behavioral Pediatrics, 37*(3), 179–187.

Bos, H. M. W., van Balen, F., & Van den Boom, D. C. (2004). Experience of parenthood, couple relationship, social support, and child-rearing goals in planned lesbian mother families. *Journal of Child Psychology and Psychiatry, 45*(4), 755–764.

Bos, H. M. W., van Balen, F., & Van den Boom, D. C. (2007). Child adjustment and parenting in planned lesbian-parent families. *American Journal of Orthopsychiatry, 77*(1), 38–48.

Boyarin, D. (1995). Freud's baby, fliess's maybe: Homophobia, antisemitism, and the invention of oedipus. *GLQ, 2*(1), special issue, Pink Freud, ed. Diana Fuss: 1–33.

Brewaeys, A., de Bruyn, J. K., Louwe, L. A., & Helmerhorst, F. M. (2005). Anonymous or identity-registered sperm donors? A study of Dutch recipients' choices. *Human Reproduction, 20*(3), 820–824.

Brewaeys, A., Ponjaert, I., Van Hall, E. V., & Golombok, S. (1997). Donor insemination: Child development and family functioning in lesbian mother families. *Human Reproduction, 12*(6), 1349–1359.

Britton, R. (1998). *Belief and imagination: Explorations in psychoanalysis.* Routledge.

Bronstein, C. (2001). Melanie Klein: Beginnings. In C. Bronstein (Ed.), *Kleinian theory: A contemporary perspective* (pp. 1–16). Whurr Series in Psychoanalysis.

Butler, J. (1990). *Gender trouble: Feminism and the subversion of identity.* Routledge.

Butler, J. (1995). Melancholy gender – refused identification. *Psychoanalytic Dialogues, 5,* 165–180.

Casey, P., Readings, J., Blake, L., Jadva, V., & Golombok, S. (2008, July). Child development and parent-child relationships in surrogacy, egg donation and donor insemination families at age 7. Paper presented at *the 24th annual meeting of the European society of human reproduction and embryology (ESHRE)*, Barcelona, Spain.

Chodorow, N. (1978). *The reproduction of mothering: Psychoanalysis and the sociology of gender*. University of California Press.

Clarke, V. (2002). Sameness and difference in research on lesbian parenting. *Journal of Community & Applied Social Psychology, 12*(3), 210–222.

Corbett, K. (2009). Nontraditional family reverie: Masculinity unfolds. In *Boyhoods: Rethinking masculinities*. Yale University Press.

Corem, O. (2015). *"Mama – heart, mama – belly": Maternal identity of Israeli raising (non-biological) lesbian mothers* [Hebrew] [PhD dissertation, The Hebrew University of Jerusalem].

Davies, J. M. (2015). From Oedipus complex to Oedipal complexity: Reconfiguring (pardon the expression) the negative Oedipus complex and the disowned erotics of disowned sexualities. *Psychoanalytic Dialogues, 25*(3), 265–283.

Dimen, M. (2002). Deconstructing difference: Gender, splitting, and transitional space. In M. Dimen & V. Goldner (Eds.), *Gender in psychoanalytic space: Between clinic and culture* (pp. 21–40). Other Press.

Durban, S. (2002). On love, hatred and anxiety – An introduction to Kleinian thinking [Hebrew]. In *Melanie Klein: Selected writings* (pp. 7–35). Bookworm Publishers.

Ehrensaft, D. (2007). The stork didn't bring me, I came from a dish: Psychological experiences of children conceived through assisted reproductive technology. *Journal of Infant, Child, and Adolescent Psychotherapy, 6*(2), 124–140.

Ehrensaft, D. (2008). When baby makes three or four or more. *The Psychoanalytic Study of the Child, 63*(1), 3–23.

Erich, S., Leung, P., & Kindle, P. (2005). A comparative analysis of adoptive family functioning with gay, lesbian, and heterosexual parents and their children. *Journal of GLBT Family Studies, 1*(4), 43–60.

Fast, I. (1999). Aspects of core gender identity. *Psychoanalytic Dialogues, 9*(5), 633–661.

Field, S. S. (2002). Coparent or second-parent adoption by same-sex parents. *Pediatrics, 109*(2), 1193–1193.

Finkelman, H. (2012). *Psychoanalysis and homosexuality: Gay men and their therapeutic experiences* [Hebrew] [M.A. dissertation, The Academic College of Tel Aviv-Yaffo].

Flaks, D. K., Ficher, I., Masterpasqua, F., & Joseph, G. (1995). Lesbians choosing motherhood: A comparative study of lesbian and heterosexual parents and their children. *Developmental Psychology, 31*(1), 105–114.

Freeman, T., Jadva, V., Kramer, W., & Golombok, S. (2009). Gamete donation: Parents' experiences of searching for their child's donor siblings and donor. *Human Reproduction, 24*, 505–516.

Freud, S. (1896). Letter 46 from extracts from the Fliess Papers. In *The standard edition of the complete psychological works of Sigmund Freud, Volume I (1886–1899): Pre-psycho-analytic publications and Unpublished Drafts* (pp. 229–232).

Freud, S. (1897). Letter 61 from extract from the Fliess Papers. In *The standard edition of the complete psychological works of Sigmund Freud, Volume I*

(1886–1899): Pre-psycho-analytic publications and Unpublished Drafts (pp. 247–248).

Freud, S. (1898). Letter from Freud to Fliess, June 20, 1898. In *The complete letters of Sigmund Freud to Wilhelm Fliess (1887–1904)* (pp. 317–319). The Belknap Press of Harvard University Press.

Freud, S. (1900). The interpretation of dreams. In *The standard edition of the complete psychological works of Sigmund Freud 4* (pp. ix–627). Hogarth Press.

Freud, S. (1905). Three essays on the theory of sexuality. In *The standard edition of the complete psychological works of Sigmund Freud 7* (pp. 123–246). Hogarth Press.

Freud, S. (1908). On the sexual theories of children. In *The standard edition of the complete psychological works of Sigmund Freud 9* (pp. 205–226). Hogarth Press.

Freud, S. (1909). Family romances. In *The standard edition of the complete psychological works of Sigmund Freud 9* (pp. 235–242). Hogarth Press.

Freud, S. (1917). Lecture XXIII the paths to the formation of symptoms. In: Introductory Lectures on Psycho-Analysis. *The standard edition of the complete psychological works of Sigmund Freud 16* (pp. 241–463). Hogarth Press.

Freud, S. (1918). From the history of an infantile neurosis. In *The standard edition of the complete psychological works of Sigmund Freud 17* (pp. 1–124). Hogarth Press.

Freud, S. (1923a). The ego and the id. In *The standard edition of the complete psychological works of Sigmund Freud 19* (pp. 1–66). Hogarth Press.

Freud, S. (1923b). The infantile genital organization (an interpolation into the theory of sexuality). In *The standard edition* of the complete psychological works of Sigmund Freud 19 (pp. 139–146). Hogarth Press.

Freud, S. (1924). The dissolution of the Oedipus complex. In *The standard edition of the complete psychological works of Sigmund Freud 19* (pp. 171–180). Hogarth Press.

Freud, S. (1925). Some psychical consequences of the anatomical distinction between the sexes. In *The standard edition of the complete psychological works of Sigmund Freud 19* (pp. 241–258). Hogarth Press.

Friedman, L. (2013). *In the footsteps of psychoanalysis: A postmodern gendered criticism of Freud.* Bar-Ilan University Press.

Ginsburg, R. (2007). Introduction [Hebrew]. In S. Freud (Ed.), *The interpretation of dreams, 1900* (pp. 11–39). Am-Oved.

Goldberg, A. E., & Smith, J. Z. (2011). Stigma, support, and mental health: Lesbian and gay male couples across the transition to parenthood. *Journal of Counseling Psychology, 58*(1), 139–150.

Goldberg, A. E., & Smith, J. Z. (2013). Predictors of psychological adjustment in early placed adopted children with lesbian, gay, and heterosexual parents. *Journal of Family Psychology, 27*(3), 431–442.

Goldner, V. (2002). Toward a critical relational theory of gender. In M. Dimen & V. Goldner (Eds.), *Gender in psychoanalytic space: Between clinic and culture* (pp. 63–90). Other Press.

Golombok, S., Brewaeys, A., Cook, R., Giavazzi, M. T., Guerra, D., MacCallum, F., & Rust, J. (2002). The European study of assisted reproduction families: The transition to adolescence. *Human Reproduction, 17*(3), 830–840.

Golombok, S., Brewaeys, A., Cook, R., Giavazzi, M. T., Guerra, D., Mantovani, A., & Dexeus, S. (1996). Children: The European study of assisted reproduction families: Family functioning and child development. *Human Reproduction, 11*(10), 2324–2331.

Golombok, S., Mellish, L., Jennings, S., Casey, P., Tasker, F., & Lamb, M. E. (2014). Adoptive gay fathers: Parent – child relationships and children's psychological adjustment. *Child Development, 85*(2), 456–468.

Golombok, S., Perry, B., Burston, A., Murray, C., Mooney-Somers, J., Stevens, M., & Golding, J. (2003). Children with lesbian parents: A community study. *Developmental Psychology, 39*(1), 20–33.

Golombok, S., Tasker, F., & Murray, C. (1997). Children raised in fatherless families from infancy: Family relationships and the socioemotional development of children of lesbian and single heterosexual mothers. *Journal of Child Psychology and Psychiatry, 38*(7), 783–791.

Gottlieb, C., Lalos, O., & Lindblad, F. (2000). Disclosure of donor insemination to the child: The impact of Swedish legislation on couples' attitudes. *Human Reproduction, 15*(9), 2052–2056.

Grotjahn, M. (1951). 'Historical notes: A letter from Freud.': *The American Journal of Psychiatry*, April, 1951, 107, No. 10, pp. 786 and 787. *International Journal of Psychoanalysis, 32*, 331.

Hargreaves, K., & Daniels, K. (2007). Parents dilemmas in sharing donor insemination conception stories with their children. *Children & Society, 21*(6), 420–431.

Harris, A. (2002). Gender as contradiction. In M. Dimen & V. Goldner (Eds.), *Gender in psychoanalytic space: Between clinic and culture* (pp. 91–115). Other Press.

Hartman, T., & Peleg, A. (2019). Minority stress in an improved social environment: Lesbian mothers and the burden of proof. *Journal of GLBT Family Studies, 15*(5), 442–460.

Horney, K. (1926). The flight from womanhood: The masculinity-complex in women, as viewed by men and by women. *International Journal of Psychoanalysis, 7*, 324–339.

Hunter, M., Salter-Ling, N., & Glover, L. (2000). Donor insemination: Telling children about their origins. *Child Psychology and Psychiatry, 5*(4), 157–163.

Ioverno, S., Carone, N., Lingiardi, V., Nardelli, N., Pagone, P., Pistella, J., Salvati, M., & Baiocco, R. (2018). Assessing prejudice toward two-father parenting and two-mother parenting: The beliefs on same-sex parenting scale. *The Journal of Sex Research, 55*(4–5), 654–665.

Jadva, V., Freeman, T., Kramer, W., & Golombok, S. (2010). Experiences of offspring searching for and contacting their donor siblings and donor. *Reproductive Biomedicine Online, 20*(4), 523–532.

Jadva, V., Blake, L., Casey, P., & Golombok, S. (2012). Surrogacy families 10 years on: Relationship with the surrogate, decisions over disclosure and children's understanding of their surrogacy origins. *Human Reproduction*, *27*(10), 3008–3014.

Jadva, V., Freeman, T., Kramer, W., & Golombok, S. (2009). The experiences of adolescents and adults conceived by sperm donation: Comparisons by age of disclosure and family type. *Human Reproduction*, *24*(8), 1909–1919.

Johnson, S. M. (2012). Lesbian mothers and their children: The third wave. *Journal of Lesbian Studies*, *16*(1), 45–53.

Klein, M. (1923). The role of the school in the libidinal development of the child. In *Love, guilt and reparation and other works 1921–1945 (The Writings of Melanie Klein, Volume 1)*. Hogarth Press.

Klein, M. (1929). Personification in the play of children. In *Love, guilt and reparation and other works 1921–1945 (The Writings of Melanie Klein, Volume 1)*. Hogarth Press.

Klein, M. (1945). The Oedipus complex in the light of early anxieties. In *Love, guilt and reparation and other works 1921–1945 (The Writings of Melanie Klein, Volume 1)*. Hogarth Press.

Klein, M. (1952). Some theoretical conclusions regarding the emotional life of the infant. In *Envy and gratitude and other works 1946–1963 (The Writings of Melanie Klein, Volume 3)*. Hogarth Press.

Klein, M. (1957). Envy and gratitude. In *Envy and gratitude and other works 1946–1963 (The Writings of Melanie Klein, Volume 3)*. Hogarth Press.

Laplanche, J., & Pontalis, J. B. (1973). *The language of psycho-analysis* (D. Nicholson-Smith, Trans.). W. W. Norton.

Laur, L. (2011). On performative mothering [Hebrew]. *Hamishpat*, *27*, 411–440.

Levi-Hazan, Y. (2020). "Not confusing the kids": Queer parenthood and the double demand for heteronormativity [Hebrew]. *Mafte'akh*, *15*, 35–44.

Lick, D. J., Tornello, S. L., Riskind, R. G., Schmidt, K. M., & Patterson, C. J. (2012). Social climate for sexual minorities predicts wellbeing among heterosexual offspring of lesbian and gay parents. *Sexuality Research and Social Policy*, *9*(2), 99–112.

Limentani, A. (2003). To the limits of male heterosexuality: The vagina-man. In D. Birksted-Breen (Ed.), *The gender conundrum: Contemporary psychoanalytic perspectives on femininity and masculinity* (pp. 275–286). Routledge.

Livni, T. (2004). *Parenthood on a rocky road: Lesbian motherhood in Israeli society* [Hebrew] [M.A. Dissertation, Haifa University].

Lycett, E., Daniels, K., Curson, R., & Golombok, S. (2005). School-aged children of donor insemination: A study of parents' disclosure patterns. *Human Reproduction*, *20*(3), 810–819.

MacCallum, F., & Golombok, S. (2004). Children raised in fatherless families from infancy: A follow-up of children of lesbian and single heterosexual mothers at early adolescence. *Journal of Child Psychology and Psychiatry*, *45*(8), 1407–1419.

MacCallum, F., & Keeley, S. (2012). Disclosure patterns of embryo donation mothers compared with adoption and IVF. *Reproductive BioMedicine Online*, *24*(7), 745–748.

MacDougall, K., Becker, G., Scheib, J., & Nachtigall, R. (2007). Strategies for disclosure: How parents approach telling their children that they were conceived with donor gametes. *Fertility and Sterility*, *87*, 524–533.

May, R. (1986). Concerning a psychoanalytic view of maleness. *Psychoanalytic Review*, *73*(4), 175–193.

McDougall, J. (1995). *The many faces of Eros: A psychoanalytic exploration of human sexuality*. W W Norton & Co.

Meltzer, D. (1973). *Sexual states of mind*. Clunie.

Ofer, M. (2014, July). "Rumours of the father's death have been greatly exaggerated": Some thoughts on the Oedipal conflict in children conceived through sperm donation [Hebrew]. *A paper presented in the Israel psychoanalytic society conference*.

Oswald, R. F., & Holman, E. G. (2013). Place matters: LGB families in community context. In A. E. Goldberg & K. R. Allen (Eds.), *LGBT-Parent families: Innovations in research and implications for practice* (pp. 193–208). Springer.

Owen, L., & Golombok, S. (2009). Families created by assisted reproduction: Parent – Child relationships in late adolescence. *Journal of Adolescence*, *32*(4), 835–848.

Oxenhandler, N. (2001). *The eros of parenthood: Explorations in light and dark*. St. Martin's Press.

Paldron, M. (2014). *The other mother: An exploration of non-biological lesbian mothers' unique parenting experience* [PhD Dissertation, University of Minnesota].

Palgi-Hecker, A. (2005). *Mother in psychoanalysis: A feminist view* [Hebrew]. Am-Oved.

Patterson, C. J. (2006). Children of lesbian and gay parents. *Current Directions in Psychological Science*, *15*(5), 241–244

Patterson, C. J. (2009). Children of lesbian and gay parents: Psychology, law, and policy. *American Psychologist*, *64*(8), 727–736.

Patterson, C. J. (2017). Parents' sexual orientation and children's development. *Child Development Perspectives*, *11*(1), 45–49.

Pelka, S. (2009). Sharing motherhood: Maternal jealousy among lesbian co-mothers. *Journal of Homosexuality*, *56*(2), 195–217.

Potter, D. (2012). Same-sex parent families and children's academic achievement. *Journal of Marriage and Family*, *74*(3), 556–571.

Rich, A. C. (1976). *Of woman born: Motherhood as experience and institution*. Norton.

Rosenblum, D. (2012). Unsex mothering: Toward a new culture of parenting. *Harvard Journal of Law & Gender*, *35*, 57–116.

Rosenblum, D., Ben-Asher, N., Case, M. A., & Emens, E. (2010). Pregnant man: A conversation. *Yale Journal of Law & Feminism*, *22*, 207–278.

Rosenfeld, M. J. (2010). Nontraditional families and childhood progress through school. *Demography*, *47*(3), 755–775.

Rumball, A., & Adair, V. (1999). Telling the story: Parents' scripts for donor offspring. *Human Reproduction*, *14*(5), 1392–1399.

Salman-Sagi, O. (2019, July). "Daddy is not mommy": Israeli gay fathers cope with a society which sanctifies motherhood [PhD dissertation, Tel-Aviv University].

Scheib, J. E., Riordan, M., & Rubin, S. (2005). Adolescents with open-identity sperm donors: Reports from 12–17 year olds. *Human Reproduction, 20*(1), 239–252.

Scheib, J. E., & Rubin, S. (2003). Choosing identity-release sperm donors: The parents' perspective 13–18 years later. *Human Reproduction, 18*(5), 1115–1127.

Segal, H. (2001). Symbolization. In C. Bronstein (Ed.), *Kleinian theory: A contemporary perspective* (pp. 157–164). Whurr.

Shenkman, G. (2016). Classic psychoanalysis and male same-sex parents: A reexamination of basic concepts. *Psychoanalytic Psychology, 33*(4), 585–598.

Smietana, M., Jennings, S., Herbrand, C., & Golombok, S. (2014). Family relationships in gay father families with young children in Belgium, Spain and the United Kingdom. In T. Freeman, S. Graham, F. Ebtehaj, & M. Richards (Eds.), *Relatedness in assisted reproduction: Families, origins and identities* (pp. 192–211). Cambridge University Press.

Stacey, J. (2006). Gay parenthood and the decline of paternity as we knew it. *Sexualities, 9*(1), 27–55.

Stacey, J., & Biblarz, T. J. (2001). (How) does the sexual orientation of parents matter? *American Sociological Review, 66*, 159–183.

Turner, A. J., & Coyle, A. (2000). What does it mean to be a donor offspring? The identity experiences of adults conceived by donor insemination and the implications for counselling and therapy. *Human Reproduction, 15*(9), 2041–2051.

Vanfraussen, K., Ponjaert-Kristoffersen, I., & Brewaeys, A. (2001). An attempt to reconstruct children's donor concept: A comparison between children's and lesbian parents' attitudes towards donor anonymity. *Human Reproduction, 16*(9), 2019–2025.

Vanfraussen, K., Ponjaert-Kristoffersen, I., & Brewaeys, A. (2003). Family functioning in lesbian families created by donor insemination. *American Journal of Orthopsychiatry, 73*(1), 78–90.

Wainright, J. L., Russell, S. T., & Patterson, C. J. (2004). Psychosocial adjustment, school outcomes, and romantic relationships of adolescents with same-sex parents. *Child Development, 75*(6), 1886–1898.

Warner, L. L. (1993). Family romance fantasy resolution in George Eliot's Daniel Deronda. *The Psychoanalytic Study of the Child, 48*(1), 379–397.

Welsh, M. G. (2011). Growing up in a same-sex parented family: The Adolescent voice of experience. *Journal of GLBT Family Studies, 7*(1–2), 49–71.

Winnicott, D. W. (1960). Ego distortion in terms of true and false self. In *The maturational processes and the facilitating environment* (pp. 140–152). London: Hogarth Press; New York: International Universities Press, 1965.

Wojnar, D. M., & Katzenmeyer, A. (2014). Experiences of preconception, pregnancy, and new motherhood for lesbian nonbiological mothers. *Journal of Obstetric, Gynecologic & Neonatal Nursing, 43*, 50–60.

Ziv, A. (2020). Querying lesbian fatherhood. In H. W. Henriksson & K. Goedecke (Eds.), *Close relations: Critical studies of family and kinship* (pp. 21–36). Springer.

Ziv, I., & Freund-Eschar, Y. (2014). The pregnancy experience of gay couples expecting a child through overseas surrogacy. *The Family Journal, 23*(2), 158–166.

Part I

What does Oedipal development have to do with the parents' sex, anyway?

Chapter one

"I want to marry you, Mommy"

On Oedipal configurations in same-sex families

Upon arrival at the home of the Neuman-Amram family, I noticed a colorful drawing hanging on the front door with a dedication that read: "I love you, Daddy Elijah! – Abigail." Entering inside, I met Joel and Elijah, the parents of three children, Ben (13), Yahli (5), and Abigail (5). Their daughter, the two fathers subsequently reported, had always favored Daddy Elijah, but recently this preference had taken on the air of a romantic courtship.

During our interview, I asked Abigail to draw a picture of a family, any family that came to mind, as long as every family member was engaged in some activity. Abigail produced the following drawing:

Drawing 1 "The princess's family": Abigail's family drawing.
(From left to right: Ricki/the queen; Abigail/the princess; Elijah/the prince; Joel/the king.)

DOI: 10.4324/9781032663333-3

Abigail's drawing depicts the princess's wedding day, in a manner reflecting the egocentric perspective appropriate to childhood: first she drew the princess, placing her in the center of the page where she takes up more than half of the space, her figure richly embellished in graphic detail. In the corresponding narrative of Abigail's invention, the other figures will be assessed in relation to the influence they exert on her.

Once the princess was done, Abigail began to draw the queen to her left. The five-year-old artist stationed the prince, the intended groom to the princess's right, "at her same height," and to the prince's right, she placed the king. Abigail related how the queen was decorating her daughter with flowers to prepare her for her wedding with the prince. But the preparations were brutally interrupted when:

> "The king pounces on the prince, because he loves him so much, but the prince nearly lands on the princess, because of the king." After this incident, the princess shut herself in at home: "She was really hurt!", Abigail explained. As for the king, "He stayed in the desert all day, and they didn't love him anymore, because it was his fault. That's how it is in their family; they never ever forgave him."

Abigail turned to me with a question, as if posing a riddle: "Tell me what she did – the queen."

Me: "Tell you? You mean I should guess?"
Abigail: "Yes!"
Me: "Maybe, hmmm . . . I don't know, maybe you can tell me?"

At this point, Abigail turned her back to me, as if revealing the secret to someone else.

Me: "Oh, you're whispering in secret, and you're not telling me? Do tell me."
Abigail: "Only if you're smart: then you'll know and find out."

After much entreating on my part, Abigail acquiesced to my request and revealed that:

She is really furious – her anger is sky-high! And it's not the princess she's angry at, because it wasn't her fault, it's the king's fault. In the end, she didn't love him at all, nobody loved him. Only he loved himself. Then an unbearably hot rain poured on the desert. God created it. He didn't like the king either, because he had heard all about it.

Abigail rehearsed to me a typical Oedipal tragedy: the princess is about to marry the prince (whom she would later identify as Daddy Elijah), but the person (later to be identified as Daddy Joel) who sabotages the event is the king, who, in his love for Elijah, pounces on him, and causes him to injure Abigail.

In the apperception task, in response to an image intended to stimulate representations of parental coitus (Card 1), Abigail used the term "pounced on" to describe the sexual act:

One puppy pounced on another puppy, and then he realized he was no puppy – he is a wolf!

Card 1 Parental coitus.

Be that as it may, the story clearly indicates that Joel's love for Elijah and his desire to be close to him are a source of pain for Abigail and provoke feelings of hostility and revenge. The story ends with the exile of the king to the desert, where he dies in torment, loved by none, and left only to love himself. Abigail's description resonates with John Steiner's reading

42   What does Oedipal development have to do with the parents' sex, anyway?

of *Oedipus at Colonus*, which portrays Oedipus in exile as barricaded in a defensive organization of self-righteousness and self-love (Steiner, 1993). The punishment fits the crime: Abigail's revenge against Joel, as the one obstructing her from realizing her desire for Elijah, is a death sentence of tormented loneliness, which may reflect Abigail's phantasy that she is being sent to her death so that her parents can sleep together (cf. Britton, 1998).

Abigail's love wishes toward Daddy Elijah and her hostility toward Daddy Joel also came up in overt interaction with her parents. When I suggested to Abigail that she show the drawing to her fathers, she first turned to Elijah:

Abigail: "Daddy, guess what I have behind my back."
Elijah: "A drawing! But what drawing? Wow. Come show me, Abigail. Come tell me what's in the picture."
Abigail: "It's for you!"
Elijah: "Thank you. And who is this here? And who is she?"
Abigail: "That's Ricki, the queen, and this is me, and this is Joel the king, and this is you."
Elijah: "Tell her who Ricki is."
Abigail: "Ricki is a friend of ours."
Elijah: "Correct, she's a friend of ours that you kids spend a lot of time with. Right?"
Abigail: "Right, and I love her a lot. And then he jumped on the prince, and then it really hurt the princess, and the prince too, and then everyone was angry at him . . . give it to me."

Abigail took the drawing and approached Joel.

Abigail: "Daddy, guess what I've got behind my back."
Joel: [in a playful tone] "What is this? What have you got there, a sweater?"
Abigail: "Wrong!"
Joel: "A drawing!"
Abigail: "Yay! You lose! You lose! Elijah didn't lose, he said it was a drawing, and it *is* a drawing. You lost!"
Joel: "Where am I in the picture? Did you draw me?"
Abigail: "I'm not telling! If you guess then I . . ."
Joel: "Please, I'm begging. Show me."
Abigail: "I won't show you, because you're not Elijah!"

Abigail's attitude toward her fathers is sharply polarized: Elijah is presented the drawing as a gift as she summarizes for him the emotional gist of the plot and identifies each of the figures; Joel is approached defiantly, as she relishes his defeat (although presumably aware that he wasn't really mistaken, but was only playing along with her). Finally, Abigail abandons Joel in a state of ignorance and loneliness, excluding him from the experience she has shared with Elijah.

Nonetheless, Joel is not a passive subject in Abigail's psychic drama. Indeed, his curiosity as to how *he* is represented in her drawing – unlike Daddy Elijah's interest in *her* emotional experience – might provide realistic grounds for her characterization of the king's selfishness. In addition, observation of the family interaction elicited several spontaneous expressions of competition and hostility on Joel's part toward Abigail. For instance, when Abigail was showing off her dance abilities to me and ignored him when he called out to her, he proclaimed (in English)[1] with a mixture of admiration and bitterness: "The queen, the queen of the house!"

The term "queen" is likely a double-entendre. "Queen," in the sense of the uncontestable ruler of the household is also gay male argot for a flamboyant homosexual, with perceptible feminine attributes. In both respects, Abigail may be competing with Joel and securing for herself a position that arouses his envy.

Abigail's immersion in Oedipal dynamics appeared to pervade everything. Even in her interaction with me she created – out of thin air – an imaginary "third" with whom she shared a secret, leaving me on the outside with a sense of humiliating ignorance. Thus, by means of enactment, Abigail turned me into an active player in her psychic drama and taught me that she experiences her parents' exclusive relationship as sadistic and brazenly defiant.

The queen's role in Abigail's psychic life

To the princess's left – the side of drawings that represents phantasy (Urban, 1963) – stands the glorified queen at a towering height. To her right, the prince and the king (her actual parents), are huddled together on an area equal to that which the queen occupies alone. They are reduced from their realistic stature to the princess's height, and in the drawing's accompanying narration they are utterly stripped of their power. Just as the princess

---

1 Parents in Israel tend to converse in English when they don't want their children to understand what they are saying.

is depicted in the drawing as turning her back to the king and the prince, following in the queen's footsteps, Abigail turns her back to her actual fathers and attaches herself in phantasy with a female mother figure. This is an encounter with Abigail's conflict of loyalties: between her actual parents and a phantasmatic mother figure, who is later identified by her as Ricki, a family friend.

In his essay "Family Romances" (Freud, 1909), Freud describes a child's tendency to invent alternative parent figures as a common phantasmatic construction in service of the process of their emancipation from the shackles of parental authority. The realistic circumstances encountered by the child – including their gradual apprehension of the social categories to which their parents belong and comparison with other parents, who are in some aspect or another preferable to their own – nourish the phantasy and help the child develop a critical perspective that facilitates the construction of their autonomous identity. A child who grows up in a same-sex family encounters from a very young age their family's difference vis-à-vis the heteronormative social category. This external viewpoint on their family may in some cases nourish the child's phantasy that their parents are replaced by a heterosexual couple, or that one of their parents is replaced by a parent of the opposite sex.

Abigail's rich creation weaves together, as in dreamwork, the common infantile phantasy of being heir to a royal family, Oedipal wishes, and a longing for a female parental figure.

The visual details accentuate the similarities between the princess and the queen: both are depicted in profile, wearing a long gown decorated with flowers (in the narrative, they are described as sharing a passion for flowers), and sporting identical hairstyles. The queen is presented as the person who initiates the princess into the mysteries of womanhood and readies her for her marriage to a man, and finally, as having the power and capacity to judge and punish the king, to avenge her injury on her behalf. Most of the children in this study, as the remainder of this chapter will make clear, did not feel the need to introduce another parental figure of the opposite sex into their family configuration. In fact, one of the more interesting observations that emerged from my encounters with same-sex parents and their children was that Abigail's family circumstances, as a single girl in a family with two fathers and two brothers, may have increased her need for a female identification figure. These circumstances and their consequences, which due to a lacuna in the literature I shall designate as "gender solitary," will be elaborated in Chapter Eight.

It should be emphasized that Abigail does not require a mother figure in order to establish Oedipal relationships; the complete Oedipal drama plays out between her and her two fathers. Indeed, as Freud points out, the Oedipal situation – with its sense of injury and insult stemming from the child's inability to attain the parent's exclusive love and their being obliged to share it with a sexual rival and with their siblings – is one of the contributing factors to the formation of a family romance. It would seem, then, that Abigail's reliance on an imaginary parental figure who is extraneous to the Oedipal triangle helps her maintain a narcissistic equilibrium in the face of the Oedipal turmoil that she experiences. This interpretive angle receives support from the queen's functioning in the story as a narcissistic extension of the princess, who avenges her injury on her behalf and thus exempts her from the burden of guilt toward Daddy Joel.

No less important is the fact that parental environments differ in their degrees of openness and toleration for the child's phantasies regarding an alternative parent figure, or to the child's emotional attachment to real figures outside the nuclear family. In Abigail's case, reality appeared to collapse into phantasy as she presented the drawing to her parents. The liberated transitional space that she had earlier indulged in was reduced due to feelings of guilt and anxiety, and the primary process was replaced by a secondary process. She seemed to avoid sharing her longings for a mother figure with her fathers. A similar process of reality collapsing into phantasy is suggested by the drawing itself, in which the right side of the image – which, as noted, represents reality – collapses toward the left: the king falls onto the prince, who in turn tumbles onto Abigail.[2] Still, her parents exhibit a visible interest in her inner world and allow her the liberty to identify with Ricki, the family friend, whereas Abigail, on her part, does openly share the affection she feels for Ricki, even if she chooses to avoid the loaded word "mother," which she had used freely when meeting with me privately. This suggests that the conflict of loyalties displayed by Abigail, could, under other circumstances, become complicated by feelings of guilt and anxiety and result in inhibition of curiosity and of the ability to play and phantasize. Complications of this kind will be described in Chapter Eight (cf. Vanfraussen et al., 2001; Ehrensaft, 2007, 2008; Corbett, 2009; Ofer, 2014).

---

2 I am indebted to Prof. Geva Shenkman for this insight, and for drawing my attention to the effort children invest in protecting their parents from recognizing a sense of lack.

Abigail's case makes evident the fact that a parent's homosexual desire (in this instance, Elijah attests that he is not attracted to women) does not foreclose romantic infatuation on the part of their daughter. How does one make sense of this fact? Is this evidence of Abigail's heterosexual orientation? Might a gay father unconsciously feel an attraction to his daughter? Do homosexual parents, like heterosexual parents, convey enigmatic messages (Laplanche, 1987), which organize their children's desires in accordance with heteronormative expectations? These possibilities will be discussed in the next chapter.

In addition, Abigail's case makes clear that having same-sex parents does not in any way preclude an Oedipal construction of the relationship. If so, what was the basis for Abigail's choice of Elijah over Joel as an Oedipal object of desire? Do same-sex parents somehow fit into complementary male and female roles, such that the system of gender identifications of each parent, or the parental distribution of roles, might provide alternative grounds, other than biological sex for choosing an Oedipal object?

Heteronormative expectations would likely construe Elijah as the more "paternal" or "masculine" of the two fathers, whereas Joel, according to the same logic, would be expected to be more "feminine" or "maternal," and thus to "naturally" fulfill the role of an Oedipal rival for the daughter. However, in Abigail's family, the fathers manage the household by egalitarian standards and are even business partners. Joel is eight years older than Elijah, and he projects a more authoritative and decisive demeanor so that it is difficult to associate him with maternal stereotypes. In fact, most of the couples I met escaped facile categorization according to traditional binary gender roles. Even if the couple fulfilled certain complementary maternal and paternal roles, for the most part, the distribution of roles did not fall into a consistent pattern across different areas of functioning.

Kath Weston (1991), who studied San Francisco's gay and lesbian community in the 1980s, showed in the context of lesbian parenting that not only did most couples not identify with the complementary "butch" and "femme" roles, but that even among couples who did embrace these identities, there was not a coherent fit between the gender identification of each member of the couple and the division of parenting roles that they had established between them; and, even more surprisingly, their gender identification did not at all dictate the choice of which of the two would serve as the biological mother. In this respect, same-sex parenting manages to produce "Gender trouble" (cf. A. Ziv, 2020; Glassman, 2015). One may wonder to what extent the traditional gender roles are valid even among 21st-century heterosexual couples.

What factors, then, are involved in the choice of an Oedipal love object? And does an Oedipal situation such as that presented by five-year-old Abigail characterize all children growing up in same-sex families?

Classification of the different patterns exhibited by the children I met has led me to identify three distinct Oedipal configurations:

a A full-blown Oedipal configuration (15 children): this is the stereotypical Oedipal pattern commonly presented in the classic psychoanalytic literature as well as in popular culture. In this configuration, one parent serves *continuously* as the object of *romantic* longings while the other parent constitutes a rival to whom expressions of hostility and attempts at exclusion are directed. This group, in which I include Abigail, comprises children who stated explicitly that they wished to marry one of their parents, to have a child with this chosen parent, or to take the place of the rival parent in the conjugal bed.

b A Platonic Oedipal configuration (nine children): In this configuration, one can identify a consistent preference for one of the parents, which is accompanied by attempts to exclude the other parent, but without the apparent involvement of *romantic aspirations*. In some cases, the libido will be directed simultaneously toward a sibling or a friend of the opposite sex; in other cases, it appears that the child's sexuality is articulated mostly in oral or anal terms.

c An alternating Oedipal configuration (three children): This Oedipal configuration organizes the relationship with the parents according to a split between the feelings of longing (whether romantic or Platonic) which are directed toward one parent, and feelings of rivalry and hostility which are directed toward the other parent; however, the figures who occupy each of these roles are *frequently exchanged* according to emerging needs.

Common to these configurations, which I have recognized as Oedipal, is a split-based organization of the relationship with the parents: the child directs warm feelings toward one of the parents and seeks their closeness, whereas the other parent is the target of hostile feelings or rivalry and attempts at exclusion; the parents' "couplehood" provokes jealousy and envy and is thus accompanied by psychological attempts to deny its exclusive nature, and by behavioral efforts to interfere with the couple's union, to separate the parents, or to join them as an equal partner.

In addition to these Oedipal configurations, into which most of the children (27 out of 33) were categorized, I identified two other non-Oedipal configurations:

a An anti-competitive configuration (four children). In this configuration, there are no indications of preference for any one parent. The child behaves as though the two parents are identical or interchangeable and is preoccupied with maintaining balance: protecting the parents from feeling jealous of the child's greater intimacy with the other parent. The parents, on their part, exhibit an effort to neutralize any element of rivalry within the family relations, in a manner that undermines the development of an Oedipal dynamic.

b A multiple configuration (two children). This is an alternate configuration to the Oedipal triangle, based on the children's relationship with more than two parental figures, without a hierarchy or preference among them.

One of the central criticisms of psychoanalytic theory concerns the way in which the theory attributes to each of the parent's pre-ordained psychological functions based on their biological sex. Thus, for example, the mother is expected to be the child's primary attachment figure, to develop a symbiotic relationship with the child, to provide holding and containing, whereas the father is expected to occupy a position outside the mother-child dyad, and from this position to promote separation and independence. In terms derived from Oedipal theory, the father is identified as "the third." Current revisions of the Oedipal theory, which seek to apply it to same-sex families, maintain that we must first free ourselves of the automatic conflation of sex, gender, and parental functions[3] (Shenkman, 2016). How can this be achieved?

There are three central theoretical solutions for coping with the problem: the first is the return to the complete Oedipus complex, which contains an implicit assumption regarding the bisexualism and polymorphism of human love life (McDougall, 1995; Naziri & Feld-Elzon, 2012; Davies, 2015). The second solution is the reduction of the drive element in the Oedipal constellation – while placing at the center of the Oedipal drama, instead of issues of desire and rivalry, a developmental process leading from a dyadic relationship, or a series

---

3 Many theoreticians, including Ferenczi, Winnicott, Lacan, or Britton, spoke about feminine or masculine functions that are not dependent on the sex of the performer, but still failed to eschew essentialist formulations.

of parallel dyadic relationships, to a triangular relationship – a process that is independent of sex or gender (Britton, 1998; Heenen-Wolff, 2014; Heineman, 2004). The third solution is to view the psychic functions derived from the Oedipal model as symbolic ones, and attribute them to parent figures irrespective of biological sex (Laur, 2011); these parental functions may also be embodied by social agents who are extraneous to the family, and by the social discourse itself, such that the triangular formation would be comprised of the relations between the triad of child-parent-law (Glocer-Fiorini, 2018; Godelier [2004] as cited in Naziri & Feld-Elzon, 2012).

Another notion, deriving from Kleinian thought, is that the Oedipal unconscious structure of a child raised by a same-sex couple will refer not to their two parents, but to their genitor and genetrix, i.e., the genetic parent and the birth other (Ofer, 2014).

The validity of these propositions will be examined in light of the findings.

"I want to marry you, Mommy": the full-blown Oedipal configuration

"If a man and woman can get married, as boy and girl, then I want to marry you, Mommy," announced Omer, Esty and Rona's four-and-a-half-year-old son, to his biological mother, Esty. His twin brother, Eran, also woos Esty and proposes marriage often. "Eran kisses a lot, I like that too, he is always kissing me on the mouth, he loves it," Esty observed. "They often feel incredibly embarrassed when Rona and I kiss, they kind of stand there watching and say, 'I want one too'."

Rona: "One time when we were kissing, Eran said, 'I don't know how to kiss like that'."
Esty: "But I think more often it's that when we kiss, they are like: 'What are you doing?!'"
Rona: "They were embarrassed by it."
Esty: "And it seemed as if they want to separate us."

Esty spoke about a love-fest atmosphere in which "Everyone loves everyone" – which had characterized the family in the past. "And now," she explained, "recently, around age four more or less, it kind of bothers them that we're close, us two."

- "I'll be the baby's father, and Mommy will be the mother," declared four-year-old David in reference to the fetus that Ayala – his biological mother and primary caregiver – was carrying in her womb. The mothers, Ayala and Michelle, reported that they had no recollection of similar statements about his one-year-old sister, Hodaya, to whom Michelle had given birth.

- "What do you know, Ron's got a lover!", Ron's friends teased him, witnessing his intense wooing by Libby, his four-and-a-half-year-old daughter. For a year now, Libby has been declaring day and night that she will marry none but Ron. She clings to him at every opportunity, begs to sit on his lap, and to sleep in her parents' bed, between him and Daddy Gabriel.

"It came to a point where she was so obsessive that she was paying a price for clinging to me," Ron recalled. Gabriel added in agreement: "She is also jealous at this very moment that we are sitting with you and not with her."

Libby has a twin sister named Anna. The twins were conceived by egg donation and the pregnancy was carried by a surrogate. Libby was conceived by Ron's sperm, and Anna by Gabriel's. Anna also declares that she will marry Ron but woos him in ways that are more subtle and allusive. For example, Anna chose to present the pictures she drew during the interview as a gift to Ron. In the following, Ron describes the difference between their two daughters; as he spoke, Gabriel nodded quietly with agreement:

Ron: "Libby has a domineering character. If she sees Anna having a 'moment' with me, or with him, then – oh, boy! Anna is more independent, she is less needy of us. We hug her a whole lot and kiss her and all that, but you can give Anna a hug and she'll move away – 'not now.' With Libby, on the other hand," Ron says, "that won't happen. No matter how much . . . she'll always want more, more, more. So this whole falling in love thing was more apparent with her."

The difference between the two did not amount merely to the fact that Libby's style is more extroverted and dramatic compared to Anna's. The unconscious materials revealed upon scrutiny that whereas Anna drifted back and forth from womb-related phantasies and dyadic longings to Oedipal contents, Libby was intensively absorbed in Oedipal issues. For example, in the family drawing task, Anna drew two pictures: in her first drawing, Anna portrayed a princess figure, and to its left side – the area known to represent phantasy – she located a "mother-kangaroo" with a baby in its pouch. Her second drawing presents a character she identified as "the queen of the cats," carrying a baby in its tummy.

"I want to marry you, Mommy" 51

Drawing 2 "A princess who found a kangaroo and they ended up being a family": Anna's first family drawing.

Drawing 3 "The queen of the cats with a baby in her tummy": Anna's second family drawing.

Anna's family drawings evidence a longing for a mother figure and a preoccupation with womb phantasies. In the apperception task, too, most of Anna's responses were concerned with mother-infant relations. It appears that Anna has the ability to recognize her parents' couplehood, but it is a painful recognition that leads her to retreat into dyadic relations. Card 2, for example, in response to the picture of the lionesses and cub (Card 2), an image intended to elicit contents relating to triangular relations within a same-sex family, Anna began by describing three figures, but was quick to drop one of the parental figures and was left with a description of dyadic relations between a mother and baby: "Those are lionesses. There was a baby girl and two mothers who were taking a walk on the road. The baby was run over and then the mother took care of her."

Card 2 Two lionesses and a cub.

Still, Anna also showed an interest in Oedipal matters. She often proposed marriage to Ron, and called him "Daddy," while calling Gabriel "Daddy Gabi," in a manner indicating a hierarchy of closeness. She confessed she had also proposed marriage to one of the boys in her kindergarten.

If Anna appears to drift between the dyadic and Oedipal spheres, Libby's entire being is absorbed by the Oedipal regions. In the family drawing task, Libby drew a queen wearing a crown and veil who is lording it over two hedgehogs. In her own words: "She is their queen and they obey her."

"I want to marry you, Mommy" 53

Drawing 4 "A queen and two hedgehogs": Libby's family drawing.

When Libby showed me her drawing and began to describe the hedgehogs' prickly spines, she said: "They have a . . . like a rooster's comb." Libby's realization alarmed her and she quickly drew hats on the hedgehogs to cover the spines poking out of their heads. To one side of the queen she drew a snake which she claimed was not part of the family, and on the queen's other side she drew "something that the snake made."

Like Abigail, Elijah and Joel's daughter, Libby also positions a royal female figure wearing a veil in the drawing's center. Similarly, this figure is the largest and most graphically elaborate one. But whereas in Abigail's drawing the princess shelters under the power of a phantasmatic mother figure, in Libby's drawing the main figure is a queen who rules imperiously over the two hedgehogs: "She is their queen and they obey her." The pair of hedgehogs are positioned to either side of the queen, and her body seems to separate them, in a mode of "divide and conquer." The dimensions of the two hedgehogs are slight, they have no arms or legs, are more schematically drawn, and yet are distinct from one another. In her words: "One is like a baby and one is like a kid." The drawing of the queen features Libby's own distinguishing mark – her long blond hair – which is the object of great admiration and has never been cut.[4] The veil attests to Libby's preoccupation with romantic phantasies. The presence of the snake, and "what the snake made," indicate phallic sexuality and a preoccupation with the primal scene.

The queen is colored pink, whereas the parts of the drawing that can be identified as phallic representations – the hedgehogs, the snake, and the snake's creation – are green. Just as she alarmingly hemmed in the hedgehogs' spines with an addition of pink hats, she also enclosed in pink the spikes poking out of the queen's crown – a correspondence suggestive of phallic identification. It should be noted that whereas Anna said that when playing "house" she usually chooses to be the baby, and sometimes the mother, Libby declared that she prefers the role of the mother and emitted an embarrassed laugh when mentioning that she sometimes chooses to be the father.

Libby's family drawing reveals her way of coping with the intense jealousy aroused by the exclusivity of a relationship between two others that leaves her out, whether this be her parents' relationship or an intimate moment that one of her parents shares with her sister. The emotional solution offered by the drawing is to deny the legitimacy of the relationship that excludes her and impose separation on the couple to seize the focal position within the triangle. The feeling of helplessness that is inherent to the Oedipal situation is projected onto others so that they are experienced as being under her domination.

A similar solution was proposed by Libby in response to the following picture, which is designed to evoke issues of jealousy, exclusion, and triangular space (Card 3): "Three . . . they're hugging. The father wants the baby and the mother wants the baby."

In this response, the projection mechanism is in full view. The picture clearly shows the parents hugging and kissing, while the baby is trying to squeeze in; but Libby proposes a reversal of roles, in which not only is the parents' relationship not exclusive, but they are also fighting over the offspring, who is the focus of their desire.

---

4 Notably, this is also an identifying feature of the girls' egg donor, from whom – as her parents explain to her – Libby has inherited her hair and her beauty. More will be said about this in Chapter Eight, which discusses the representations of the birth other among children.

"I want to marry you, Mommy" 55

Card 3 A family hug.

Libby's response to Card 4, which is intended to elicit primal scene phantasies, reflects a denial of the parental bed which occupies the majority of the picture frame.

Libby: "A baby's bed, which is nice."
Me: "Is there only a baby's bed here?"
Libby: "And a lamp."

During the parents' interview, Gabriel mentioned Libby's desire to sleep in bed with them every night as well as their engagement in an ongoing struggle over this. This report implies that in reality, too, Libby attempted to block the parental union with her own body and her preceding response to the image similarly suggests that the thought of the parental bed standing apart from the baby's bed arouses unbearable distress. When I asked Libby whether there was anything that Daddy and Daddy liked to do just the two of them alone, she replied: "They like to be alone a little bit. To rest. They fall asleep."

These examples illustrate the point that parents of the same sex can provide the foundation for the development of Oedipal dynamics in children, and that having parents of opposite sexes is not a necessary basis for the formation of a split between a loved and a rival parent. It is therefore tempting to think, as some contemporary theories suggest, that an Oedipal

56   What does Oedipal development have to do with the parents' sex, anyway?

Card 4[5]   The Bedroom.

configuration is an inevitability deriving from the very existence of two parents, regardless of their sex. However, from among the 15 children who exhibited a full-blown Oedipal configuration, 12 were of the opposite sex to their parents, (i.e., boys of lesbian mothers, or girls of gay fathers). One must therefore consider the fate of Oedipus in the case of children whose biological sex is the same as that of their parents – what dynamics are to be expected here? This is the moment to make acquaintance with the two alternative Oedipal configurations.

"Mommy and Mommy, I want to marry a boy": the Platonic Oedipal configuration[5]

When I came to visit four-and-a-half-year-old Nina's family, she was home with her baby brother, Tomer, and their birth mother Tali. An hour later, Inbal,

---

5   Card #5, CAT-A (Children's Apperception Test). © CPS Publishing LLC, All Rights Reserved

the children's social mother, came home from work and joined us. Inbal's three teenage children from a previous heterosexual marriage were staying that day at their father's home as part of their joint custody arrangement.

During their interview, the two mothers described Nina's unmistakable preference for Tali, the birth mother, and attested that she is possessive of Tali and constantly seeking to distance Inbal. Throughout the encounter, Nina displayed a conspicuously different communicational style with each of the mothers: she approached Tali in a childish tone of voice, using cuddly physical contact, whereas any contact with Inbal tended to be more matter-of-fact. Inbal seemed to play the role of the "third," associated with the function of setting boundaries and introducing the reality principle. Now and again Inbal would interrupt the cuddling between Tali and Nina, possibly motivated by unconscious jealousy. For example:

Nina: "Mommmmy."
Tali: "What, dear?"
Nina: "Cuddle!"
Inbal: [sternly] "Nina, dear, you have to go to sleep!"

Nina continued to demand Tali's attention even during the interview I was conducting with the mothers. Tali tried to divide her attention and respond to Nina's pleadings, explaining to her gently that she was in the midst of a conversation. Inbal's approach was quite different:

Inbal: "Nina, you are going to bed. If you don't stop driving us crazy, you're going to bed. Enough!"
Nina: [ignoring Inbal and addressing Tali again] "Cuddle!"

In Nina's family drawing, abounding in graphic and verbal detail, she positioned Mommy Inbal on one page and depicted herself embraced by Mommy Tali on another page, standing next to what she called their "private house."[6]

---

6 Translator's note: The term used by Nina to describe the depicted house, "*bayit prati*" – here translated literally as "private house" – is linguistically ambiguous. In standard usage, *bayit prati* refers simply to a single dwelling house (privately owned, as opposed to a flat in a *bayit meshutaf*, the more prevalent co-owned housing type). However, *bayit prati* can also imply a house that is private. The ambiguity is symbolically significant here, underscoring Nina's desire for exclusivity with her preferred mother.

58 What does Oedipal development have to do with the parents' sex, anyway?

Drawing 5a "Mommy Inbal holding a royal family of birds": Nina's family drawing, first part.

At first, Nina drew Mommy Inbal standing alone in the center of the page. She then added a bird perched on her arm, and then another one beside the first, and then another – "a royal family of birds," as she put it. Next came the addition of more birds, an entire other family on the mother's second arm. The atmosphere in the drawing began to grow uncanny (*unheimlich*). In the background, the mothers joked that Nina was drawing a scene from Hitchcock's *The Birds*. At Inbal's feet, Nina drew a baby snail and a beetle. On her other side, she drew a nectar-filled flower that had wilted, because, as she explained, Nina had picked off its petals and used them for her birthday party decorations. The representations on the page multiplied and it seemed that Nina was having difficulty regulating the flow. In the sky she drew a "Mommy butterfly," fluttering alone, and "a bee with a sting." Only after an organizing intervention on my part, was she able to stem the outpouring. At this point, she realized that she had left no room for the other family members and decided to draw them on a separate page.

On the second page, Nina herself appears, celebrating her birthday. Nina is standing on the birthday girl's chair and Mommy Tali is sitting beside her, hugging her. To the right stands the "private house" of Nina and her mothers. It is decorated with leaves that she had apparently picked from the flower featured in the drawing of Mommy Inbal.

Drawing 5b "Nina, the birthday girl, embraced by Mommy Tali": Nina's family drawing, second part.

If Abigail sentenced Daddy Joel to a desert exile, Nina's need was to exile Mommy Inbal to a separate page, at a remove from her snug dyad with Tali. The page that depicts Mommy Inbal overflows with images that suggest procreation: birds, various insects, and a flower brimming with nectar. The excess of stimuli indicates anxiety, which in light of the procreative contents can be described in terms of castration anxiety. This interpretive direction is supported by Nina's self-blame for the wilted flower – it was she who picked it for her own birthday party. Since the depicted celebration is an intimate one, including only herself and her birth mother, this might indicate that Nina's anxiety concerning Mommy Inbal is related to her guilt over invading the intimate space that Tali and Inbal had shared as a couple prior to her birth, and over her phantasies of Oedipal triumph. Another possible interpretation is that the insects represent Inbal's children from her previous marriage. Either way, the page where Nina drew herself with Mommy Tali is calmer and more organized compared to the page that depicts Inbal; it contains a house with neither door nor windows, perhaps representing the prenatal environment, and a birthday party, which may reflect her preoccupation with the mystery surrounding her birth.

Nina's relationship with her mothers is organized along a split between a tender, containing mother (Tali), who is the object of her longings, and a mother (Inbal) who represents the law and boundaries, and who constitutes a rival for the attentions of her beloved mother. This split accords well with theoretical models such as that of Britton or Lacan, while also illustrating how maternal and paternal parental functions can be performed independently of the sex of the performer (Laur, 2011).

The distinction between the cases of Abigail and Nina rests on the fact that, whereas phantasies of Abigail's union with Daddy Elijah were colored by romantic hues, Nina's preference for Mommy Tali is devoid of such coloring. Parallel to the triangular Platonic dynamic with her mothers, it was apparent that Nina was also invested in romantic phantasies, which, however, were directed toward her male peers:

Me: "Did you ever get married?"
Nina: [visibly excited] "Yes! With Noam Orgad. He's a boy from my kindergarten. I almost wanted to give him a kiss, but they don't like kisses in our kindergarten."

Later in our conversation, Nina mentioned other marriage candidates she was contemplating. Her mothers described her as a "heartbreaker," a girl who enjoys the rivalry of several boys for her affection. In response to my question whether Nina had ever proposed marriage to either of her mothers or spoken of such a possibility, they replied:

Tali: "She has no wedding business with us. None at all."
Inbal: "No. Because she wants to marry a man. That's the principal reason."

One day, recounted Tali and Inbal, when they were all driving together in the car, Nina announced out of the blue, as if seeking their approval: "Mommy and Mommy, I don't think I'm going to want to marry a girl. I think I'll want to marry a boy." It appears that Nina's experimentation with romantic desire, courtship, and betrayal was directed toward boys who were her peers, whereas Oedipal preoccupations surrounding her mothers were painted in non-romantic yet clearly dramatic tones.

The Platonic Oedipal group included nine children, seven of whom were children of lesbian mothers, and two children of gay fathers. More than half of the children in this group exhibited an organization that matched Nina's – a Platonic preference for one of the parents accompanied by romantic longings that were directed toward a relationship with a sibling or a friend. The remainder of the children in this category displayed a clear preference for one of the parents and exhibited feelings of competitiveness, without any accompanying interest in romantic content, or alternatively manifested erotic preoccupations associated with the oral or anal domains.

"It depends on the season": an alternating Oedipal configuration

Besides himself, the family of four-year-old Eithan includes four female figures: his mothers Mali and Rina, and his twin sisters, Lizzie and Lia, who are 12. During my visit to their home, Eithan seemed to be most attached to Mali, whispering secrets into her ear and approaching her in moments of distress, while utterly ignoring Rina. However, according to his two mothers, Eithan is actually involved in an intense alternating courtship of both mothers.

In his family drawing, Eithan chose to depict an "amusement park." He first drew a "red water slide," and to its left a light blue trampoline, which quickly morphed into a figure of a "pig-boy" that made him laugh, and which he eventually identified with his Mommy Mali. Later, Eithan wanted to draw a child sliding down the water slide. At first, he drew the child in red, merging with the color of the slide. Realizing that the child was imperceptible this way, he colored him green and even expressed amusement at his resemblance to a cypress tree. Later, Eithan identified the figure of the cypress-tree-boy as himself. Noticing that the trampoline had become a pig-boy, he asked me to help him draw another trampoline, on which he placed a jumping boy, who soon turned into a girl, who was later identified as Mommy Rina.

62   What does Oedipal development have to do with the parents' sex, anyway?

Drawing 6 "Amusement park": Eithan's family drawing.
(From left to right: a boy jumping on a trampoline/Mommy Rina; a "pig-boy"/Mommy Mali; "cypress-tree-boy"/Eithan; Eithan's sister hiding behind the slide.)

As appropriate for a child growing up with two mothers and two sisters (a case of "gender solitary," see Chapter Eight, pp. 199), Eithan exhibited a preoccupation with the gender of the figures and with the question of whether there was room for a male figure in a family comprised purely of women:

Eithan: "They're all girls. Right?"
Me: "It's whatever family you say. Who is in the family you made up?"
Eithan: "Only girls?"
Me: "Whatever you say, whatever you invent."
Eithan: "Just girls!"

Throughout the task, Eithan expressed anxiety about the possibility of coloring outside the lines and required much soothing on my part in order to carry on drawing. Thus, for example:

Eithan: "What if I go outside the lines by mistake?" [rotating the drawing toward me to ask for my help] "Oy, I went outside by mistake, but maybe it's okay to, a little . . . I went a little bit outside. Does it look nice?"

When asked to make up a story about the family in the picture, Eithan said: "I'm sliding down the slide, Mommy Mali isn't doing anything, she's watching over us. And Mommy Rina is jumping. And we forgot Lia and Lizzie underneath the slide. They're hiding from Mommy Mali."

Eithan went back to the drawing to add the figures of Lia and Lizzie behind the slide, and then relented and wanted to draw another family. He was only appeased after I promised to white out the one figure peeking out from behind the slide; this, it seems, was an expression of his wish to erase his rivals for parental attention.

Eithan chose to depict his family in an amusement park. As the connotations of an amusement park suggest, the levels of arousal associated with his family relationships appear to be high. His choice of a water slide or a trampoline as maternal representations contains a dimension of instability or emotional upheavals, along with a dimension of excitement, enchantment, and enjoyment. The great fluidity characterizing his objects produces a sense of chaos, which in certain moments becomes a source of dread. This was evidenced in the intense anxiety he exhibited around the possibility of "going outside the lines" and his great need for soothing and reassurance on my part. Yet, to no less degree, this fluidity forms the basis for a playful and humorous emotional stance, reflected in a mood of joyful creativity and in the drawing's colorful exuberance. Like in Wonderland, anything can be anything else: a trampoline changes into a pig-boy, which ends up being labeled as "Mommy Mali"; a child merges into a slide to the point of imperceptibility, and then changes color to become a cypress tree; sisters appear and disappear, hide and are erased; a boy changes into a girl, who changes into a mother. Hence in his inner world, a considerable degree of fluidity exists between the sexes as well as between generations.

Despite the grotesque representation of his birth mother, "Mommy Mali," as a "pig-boy," there were also signs of his special connection to her: for instance, the placement of her figure on the page next to his own and near the water slide with which his own figure had been merged before; her passive representation as a kind of "environmental mother" (Winnicott, 1963), who protects both him and Mommy Rina, who is engaged in child-like play; and finally, his reference to her as "Mommy," the term he used in his verbal explanations unqualified by her personal name. The more removed location of Mommy Rina, to Mali's left, places her unconsciously as the mother's partner who has no direct relation to Eithan. But a motif of identification with Mommy Mali is also present: they both enjoy the amusement park rides and engage in playing.

When the two mothers asked Eithan what he had drawn, he declared:

Eithan: "This one is prettier, so it's Mali because she's prettier!" [Cuddling with her.]
Rina: "She's prettier." [Laughs.]
Mali: "Bless your heart!" [Kisses him.]

As noted earlier, according to the mothers' reports, Eithan is engaged in a romantic pursuit of both, alternatingly.

Rina: "He's always doing this to us, this kid . . . sending us hearts."
Mali: "This is how I wake up in the morning, he does this to me." [Demonstrates a caress.]
Me: "Does it ever happen that he says 'I love one of you more than the other'?"
Mali: "It depends on what he needs."
Rina: "It depends on the season, on the reason, and his mood. Often, if he is angry with me, he will go to Mali. But it isn't something consistent. One time it's me, another time, her."

Although Eithan was showing a clear preference for Mali on the day of my visit, it could well be that given a different mood, on a day when his romantic overtures were focused on Rina, or perhaps when angry at Mali, he might have identified the parental figures in an opposite manner or positioned them differently on the page. In any case, the fluidity of the objects and the levels of arousal and excitement manifested in the relations with his parent figures – in which enchantment and dread were both present – give a sense of the type of experience that might attend the organization of relations in an alternating Oedipal configuration marked by romantic overtones.

Besides Eithan, an alternating Oedipal configuration was manifested by two girls whose parents were also lesbian mothers. Whereas in Eithan's case, the possibility of attraction to both mothers was accompanied by high levels of arousal, and the alternation between the mothers as a preferred object appeared motivated by passion and rage, in the girls' case, the alternating pattern seemed to serve as a cover for a preference for one of the mothers, which was accompanied by guilt and attempts at reparation.

In her article on triangulation, Tony Heineman (2004) described three possibilities that are available to the children of lesbian couples. The first possibility is to treat their mothers as a mother and the "other," or the "third." This structure can be identified both among children who displayed a full-blown Oedipal pattern and among children who were classified as displaying a Platonic Oedipal configuration. The distinction between the first two configurations is not structural but is rather related only to the object to which the child's romantic yearnings are oriented.

The second structure that Heinemann described is based on the child's perception of the parental couple as two mothers, as opposed to a clearly designated mother and other. In this case, each of the two mothers must at times accept the role of the "other" – an adult with whom one can identify but who is "not mother," and thus to advance a more autonomous relationship with each of the mothers. Such a structure coincides with the alternating Oedipal configuration. Eithan's case provides a felicitous illustration of Heineman's characterization of a state of affairs in which a child may on one day be enchanted by and act seductively toward one of the mothers while rejecting the other, and the next day reverse their behavior towards them.

The third structure that Heinemann identified is based on the merging or melding of the two parental figures into a single object representation so that the child behaves as if the parents were identical or interchangeable. This state of affairs, in which the child is obliged to either enchant or reject both parents simultaneously, I will define as a *non-Oedipal* dynamic.

Non-Oedipal configuration

Classification of the children's patterns led me to identify two non-Oedipal configurations. The first, which I designate the anti-competitive configuration, will be used to characterize families in which one perceives an attempt on the parents' part to neutralize any element of competitiveness in family relations, in a way that undermines the development of an Oedipal dynamic. The children in these families are engaged in maintaining equilibrium and protecting parents from possible feelings of jealousy. The desire to minimize competition and jealousy also manifested in families that were classified as exhibiting an Oedipal dynamic. But in this case, there is a more comprehensive attempt, which involves denial and an expectation of absolute control of conflictual factors that are uncontrollable.

66 What does Oedipal development have to do with the parents' sex, anyway?

"The moment you neutralize it, it doesn't exist": an anti-competitive configuration

Barak and Niv live with their four-year-old son Dori in the residential expansion quarter of the kibbutz where Barak grew up, and where his parents and sister still live. Both fathers grew up on kibbutzim, but whereas Niv was raised in a communal children's home (where children slept together, away from their parents, a practice that characterized all the kibbutzim until the 1980s), Barak, the younger partner, grew up at home with his parents. The couple was in the midst of a second surrogacy process, planning the birth of a second child.

I spent the afternoon with Dori and his father, Niv. Later, in the evening, his other father, Barak, came home from work and took over from Niv as primary caregiver, while Niv retired to his study. When the activity with Dori ended, I presented him with a prize: a ball that when bounced off the floor, breaks open to reveal a surprise. It is a one-off amusement: once broken, the ball cannot be put back together. After throwing the ball and relishing the moment with Daddy Barak and me, Dori realized that Daddy Niv had missed out on the thrill:

Dori: "I want to show Daddy Niv. I'm going to call him, okay?"
Barak: "No problem, great."
Dori: [running excitedly to the father's study] "Daddy Niv, do you want to see a surprise?"
Niv: "Sure."
Dori: "I need to put it back in, and it will explode."
Barak: "Wait, let's see if we can do a re-run." [Attempts to put the parts back together.]
Niv: [curious] "What is it?"
Dori: "It's a ball that explodes . . . I'll show you in a second! I want to put it back in, I've got to put it back in!"
Niv: "That's what Daddy's trying to do."

There was something poetic about this family moment. Barak labored in vain to restore the ball to its previous state and had a hard time accepting that this was impossible. Dori and Barak's regret was palpable: they had shared an exciting moment in Niv's absence. The two of them tried to rewind time and re-experience the moment that had passed forever, this time with Niv. Barak's efforts to reassemble the smashed pieces is a

"I want to marry you, Mommy" 67

fitting image for the act of magical reparation. It includes an element of denial because even if it had been possible to reconstruct the pieces of the ball, the novelty and excitement of the first experience could not be reclaimed.

During the couple's interview, Niv harked back to this moment and described it as representative of the family dynamic. Thus, when I asked Barak and Niv whether Dori sometimes tries to separate them, the couple responded:

Together: "No, no, no."
Barak: "No. He doesn't have that bit."
Niv. "None of that, he's a good boy. He's *really* a good boy. He has a kind spirit. So, it's just like it was here with the toy, wanting me to come and see, because I hadn't seen it."

Barak and Niv also attempt to neutralize any possible feelings of competitiveness concerning the fact that Dori is related genetically only to one of them. As a matter of fact, Barak and Niv were the only couple among all the research participants who chose not to know their children's genetic affiliation:

Niv : "We are not in the least interested in whose he is. He is not affiliated to me or to Barak. There is no issue of affiliation here."
Me : "Some couples do describe some kind of tension around this."
Niv : "Not for a moment. Were you tense?"
Barak: "No."
Me: "Curious?"
Barak: "No. No."
Me: "And didn't it make a difference for the families?"
Barak. "Of course it did. The curiosity was *theirs*. 'This one was like this as a kid, this one was like that,' there's a kind of competition [laughs] between the families. They're trying to spot the resemblance and figure it out."
Me: "Ah, they don't know?"
Barak: "They don't know, no. We don't know either."
Niv: "We left the matter to the attorney. Only if, God forbid [knocks wood] there is some medical incident, then we can pull it up."
Me: "Wow, that's mind-blowing. So, you simply don't know."
Niv: "Because it isn't interesting."

Barak:	"We created a family in order to be all together, not for 'This is mine, this is yours.' This game does not exist. The moment you neutralize it, it doesn't exist."
Me:	"But in the day-to-day, as you mentioned, the families that compete? Don't you ever have moments where you wonder, is that like me, what he's doing?"
Niv:	"No. We are partners. We are partners in the child-rearing, and we are partners in failures. We are partners in successes. We are partners in everything. What you see here is a structure of two, a couple. A quite strong one. Maybe it will fall apart, and you'll find some hot thing, just kidding . . . it's quite strong indeed. And once again, since we've already discussed it, we exhausted the subject. We've unburdened ourselves, like, we are at peace with it . . . we have no conflict."

Joking about the possibility that a "third" might undo their couple relationship reveals an unconscious fear that an Oedipal romance of one of the parents with Dori might jeopardize the couple's union. It is this fear that presumably leads them to close ranks and maintain a united front. At times, one can even hear echoes of the communal kibbutz ideology in the couple's voice. They seem to employ rationalization and denial to cope with negative feelings and tensions that are inherent to family relations, as though conflicts can be subdued and their impact wiped out through discussion and rational negotiation:

Niv:	"We made a *decision*. That's exactly what our relationship is about. It isn't one person making the decisions. If we disagree, we talk it over and then if we come to an agreement, then that's the agreement. Case in point: deciding to have a child. I didn't have my whole heart in it, no. Barak knows where I stand, but if we come to a decision that this is what's right for our relationship, then at this moment, the 'me' that had been opposed is no longer relevant. Because a decision was made, and that's the joint decision, and the moment we made the decision I'm 100% with that decision. There isn't even the slightest doubt about it."

In what ways did Dori's reaction patterns fit the anti-competitive dynamic exhibited by his parents? First, as suggested by the scene in which Dori called Niv to share the missed experience with him – the observations did not indicate a preference for one of the parents. During the interview, Dori told me that in kindergarten he doesn't play "house" with other children, and when I asked him whether he would like to get married when he grows up, he replied adamantly that he would not. In the apperception task, Dori tended to stick with concrete descriptions of the pictures in the cards and found it difficult to produce stories that involved phantasmatic activity: a plot composed of past-present-future, or the attribution of feelings and thoughts to the figures presented.

Card 5 Tug-of-war.[7]

In response to Card 5, which is supposed to elicit responses related to Oedipal rivalry and competitiveness generally, Dori found it difficult even to produce a concrete description of the depicted event. Dori gazed at the picture as if he were an anthropologist encountering for the first time an exotic practice of which he was unable to make any sense:

Dori: "What is this, what are they doing? I've never seen anything like it."

Unlike his reserved attitude to the apperception test, in the drawing task, Dori seemed to engage freely in the creative activity. Once a playful space was established, enabling him to share his phantasies with me,

---

7 Card #2, CAT-A (Children's Apperception Test) © CPS Publishing LLC, All Rights Reserved.

an internal representation merging the two fathers into a single object emerged. Dori squiggled several indistinct objects, which he described as a "family of tractors" and announced: "I am drawing Daddy and *their* baby." A similar syntactical leap from singular to plural occurred when I asked him: "Who do you think loves you the most in all the world?" He responded:

Dori: "Daddy."
Me: "Which Daddy?"
Dori: "Daddy Barak and Daddy Niv."

Such a merger of two parents into a single figure, the avoidance of competition, and the lack of interest in playing "house," or in age-appropriate romantic experimentation, are recurrent motifs among children classified under the anti-competitive configuration. It may be that these children's sense of freedom to differentiate between their parents, to desire or reject them, or to use them playfully, is constrained by guilt and a need to protect their parents from conflictual feelings they are trying to avoid.

Heineman (2004) points out that if the child feels compelled to treat the two adults as one, then they are doing too much of the psychological work on their own – there is no parent available to help them manage their sexual excitement, their fears of being seduced or their rage at being excluded. However, these aspects of the relations tend to be obscured anyway in an anti-competitive family climate. Despite Heineman's warning, the encounters did not reveal any evidence of emotional distress among children who were classified under the anti-competitive configuration. The inhibitions evidenced were limited to issues of competition, romantic courtship, and curiosity about sexual and romantic contexts, and in any other respect, these children seemed well-developed and nurtured children, who displayed joie-de-vivre, self-confidence, and secure attachments to their parents.

"Smurfette in the Smurfs' village": a multiple configuration

An additional non-Oedipal configuration identified as the "multiple configuration" appeared in just one family. Similar to the anti-competitive configuration, the multiple configuration does not contain indications of a hierarchy or preference between the parent figures, but in this instance, the relational configuration includes more than two parental figures.

Gili and Noah, four-year-old twins, live with their fathers Avi and Nathan in a residential unit adjacent to the home of Nathan's mother, whom the boys know as "Grandma Yardena." When I entered their home, the children approached me excitedly, extending a book from the Smurfs series, and asked me to read aloud to them. They sat to either side of me, nestling close. Their comfort level was apparent, and they surrendered easily to my narrating voice. The story they asked me to read is about the entrance of Smurfette, the female Smurf, to the Smurfs' village. Excited by her female presence, the entire village falls in love with her, unaware that she is actually an emissary of the evil Gargamel. A moment of dread ensues, but the story's happy end has the Smurfette falling in love with the rest of the Smurfs and joining their home in the village. While reading aloud to Gili and Noah, I felt that the story accurately reflected the scenario of my own entry into their home: a home of four boys. I, the seductress, had piqued their curiosity – but was I a messenger of evil sent their way to lay a trap for them? Or might we all fall in love with each other and live together happily ever after?

The latter possibility seemed not too far removed from their own family situation, since Grandma Yardena in whose courtyard they lived was deeply involved in their lives, and in many respects acted as a third parent. This arrangement certainly answered concrete needs, because raising twins requires a great deal of help from the environment, but to no less degree it reflected Nathan's separation issues vis-à-vis his mother. Throughout our meeting, Nathan expressed ambivalence toward his mother and the foothold she maintained in his emotional and familial life; yet at times it seemed that he had nevertheless succeeded in fulfilling his infantile Oedipal phantasy: to have children and raise them together with his mother. In the course of the couple's interview, Nathan credited his mother with many of the crucial decisions they had made in the process of creating their family. He reported, for example, that it was only for his mother's sake that he had not from the outset relinquished the possibility of genetic fatherhood, because of the importance she attaches to genetic kinship. Even their decision to conceal from their social environment the fact of the boys' genetic affiliation to Avi was explained by Nathan as a fulfillment of his mother's wish. Avi and Nathan's children also perceive the special character of Nathan's relationship with his mother. When, for example, I asked Noah who Daddy Nathan loves more than anyone in the world – a question most children answer by indicating the parent's partner or children – he replied decisively: "Grandma Yardena." And when Nathan himself was asked who he loves most in the world, he replied: "My family, Noah, Gili, Avi, and my mother and father." Nathan's merging of the family he created with his family of origin was surprising and atypical for a man in his 40s who already has a family unit of his own. Grandma Yardena was mentioned frequently in the children's descriptions as a de facto parent figure. When I asked Noah to whom he turns in distress, he answered: "Sometimes Daddy Avi, sometimes Daddy Nathan, or Grandma Yardena." Gili also repeatedly mentioned the grandmother, both in the apperception task and in the interview. When I asked him: "Who do you think loves you most in the world?" he replied: "Daddy and Daddy. And Grandma! Grandmommy is the funniest!"

In a striking correspondence to the configuration of the actual family relationships, Gili's primal scene phantasy includes three parent figures – two fathers and a mother:

Daddy Avi:	"Whose tummy were you in?"
Gili:	"Iman's." [Sounds like "In mom's."]
Me:	"Whose?"
Daddy Avi:	"Iman's, Iman is the surrogate's name."
Me:	"Ah, yes?"
Gili:	"She even got married to Daddy and Daddy."
Daddy Avi:	"What? What???"
Gili:	"She was in the middle. And Daddy and Daddy (laughs) were on the sides."
Daddy Avi:	"She was photographed. She didn't get married. She was pho-to-graphed!"[8]

Like Gili – who maintains the phantasy that the surrogate who carried him in her womb had actually married his two fathers, and who may actually believe that he was created by the sexual union of two men and one woman – Noah, his twin brother, related that he likes to play "house" at kindergarten. When I asked him what role he chooses, he replied: "The father. Lia is the mother. She allows [there to be] two fathers! My favorite is two fathers and one mother!"

---

8 In Hebrew, the verbs "got married" and "was photographed" vaguely rhyme due to the shared vowel pattern of the verbal conjugation.

"I want to marry you, Mommy"   73

It seems then, that in the inner worlds of both Noah and Gili, the primary relational configuration is not one of a father and a father, nor of a mother and a father, but of two fathers and a mother. Another significant factor is that the two brothers are twins. Since their uterine experience was of two boys sharing the body of the same woman (the same surrogate), one cannot rule out the possibility that their primary experience, or at least the phantasy aroused retrospectively (Nachträglichkeit) in regard to that primary union between three partners – two boys and a woman – also seeps in and shapes the phantasy of a primal scene with multiple participants, which both children evoked.

While the multiple configuration was observed only among two children, twin brothers, in unique familial circumstances, it is quite conceivable that, in families including more than two parent figures, this configuration might be found to a greater degree. Its appearance raises questions about an alternative developmental trajectory to the Oedipal one, which may include a bisexual and polyamorous object choice.

References

Britton, R. (1998). *Belief and imagination: Explorations in psychoanalysis*. Routledge.

Corbett, K. (2009). Nontraditional family reverie: Masculinity unfolds. In *Boyhoods: Rethinking masculinities*. Yale University Press.

Davies, J. M. (2015). From Oedipus complex to Oedipal complexity: Reconfiguring (pardon the expression) the negative Oedipus complex and the disowned erotics of disowned sexualities. *Psychoanalytic Dialogues*, *25*(3), 265–283.

Ehrensaft, D. (2007). The stork didn't bring me, I came from a dish: Psychological experiences of children conceived through assisted reproductive technology. *Journal of Infant, Child, and Adolescent Psychotherapy*, *6*(2), 124–140.

Ehrensaft, D. (2008). When baby makes three or four or more. *The Psychoanalytic Study of the Child*, *63*(1), 3–23.

Freud, S. (1909). Family romances. In *The standard edition of the complete psychological works of Sigmund Freud 9* (pp. 235–242). Hogarth Press.

Glassman, N. S. (2015). "The baby with the cream puffs": Further complications in Oedipal complexities, commentary on paper by Jody Messler Davies. *Psychoanalytic Dialogues*, *25*(3), 295–305.

Glocer-Fiorini, L. (2018, September). *Psychoanalysis and sexual & gender diversity studies committee*. International Psychoanalytical Association. www.ipa.world/IPA/en/IPA1/Webinars/Sexual_and_Gender_Diversity_Studies.aspx.

Heenen-Wolff, S. (2014). Same sex parenthood. *Rivista di Psicoanalisi*, *60*, 147–158.

Heineman, T. V. (2004). A boy and two mothers: New variations on an old theme or a new story of triangulation? Beginning thoughts on psychosexual development of children in non-traditional families. *Psychoanalytic Psychology*, *21*(1), 99–115.

Laplanche, J. (1987). *New foundations for psychoanalysis*. Blackwell.

Laur, L. (2011). On performative mothering [Hebrew]. *Hamishpat*, *27*, 411–440.

McDougall, J. (1995). *The many faces of Eros: A psychoanalytic exploration of human sexuality*. W W Norton & Co.

Naziri, D., & Feld-Elzon, E. (2012). Becoming a mother by "aid" within a lesbian couple: The issue of the third. *The Psychoanalytic Quarterly*, *81*(3), 683–711.

Ofer, M. (2014, July). "Rumours of the father's death have been greatly exaggerated": Some thoughts on the Oedipal conflict in children conceived through sperm donation [Hebrew]. *A paper presented in the Israel psychoanalytic society conference*.

Shenkman, G. (2016). Classic psychoanalysis and male same-sex parents: A reexamination of basic concepts. *Psychoanalytic Psychology*, *33*(4), 585–598.

Steiner, J. (1993). *Psychic retreats: Pathological organizations in psychotic, neurotic and borderline patients*. Routledge.

Urban, W. H. (1963). *The draw-a-person catalogue for interpretive analysis*. Western Psychological Services.

Vanfraussen, K., Ponjaert-Kristoffersen, I., & Brewaeys, A. (2001). An attempt to reconstruct children's donor concept: A comparison between children's and lesbian parents' attitudes towards donor anonymity. *Human Reproduction,16*(9), 2019–2025.

Weston, K. (1991). *Families we choose: Lesbians, gays, kinship*. Columbia University Press.

Winnicott, D. W. (1963). The development of the capacity for concern. In *The maturational processes and the facilitating environment* (pp. 73–82). London: Hogarth Press; New York: International Universities Press, 1965.

Ziv, A. (2020). Queer kinship [Hebrew]. *Mafte'akh*, *15*, 135–154.

Chapter two

Oedipal configurations

Mutual illumination of theory and research findings

Chapter One introduced three Oedipal configurations and two non-Oedipal ones. As previously discussed, Freudian theory is premised on the assumption that it is the child's recognition of the parents' sexual difference that initiates the Oedipal developmental process and dictates the organization of their systems of desire and identification. However, most of the children that I met and interviewed (27 out of 33) manifested Oedipal patterns, i.e.: organized their relations with their parents according to a split between a parent to which they directed feelings of love and a parent who became the object of feelings of hostility and rivalry – despite the fact that their parents are not of different sexes. How is this fact to be understood?

Triangulation and triangular space

Ronald Britton is a contemporary Kleinian psychoanalyst whose thinking has been embraced by the relational community due to his highly creative ability to reconstruct familiar psychoanalytic ideas. While not addressing the realities of new families, his reformulations have been adopted at the cutting edge of the effort to rethink the Oedipal situation within same-sex families.

According to Britton (1998), the primal family triangle equips the child with two links that connect them separately to each of their parents. At the same time, it confronts them with a third link that connects their two parents, or in other words, with the inevitable experience of exclusion. The child's increasing ability to tolerate the exclusive connection between the parents, with all the emotional complexity this entails, engenders object relations in which the child acts as an observer and not as a participant. The internalization of this observer position lays the ground for the development of such

DOI: 10.4324/9781032663333-4

capacities as empathy and introspection. Absent this function, which Britton calls "triangular space," the connection between the object and a third object becomes intolerable – and is dreaded as a catastrophe.

Britton goes a step further and argues that what we recognize as a classic Oedipus complex is no more than an *Oedipal illusion* – a defensive phantasy meant to deny the misery entailed by the actual Oedipal situation – the child's experience of exclusion, jealousy, and inferiority vis-à-vis the parental union. Based on Steiner's reading of Sophocles' *Oedipus Rex* (Steiner, 1993), Britton proposes viewing Oedipus' occupation of the throne alongside his mother-wife – surrounded by courtiers who turn a blind eye to what they half-know but choose to disavow – as the epitome of such Oedipal illusions. The parallel of this scenario in the tragedy is a psychological state of affairs in which the parental bond is known to the child, but there Is an avoidance of full recognition of its meaning and nature – which accentuates the difference between the parental relationship and the parent-child relationship. Underlying the Oedipal illusion is the unconscious claim that a union with the loved parent is not a mere wish, but an actual – either pleasurable or dangerous – possibility. As long as the Oedipal illusion is ascendant, Britton argues, curiosity is experienced as if it harbors disaster: the discovery of the Oedipal triangle is experienced as a "murder" threat to the dyadic bond – in other words, as a threat to the survival of the parent-child dyad or of the parental couple. Britton believes that the child's recognition of their realistic place within the family system involves cycles of illusionment and disillusionment. In cases where this movement is obstructed and Oedipal illusions persist as solid beliefs, they prevent the resolution of the complex through processes of rivalry and relinquishment.

Returning to the case of Abigail, as representative of the full-blown Oedipal configuration, we can observe that her relations with her parents Elijah and Joel are organized according to the prevalent Oedipal split. Despite the fact that both of her parents are men – i.e., both parents could present as potential objects of heterosexual desire, whatever the sources of that desire may be – Abigail nevertheless chose Elijah as a continuous object of desire and cast Joel in the role of rival. This finding implies that a split between a desired parent and a rival parent, or in other words, the classic version of the Oedipus complex, does indeed serve as a defensive structure in the face of the painful recognition of the exclusive bond between the parents.

The fact that most of the children (27 out of 33) could be classified into one of the Oedipal configurations, i.e., that they organized their relations with their parents by means of some version or another of a split between a loved parent and a rival – suggest that such an infantile split-based organization serves a basic emotional need, which is prior to questions of sex and gender. It might also imply that, due to the cultural centrality of gender dichotomy, the gender system presents itself as a ready-made split construction for children of heterosexual parents. However, as the research findings suggest, it is not the parent's sex that motivates the split. The splitting may occur on the basis of the parents' personalities or on the basis of the quality of each parent's relationship with the child. In fact, as the next chapter will clarify, most of the children who chose a continuous object of desire cast in this role the parent who was their primary caregiver during infancy – a choice that aligns with the Oedipal development that Freud attributes to boys only, in reference to a reality in which the mother is identified with the primary caregiving role. This finding indicates that a reality in which men fulfill the "mother" role, or women fulfill the "father" role does indeed affect the child's internalized representations (e.g., Benjamin, 1988; Chodorow, 1978; Laur, 2011).

In what way are Oedipal and non-Oedipal configurations different?

Heineman (2004), whose revisions of Oedipal theory aim to include same-sex families, emphasized the fact that the internal triangular space can only be maintained when each point exerts sufficient tension to prevent the collapse into a dyad. Thus, when a couple decides to have a child, the shift to a triadic structure provides an opportunity to enrich the couple's relationship by means of an exclusive dyadic bond of each of the parents with the child, alongside their shared experience of parenting; but if for some reason the child exerts too much or too little emotional gravitational pull in relation to the parental couple, the emotional currents of the family will be dyadic, even if it is composed of three partners.

The notion of triangulation processes, as depicted by Britton (1998) and Heineman (2004), allows us to distinguish between Oedipal and non-Oedipal configurations according to the degree of the child's or the family's capacity to tolerate the complexity entailed in triadic relations. This capacity depends on prior developmental achievements – of both child and parents – such as the capacity to differentiate between the two parents, to acknowledge their exclusive relationship including its sexual nature, and to move between moments of victory and defeat, between a participatory position and an observing one.

In the drawing by Abigail (Drawing 1, p. 39), the representative of the full-blown Oedipal complex, the figures are detailed and distinguished from each other, and the recognition of the nature of the parental bond is also apparent. This recognition of the love that Joel and Elijah share for each other inflicts emotional pain on Abigail and produces narcissistic rage; which, in turn, evokes a defensive phantasy that can be viewed as an Oedipal illusion, since it is rooted in the belief that Joel's presence is the only thing that is preventing the romantic union between her and Elijah. In other words, Abigail is invested in the working through of the Oedipal conflict by means of what Britton (1998) terms "cycles of illusion and disillusionment" (pp. 37). On the other hand, we may say of children like Dori, who were classified under the anti-competitive configuration, that their curiosity – whether about the differences between the parental figures or about the nature of their exclusive relations – is inhibited by anxiety. This anxiety stems from the unconscious belief that full recognition of the significance of the triadic bond is tantamount to the murder of the dyadic relations. It characterizes not only the child, but the entire family atmosphere.

It is very tempting, therefore, to conclude that the development of an Oedipal structure is a psychic achievement unto itself, independent of questions of sex, gender, and sexuality. However, as mentioned in Chapter One, a full-blown Oedipal configuration appeared mostly among children whose parents are of the opposite sex (of the 15 children who displayed a full-blown Oedipal complex, 12 were of the opposite sex from their parents: six of the 12 were daughters of gay fathers, and six were sons of lesbian mothers); whereas the other configurations were characteristic of children whose parents' sex was the same as theirs, i.e., daughters of lesbian mothers and sons of gay fathers. Therefore, even if most of the children constructed some type of Oedipal configuration that related to both their parents, an explicit expression of sexual or romantic desire toward one of the parents almost always entailed a heterosexual object choice.

This book does not aspire to decipher the etiology of sexual orientation. The empirical evidence it relies on points to various factors that may contribute to the heterosexual object choice which most of the children displayed. These may include: (a) constitutional factors that orient the child's object seeking (not a few parents described their child as having innate heterosexual tendencies, or a stereotypical cisgender identity which they perceived as alien to their own experience, and which they felt was not acquired through the child's identification with or imitation of them); (b) environmental influences, such as entering public preschool, on the child's formation of heteronormative internalizations; (c) the parents' own overt and covert heteronormative expectations, which may be variously conveyed: as knee-jerk heteronormative scenarios offered in conversations with the child; through a general aspiration to lead as normative a life as possible, motivated by concern for the wellbeing of the child whose mere family association – so the parents assume – will force them to deal with a sense of being different; by ascribing romantic meanings to their child's interaction with children of the other sex, or by encouraging the child's own heterosexual romantic expressions; or finally, through unconsciously conveying to the child the parent's deeply-held anxiety about their child potentially developing a homosexual orientation (for illustrations of these various factors, see Eitan-Persico, 2020).

My point of departure at this stage of the argument is the psychoanalytic assumption that every person is born with feminine and masculine as well as homosexual and heterosexual tendencies – even if the relative proportions of each tendency vary from one person to the next. As a result, the infantile attraction to the parent is part of the emotional attachment and is independent of biological sex. This notion is derived from the complete Oedipal model, which comprises a positive and a negative complex (see Freud, 1923; McDougall, 1995; Davies, 2015). Why, then, was the attraction to the parent of the same sex not manifested in the child's relational organization?

Butler (1995) argue that the Oedipal model embeds not only a prohibition of incest but also a prohibition of homosexuality. According to Butler, gender is acquired, at least partially, by the rejection of homosexual attachment. This rejection positions the forbidden object as part of the "ego" by means of melancholic identification. Thus, whereas a son in a traditional family relinquishes his mother as an object of desire through a prolonged process of seduction, rivalry, and acceptance of the unfeasibility of his desire, his relinquishment of his father as an object of desire usually takes place without there having been an opportunity to recognize the desire, and therefore also without an opportunity to work through the loss.

80 What does Oedipal development have to do with the parents' sex, anyway?

To take this idea further, one can regard all of the alternative configurations to the full-blown Oedipal complex – both the Oedipal and non-Oedipal ones – as different emotional solutions to the taboo on homosexual relations. The full-blown Oedipal configuration, as shown, appeared mostly among children whose parents were of the opposite sex, regardless of whether they were daughters of gay fathers or sons of lesbian mothers. But among children whose parents were of the same sex as their own, a significant difference was found: whereas daughters of lesbians organized their relations according to a Platonic or an alternating Oedipal configurations, the sons of gay fathers tended to organize their relations in non-Oedipal configurations.

Since the daughters of gay fathers display full-blown Oedipal patterns, just like the sons of lesbian mothers, one can conclude that homosexual fathers are not deficient in respect to the developmental achievement that Britton speaks of, and are indeed capable of creating a triangular space and dealing with its consequences. How can one explain this difference in relational patterns between daughters to lesbian mothers and that of sons to homosexual fathers?

To understand this difference, one must take into account the fact that the cultural taboo against male homosexuality is more severe than the taboo against lesbian relations. This asymmetry is reflected both in the grave and explicit biblical prohibition of male homosexual intercourse, which is not paralleled by a prohibition of sexual contact between women (Boyarin, 1995) and in the language of criminal law.

In Israel, up until 1988, the law prohibited "unnatural intercourse," a prohibition that was identified in practice only with sodomy, or in other words, with "any act of penetration, or more accurately the penetration of the male sexual organ into any bodily orifice other than the natural place."[1] Unlike gay men who were vulnerable to criminal lawsuits, women were never indicted for conducting lesbian relations[2] (Yonai & Spivak, 1999). Within psychoanalytic discourse, perversion

---

1 Although "unnatural intercourse," that is to say, oral and anal sex between a man and a woman are very commonly practiced, the discourse allows for pretending that heterosexual couples engage only in "natural" sex, whereas a male gay couple has seemingly no alternative but to engage in such "unnatural" practices (see Yonai & Spivak, 1999).

2 The distinction in Israeli law between homosexual and lesbian intercourse is a legacy of British Mandatory law, and accordingly characterizes both the English and American law (see Yonai & Spivak, 1999).

was traditionally associated mainly with male sexuality. Perverse constructions were perceived as defenses against castration anxiety and as conflicts related to the male Oedipus complex, bolstering the social perception that women do not develop sexual perversions (Welldon [1989], in McDougall, 1995). Similarly, the pejorative label "faggot" reflects the taboo on male homosexuality, which serves to police the gender behaviors of boys, male adolescents, and men, a word for which no parallel of equal ferocity exists in reference to girls, female adolescents, and women.

The heteronormative Oedipal process may provide an explanation for the fact that the social taboo on male homosexuality is more severe than that against female homosexuality. Since the mother is the primary attachment figure for both boys and girls in the traditional heterosexual family, the girl is expected to perform a libidinal shift toward the father, but to maintain her identification with the mother, whereas the boy is expected to develop an identification with the father, but at no point is he expected to choose the father as an object of desire.[3] As long as the function of childrearing is culturally assigned to the mother, the Oedipal process endows the collocation of son-father-desire the status of an unformulable experience.

Each of the alternatives to the full-blown Oedipal configurations provides a unique strategic defense in the face of the taboo on homosexuality. Before I discuss the solution presented by each such configuration, I wish to dwell on the predisposed internalizations, expectations, and anxieties that same-sex parents – and especially gay fathers – bring with them into parenthood.

Internalized homophobia and the demand for normal sexual and gender socialization

Yael Levi-Hazan (2020), a Queer scholar, has described the demand for normal gender and sexual socialization of children, which is imposed

---

3 In a survey I conducted about the Oedipal patterns among 48 children of heterosexual psychologist mothers, most of the children who exhibited the full-blown Oedipal pattern, chose – according the mothers' reports – a parental object of the opposite sex. A number of girls chose their mother as an Oedipal object, but not a single boy openly chose their father as an Oedipal object of desire.

on parents, and more relentlessly so on same-sex parents – due to their identification

> as perverts, who violate heteronormativity, for whom parenthood is always subject to a hermeneutics of suspicion, and by virtue of the fear of their detrimental influence on their children: the traditional association of homosexuality with disease and pedophilia and the understanding of homosexuality as "contagious". All of the above produce a perception of LGBT families as a hothouse for the cultivation of LGBT people.
>
> (Levi-Hazan, 2020, p. 5)

As a result of the severe taboo imposed on male homosexuality, gay fathers are especially vulnerable to these demands and may find themselves struggling against internalized homophobic ideas that identify homosexuality as a contagious disease, namely, one that is transmitted through seduction, or even with notions associating it with pedophilia. Such notions are clearly manifested in the following excerpt from the couple interview with Rafi and Avner:

Rafi: "There is no doubt that it won't be easy for them [their children] either, and we also will have to contend with society, with the parents. If we're to maintain contact with the other parents from the kindergarten, from the school, if we're to feel comfortable hosting children here, their friends."

Me: "What exactly is the . . . what is in doubt?"

Rafi: "I don't want to oblige the other parent to confront their child in regard to our situation."

Me: [smiling] "What is 'our situation'?"

Avner: "Let's say if he thinks that homosexuality is *contagious*.[4] Let's say he thinks that if his son spends time with our kids, he'll come home and be gay."

---

4 Gay fathers' repeated use of terms semantically related to "contagion" in reference to homosexuality brings to mind the collective trauma endured by the community during the AIDS era. As Simon Watney (1987) has shown, AIDS was disciplined in the social discourse of the 1980s as a symbolic embodiment of homosexuality itself, and thus reinstated the perception of homosexuality as a communicable disease, i.e., one that is passed on by means of seduction, a perception from which the gay liberation movement had been successful at freeing itself.

Rafi:	"Not to put homosexuality into their heads. So, if someone offers a playdate, we'd happily accept, but I'm not comfortable with offering, 'Why don't we host your child in our house today?' We don't really know the parents from the kindergarten, we don't really have social ties. I have a difficulty with that."

I met Rafi and Avner when their son Hillel was still a toddler. At that time, Avner had defined his relationship with his son Hillel in terms of being mutually in love: "I think that Hillel is quite in love with me in some way, and I am quite in love with him." In order to further validate my conclusions, I met with Avner a second time when I was analyzing my research data and asked him for his insights about the findings. During our second meeting, Hillel was seven years old. Avner's reports indicated to me that Hillel's entry into the Oedipal stage had led to a "platonicization" of their relationship. When I reflected on the change in the tenor of their relationship, Avner candidly pointed out the intense anxiety that is likely to accompany the erotic dimension of the relationship between a homosexual father and his son. During the conversation, when we jointly sought ways of understanding this anxiety, Avner associatively recalled moments in which while taking bodily care of his son he felt vigilant not to cross any line. This thought led him to recall a friend, "A fifty-something gay man who is an art therapist, who at some point avoided treating children because of the idea that someone might think he is a pedophile." Avner clarified that his friend's avoidance is based on the mistaken association between homosexuality and pedophilia: "It's like, a gay person who thinks he is a pervert, and then the perversions can be in all sorts of direction, with that [pedophilia] being one such direction. It's simply a kind of cognitive distortion."

Analysis of Avner's associative train of thought suggests that his caution not to cross any line in such intimate moments of bodily caring for his son, is associated in his own mind with his gay friend's avoidance of working with children, fearful that he might be accused of pedophilia. It would seem that Avner's homophobic internalizations regarding his sexuality bring about "cognitive distortions," as he defined it, which create a symbolic equation between homosexuality and sexual perversions such as pedophilia.

These types of symbolic equations are rooted in different discursive fields: the wording of the criminal law against male homosexual intercourse in Israel, for example, combines under the same section the prohibition of "unnatural intercourse" as well as the prohibition of bestiality – as if these

84 What does Oedipal development have to do with the parents' sex, anyway?

were different but equivalent forms of deviation from the "normal" pattern (see Yonai & Spivak, 1999). Similarly, there is a wide-ranging discursive tradition that homophobically associates homosexuality with pedophilia – centering on the figure of the older perverted man who seduces innocent young boys and irreversibly reorients their sexuality.

These homophobic notions permeate parenting via unconscious routes, as suggested, for example, by Avner's following statement:

> I do want to say something about the subject of . . . romance. This is a bit embarrassing, but, um . . . it might help you with your research. It seems to me that . . . (pauses), okay, it's embarrassing. It seems that . . . it could be that one time Hillel came into our room by mistake when we were at it, and that he saw something. And, I don't know, I constantly associate it with that, but I don't know if it's related to that – he does all sorts of stuff with me that is like, seductive. . . . Sometimes I find it funny, but at times it makes me angry and I tell him to stop doing it.

This description, culminating with Avner's embarrassed chuckle, reveals ambivalence and vulnerability to a sense of guilt. Avner relates his son's seductive, mischievous behavior – which can be seen as typical Oedipal behavior – to the fact that he was accidentally exposed to his parent's while they were having sex. During the Oedipal phase, a child requires a playful arena in which he can test his own sexual charms, his competitive abilities, and he must feel loved and desired by the parent, even if he is never to prevail in the Oedipal rivalry (Davies, 2003; Loewald, 1979; Searles, 1959). Because of the incest taboo, bodily care of the child, which unavoidably arouses sexual feelings in parents (Laplanche, 1987), always entails embarrassment and dread. As the research findings show, the emotional and physical bond between the parent and child, which is complicated in any case, may become even more complicated when a parent has internalized his sexuality as "perverted," and as a result, he unconsciously interprets expressions of intimacy with his son as a seductive act which may "sow" homosexual desire in his son.

A similar ambivalence to that reported by Avner can be observed in the countertransference[5] reactions emerging from a case study by Corbett

---

5 From Freud's perspective (1910), countertransference reflected a specific disturbance in the analyst, which arises as a response to the patient's transference, and necessitates the

Oedipal configurations 85

(2009), a relational psychoanalyst who identifies as gay. Corbett recounted that one of the phases in his treatment of Andy, a seven-year-old boy of two lesbian mothers, was characterized by Andy's increasing need for physical closeness with him. Andy frequently leaned on him, jumped in his lap, and drew him into physical rough-and-tumble play. At the same time, Andy would ask lots of questions about his personal life and repeatedly wondered whether they could meet outside the clinic, perhaps go fishing together. Corbett describes the way he initially interpreted the fishing as a metaphor for the therapeutic encounter, but Andy's insistence on the possibility of their going fishing together led him to understand that his clever interpretation was actually a defense against countertransference feelings. Corbett admitted that he too began to entertain a phantasy about going fishing together, and even found himself reading an article about fishing, which he would have normally skipped over. Gradually, Corbett began to recognize the erotic dimension that he felt he had been trying to deny until that point.

Corbett's descriptions indicate the presence of his and Andy's shared wish for a father-son relationship, which incorporates the Oedipal experience of a mutual falling in love. One of the nuances arising from his description relates to the reparative experience afforded to him – as a gay man who may not always have lived up to the social expectations ascribed to "masculinity" – by presenting as a role model and object of admiration for a boy in the process of forming his male identity. But the pleasure derived from emotional and physical intimacy with a child also brought with it discomfort and anxieties related to the erotic dimension of the relationship. Corbett writes:

> I reflected on the nonverbal limiting cues I conveyed to Andy about how he could sit with me, or the ways in which I managed his pull toward rough-and-tumble play. . . . Here, I believe we come upon an aspect of child therapy that is rarely discussed and insufficiently problematized – the subtle ways in which a child therapist is often in a position of having

analyst's continuation of his own analysis. Instead of viewing countertransference as an obstacle that interferes with analytic work, which should be blocked or overcome, most analysts today recognize that the analyst's feelings and phantasies about his patients are pervasive and hope to make use of their reactions for a better understanding of their patients (Aron, 1996, pp. 110–111).

to negotiate the muscular eroticism of children, up to and including the therapist's own erotic countertransference response. . . . For example, I was aware of the pleasure I experienced in exercising my strength in setting limits with him, and my corresponding recognition of his pleasure in feeling my strength. Or the pleasure I felt in feeling his small body (the fragility of his rib cage, the thinness of his arms) as I lifted him up so that he could reach something on a shelf in my office. . . . I had to entertain the ways in which my own experience of prohibition may have been inhibiting the development of Andy's erotic transference. Was I more comfortable presenting myself as a nurturing parent as opposed to an erotic man?

Following up on these countertransference reflections, I began to interpret more directly Andy's wish to be close to me – to observe my habits, to touch my body, to feel the excitement (muscular eroticism) of rough-and-tumble play . . . by stepping out of our previous nonverbal manner of managing his wishes, I was also stepping out of the wish.

(pp. 69–70)

As Corbett's words suggest, in order to overcome incestuous wishes, the parent and the child need to work through their shared loss, and such a working through requires an essential recognition of desire[6] (cf. Loewald, 1979). In the case of Avner and Rafi, this kind of essential recognition was attainable. It seems that both Avner and Rafi are struggling with internalized homophobic notions that engender fear about seducing their son and guiding him toward a homosexual orientation, but the very fact that they are able to recognize these feelings and discuss them suggests that their level of anxiety is benign and containable. In Avner's descriptions, one sees how along with his occasional imposition of a rigid boundary in respect to affectionate gestures and touch, he is also capable of playfully enjoying his

---

6 An interesting aspect of Corbett's case study is his choice to end his description not at the moment of termination of treatment, but with a scene of a fortuitous encounter with Andy years later, a scene that might have been taken from a heteronormative teen movie. Andy, now in his teens, is giving a ride to a girl on the back of his bicycle, in a small resort town. This picturesque scene implicitly conveys the message that the success of the treatment is evidenced in Andy's ability to consolidate a normative masculinity and realize it in a heterosexual relationship. Corbett's authentic sense of satisfaction echoes a feeling gay fathers or lesbian mothers commonly express regarding their sons and daughters respectively.

son's seductive games, and of taking pleasure from Hillel's preference for him over Rafi – a preference that Rafi is also willing to acknowledge.

The level of parental ambivalence described might be one of the factors that shape Hillel's relational organization as a Platonic Oedipal configuration, which allows him to express his preference for Avner and even be somewhat playfully seductive around him, approaching yet not crossing the boundary of expressing explicit romantic desires toward him. It could also be that the message as interpreted by the child is not limited to a prohibition of incest; because both his parents are men, the internalized message might end up as a prohibition of homosexuality, even if his parents exhibit a model of successful homosexual relations. When the level of parental anxiety is higher, or insufficiently worked through, the erotic dimension will be thoroughly denied – as suggested by the illustration of Barak, Niv, and their son Dori, the representatives of the anti-competitive configuration. In such circumstances, the unconscious message communicated to the child might be that romantic or erotic relations between a father and son are prohibited, not only in reality, but also as a phantasy, or play – which are essential for establishing an Oedipal arena. Therefore, it seems that, whereas parents of children who have organized their relations according to a Platonic Oedipal configuration are content to emphasize emotional closeness, love, and involvement, while somewhat disavowing their own and their children's erotic parts of the self, fathers to sons who have organized their relations according to the anti-competitive configuration will stress parental functioning, and perhaps even the couple's joint functioning as parents, rather than each parent's dyadic relationship with the child. They will attend to their parental roles with the utmost seriousness and responsibility, while utterly denying any erotic element of their relations.

Reenactment of traumatic Oedipal relations

In a lecture dedicated to the Oedipal dynamics among gay men whose object of desire as children was their heterosexual father, Offer Maurer (2007) described the way in which the father typically was transformed from a figure who inspires erotic arousal in the pre-Oedipal stage to one who prohibits such arousal during the Oedipal phase. The child's attraction, which had been accepted lovingly during infancy, was met at the onset of the Oedipal phase with expressions of aversion and alarm on the part of the father, who projected onto the child disowned aspects of his own psyche associated with homoerotic attraction. This painful experience has the potential of resurfacing within the current father-son relationship, such that the early Oedipal relation patterns are reenacted and expressed as a rejection of the child's emerging sexuality. Following this logic, one may expect that the more traumatic and insufficiently worked through the historical Oedipal drama was, the more it will tend toward reenactments and be accompanied by stronger denial of the very conflict.

In his lecture, Maurer presented a case study of a gay man who experiences difficulty integrating sexuality with love and tenderness. In the course of therapy, the patient recalled a moment from his childhood that became a turning point in his relationship with his father:

> Me and dad were sitting on my parents' bed one Sunday morning. Mom wasn't at home and neither were my little brothers. Dad was reading me the story about the "Puss in Boots" but I wasn't too interested in the story. I remember I just wanted him to hug me, soothe me, and kiss me. I was looking at him as he was reading and then I saw it in his eyes. He could tell that I wanted more. I swear to you that I could tell he knew it – right then and there – he knew that I'm a pervert. He freaked out, totally disgusted, jumped out of bed, muttering some lame excuse about needing to pick up mom from wherever she was, and so he just took off without ever completing the story.
>
> (Maurer, 2007, p. 10)

Experiences of shock and revulsion that were reflected in the father's gaze, the first object of desire of many gay men, were juxtaposed in Maurer's article with a benign Oedipal interaction, as described by Jonathan Slavin (2002). Slavin describes a magical moment in which a mother is reading to her four-year-old son at bedtime, when suddenly, in the middle of the story, the child puts his hand on the book and shoves it aside to get his mother to stop reading. She raises her eyes and he says to her: "Mommy, you're beautiful!", causing his mother's heart to melt upon hearing the words. Slavin addresses crucial developmental aspects of this moment shared by mother and son. The first concerns the fact that the mother-son relationship is sufficiently secure and accepting. The son feels comfortable expressing (age-appropriate) feelings of love and sexuality in a relatively direct way – a sense of security lacking in the child who felt similar feelings toward his father, in the earlier scenario described by Maurer. The second aspect concerns the mother's "melting" in response to her child's declaration of love, thus validating his emerging gender identity, sexuality, and loving feelings as basically good, desirable, and innocent – the inverted image of that received by the child who read in his father's shocked expression the notion that he was a pervert.

Anxiety concerning the child's potential homosexual orientation might also stem from the parent's wish to spare the child the pain that they have personally experienced as a result of their sexual orientation. It may be that the stronger the parent's sense of alienation has been, or the more acute their "coming out" crises have been, the more they will be burdened by anxieties about their own child's fate, and the greater the feelings of guilt about the nonconformity that they are imposing on him.

Due to the severity of the taboo on homosexuality compared with lesbianism, the sexuality of the gay father is liable to be more conflictual and generative of emotional complication in his relations with his son than the lesbian mother's relations with her daughter. But the sexual arena is not the only one that causes complications for gay fathers. As I will show presently, male same-sex parenting also clearly violates the binary gender system by which the role of childrearing is allocated to women.

"Motherhood is women's business": self-doubt among gay fathers

Eyal and Ido fathered two children: their daughter Noam was conceived by shared parenting with Dafna, a friend of Eyal's, whereas Judah, their younger son, was conceived through surrogacy. Regarding their initial choice of joint parenting, they recounted the following:

Eyal: "At that time I was still convinced that *a child needs a mother*. It was a process I went through with myself."

Ido: "Where I was coming from, it felt more *natural* to me. I think I was coming from a place, like Eyal, that 'there has to be a mom.' And then, little by little, I began to comprehend the error, because with Noam we agreed that there would be a mom and a dad and that Noam would call me by a different name: she wouldn't call me Dad. And then I understood that that was a mistake. It took me about three years almost [laughs] to understand."

Me:	"Why indeed was there no place for three [parents]? Why not, Dad, Dad, and Mom?"
Ido:	"It was truly a product of our outlook. And Dafna, of course, felt comfortable with it. I said to her, 'Eyal will be the father, and I will be, like . . .'."
Eyal:	"We were newbies then."
Ido:	"We were newbies."
Eyal:	"We all grew up and were brought up in heterosexual homes and you try to extrapolate. It was like importing that structure into this one – but no, you need to make adjustments."

The relations with Dafna quickly became troubled. The arrangement was not suitable for either party. As Eyal and Ido told it, Dafna had expected to develop closer family relations with the couple, but those hopes were dashed; Eyal learned that it was very difficult for him to separate from his daughter, especially during infancy, when he discovered how deeply immersed he was in a state of "primary parental preoccupation"; Ido, for his part, deeply regretted relinquishing recognition of his own status as an equal parent; he felt invested in a parenting relationship that carried no guarantee of his rights further down the road. These difficulties led them to the surrogacy path the second time around – a choice that they are much more at peace with.

Eyal and Ido recall the fright that seized them upon realizing how much power was accorded to Dafna due to the family court's preference for maternal custody:

Eyal:	"What is an 'agreement'? It doesn't count in real life."
Ido:	"We made an agreement. Ultimately the court doesn't care about that. It cares about the child's welfare."

The case of Eyal and Ido allows us to see the unique difficulties that gay men experience in their transition to parenthood. The couple may feel ready and fit for raising a child, but when they begin to plan and consider what family structure to choose, they find themselves battling the ghosts of their childhoods as the sons of heterosexual parents. Something deep inside refuses to accept the legitimacy of a family unit comprised of two fathers. They perceive a mother's presence as a crucial, even "natural" element. What's more, even given Eyal and Ido's choice of joint parenting with a woman, the cultural processes of Oedipalization make it difficult for them to establish a family model in which there is room for three parent figures. Like many other parents in a shared parenting arrangement,[7] the notion to which they defaulted was that if both a biological mother and father were present, Ido could not be called a father, or share equal rights, despite his having an equal role in raising their daughter in practice. Even when, based on their successful parenting experience, they wish to become disabused of such notions – that a child needs a mother, that there is no room within a family structure for three parent figures – these very same biases continue to assail them from without, in the form of the socially conservative views, represented in their account by the court, which equates the child's welfare with an a-priori preference for maternal custody and refuses recognizing the custodial rights of a third parent. It should be noted that the law does not only reflect a given socio-cultural reality, but it also (re)produces and constitutes the social subjects and their inter-relationships (see Berkovitch, 1997).

In view of the conflicts that Eyal and Ido describe, one can regard the choice of Avi and Nathan (who represent the multiple non-Oedipal configuration) to raise their children in Nathan's mother's courtyard as a kind of compromise, a configuration which on the one hand is meant to quell internal doubts about the legitimacy of a family unit lacking a maternal figure; on the other hand, since the third parental figure, Yardena, is the children's grandmother and not their mother, this kind of family structure allows the couple greater freedom to view themselves as a pair of fathers in respect to shared parenting arrangements, which, as mentioned, often produce a parenting couple comprising the genetic mother and father, according to Oedipal logic.

Similar doubts to those expressed by Eyal and Ido are reflected in a nightmare that struck terror in Niv, Dori's father, when he and Barak were dealing with the bureaucracy for authorizing a second surrogacy procedure:

Niv: "In my dream, we're travelling to Canada, and Dori isn't allowed to enter Canada because in the surrogacy procedure, there's a

---

7 During the research, I also met with four families that had children through joint parenting arrangements. In two of them, the father avoided meaningful romantic relations and built a kind of Platonic couplehood with the mother of the children, and in the other two, the genetic father had a partner who was not defined as a father within the family constellation. In other words, not one of these four cases allowed for a deviation from the classic Oedipal model of a child with two parents. The alternative configuration of multiple parents also exists of course, but one may assume that in much smaller numbers.

	mother registered on the birth certificate. She is eligible. She has to sign waivers."
Barak:	"And they require these documents in Canada."
Niv:	"But somehow we decide that we are going with Dori, and then we get a baby girl, and we aren't allowed to leave the country with Dori, because the state claims that he is Indian and has to be returned to the mother. So Dori says to me, 'It's okay, Dad, I can go back to being Indian.' And his sister appears in this dream."
Barak;	"My sister."
Niv:	"She says to the authorities, it's my child and . . . in short, at some point I woke up in a cold sweat."

Beyond the realistic concerns preoccupying Niv in regard to recognition of Dori's status as their legal child, a psychoanalytic reading of the dream suggests that he is riddled with feelings of guilt, anxiety, and doubt about the legitimacy of raising a child without a mother. His awakening from the dream in a cold sweat suggests that something about these contents resists being worked through emotionally to an adequate degree (Ogden, 2005).

As I shall show in Chapter Four, lesbian social (non-biological) mothers may also experience anxiety and report nightmares concerning their parental status. The common basis for the anxiety of the social mother and the gay father is, therefore, the assumption that the child belongs to the birth mother.

A thorough accounting of the doubts that a gay father may feel in regard to his choice to raise children without a mother figure appeared in the interview with Erez and Zohar. Erez, the biological father of Gaya and Michael, related that he was ambivalent about parenthood to begin with and that after the children were born, he suffered from post-partum depression:

Erez:	"All the symptoms were spot-on. Like, if you opened up the DSM, everything that's written in it about post-partum depression, the physical symptoms too. Maybe I wasn't experiencing a hormonal tempest, but . . ."
Me:	"I don't know, some studies show that . . ."
Erez:	"Exactly! So maybe my hormones were also going hay-wire. Because of the intimacy. Right, so absolutely, yes. That's the diagnosis I was given, and . . ."
Zohar:	"And you embraced it with both arms." [Laughs.]
Erez (laughing):	"And I embraced it with both arms . . ."

Me:	"And among the contents that came along with this depression, was there a layer of internalized homophobia that was piggybacking on top?"
Erez:	"That's a very, very good question. I think there was. Not just during the post-partum depression. My entire parental experience resonates at some level with the internalized homophobia I am combatting. First of all, just on an anecdotal level, I am a family therapist, and at my institute, I coordinate a large project dealing with families that have chosen to have a child without a mother. All this rests on some kind of assumption, that even if I utterly reject it on a theoretical level, it bugs me on the inside, that there is something about motherhood . . . that I cannot achieve as a father."
Me:	"That's amazing. Because ultimately, the post-partum depression is paradoxically a product of that, but it also proves that, here . . . you can achieve."
Erez:	"Right, even the post-partum depression. At a conscious level, I do not experience my parenthood as lesser in any shape or form. But I do have to admit that my preoccupation with it is also related to some extremely primitive assumption."
Zohar:	"That nothing compares to Mama."
Erez:	"That nothing compares to Mama – like my own mother, who is incomparable. And my own father – whom I don't want to be like. Because to be a father like my dad, well, you had better have a mother in the picture. Like, it rests on a very complex system of identifications – I call this thing a kind of internalized homophobia. Like there is something very deep inside that thinks that I am actually doing something that I shouldn't be doing. Or that isn't right for me. Or that it is improper. But it's very important for me to clarify for the record that . . .'
Me:	"That this goes against your conscious agenda."
Erez:	"Exactly."
Me:	"And these things co-exist."
Erez:	"Exactly!"

As Erez articulated so well, there is a discrepancy between his conscious recognition of his own parental capacities and the difficulty he has shaking free of primordial beliefs and feelings that he harbors which privilege the mother's exclusive role in child-rearing. Two concepts that come to mind in this context are womb envy and a debt to the mother.

"Stealing" motherhood from women: womb envy and a debt to the mother

In her book *Mother in Psychoanalysis: A Feminist View* (2005), Palgi-Hecker proposes a feminist reading of "Little Hans," one of Freud's well-known case studies. Instead of the Freudian reading that centers on the child's castration anxiety, Palgi-Hecker posits womb envy: in other words, the difficulty Hans experiences in giving up his primal identification with his mother and relinquishing his wish to be like her – i.e., to be a mother to his own children. She describes the way in which Freud and Hans' father strive together to persuade him that girls "have not"; however, Hans is preoccupied with what girls "have," and this includes the ability to become pregnant and give birth.

As early as 1926, Karen Horney (1926) objected to the positing of penis envy at the center of women's experience, in utter disregard for women's physical advantage: her ability to create new life within herself. Based on her clinical experience, Horney reported the intense envy men express toward pregnancy and breastfeeding, and proposed that the patriarchal effort to belittle women's assets, as well as the male creative and ambitious drives are rooted in this primal envy of women, or more accurately, of the mother.[8]

In her article, "Womanliness as a masquerade," Joan Riviere (1929) describes a psychological complex that afflicts successful women, characterized by a defensive use of flirtatious feminine performance and self-deprecation stemming from fear and guilt over stealing the phallus. Here I wish to propose thinking about gay fathers as liable to experience the reverse complex to that described by Riviere, i.e., a complex arising from fear and

---

8 At the heart of the critique of Horney's thought stands the claim that she set out to liberate women from the chains of male perceptions, but eventually trapped them within their biology. The symmetrical Oedipal model that she proposed obviates the possibility of a cultural critique of patriarchy that is embedded in Freud's asymmetrical Oedipal model (see Palgi-Hecker, 2005; Mitchell, 1974).

guilt related to the sense of having stolen the womb – women's childbearing capacity – from the women, or more precisely, from their own mother.[9]

A second concept that may shed light on the unconscious emotional experience of gay fathers is the sense of debt to the mother (Palgi-Hecker, 2005). Winnicott, who identified this emotional phenomenon, argued that the cultural fear of women, including the cruelty and oppression directed toward them,

> is related to the fact that in the early history of every individual . . . there is a debt to a woman – the woman who was devoted to that individual as an infant, and whose devotion was absolutely essential for that individual's healthy development.
>
> (p. 164)

If the guilt related to this debt to the mother cannot be worked through, one will encounter efforts at denial, fear of women, and perhaps a general fear of dependency. In another article, discussing the mother's contribution to society, Winnicott wonders:

> Is not this recognition of the devoted mother unrecognized precisely because it is immense? If this contribution is accepted, it follows that every man or woman . . . is in infinite debt to a woman. . . . Here a man is in a more difficult position than is a woman; he obviously cannot come to terms with his mother by becoming a mother.
>
> (pp. 142–143)

Can a man never become a "mother"? Can a gay male couple that raises a child from infancy not achieve – through their parental devotion – the same level of understanding and identification with their mothers' primary devotion? Can they not feel gratitude and come to terms with their mother in the same way that women are able to?

Most of the gay fathers that I encountered were preoccupied to some degree or another with the question of whether motherhood has a singular

---

9 These ideas may shed light on the storm caused in Israel in 2018 by the slogan "A womb for every gay man!" that was displayed by one of the demonstrators in the campaign for equal access to parenthood.

value that they would never be able to achieve. Is there a bodily experience, or some kind of maternal instinct, that is beyond their reach? Is there something forbidden about the desire to be like the mother and claim ownership over her unique functions? Some of the interviewees openly shared feelings of envy toward mothers; they felt unfortunate for their inability to experience the magic of creating life within their own body, or to feed an infant with their own bodily substance; others actively engaged in a denial of envy by eradicating any difference between fathers and mothers, or by devaluing the latter. As can be seen in the following dialogue between Erez and Zohar, while Erez was invested in active efforts to deny the belief that there is something about motherhood that is inaccessible to him as a father, his partner Zohar freely expressed envy toward the woman's maternal capacity to bear children in her body and nurse them:

Erez: "I tend to think that the issue of emotional bonding around breastfeeding is part of the realm of maternal instinct that I am very, very skeptical of. What's natural about breastfeeding is the substances, the minerals that come out."

Zohar: "I don't agree with you. I'm not talking about maternal instinct. I don't know what that is. But can you imagine that, that the child is part of your own body?"

Erez: "But the kids were here [points to his bosom area], for many months. Like this. It's quite the same, except for not being attached, I mean, except for it not biting your breasts."

Zohar: "And how about it growing in your belly . . . how about that phantasy?"

Erez: "Look, nothing ever grew in my belly except for fat and food [we all laugh simultaneously], so I don't know, I only hear reports."

Zohar: "But prior to becoming pregnant, a woman also never had something grow in her belly . . . didn't you ever phantasize about doing something like that?"

Erez: [in a repulsed tone] "Becoming pregnant?!"

Zohar: "Of course not, because you would probably worry that you wouldn't be able to shed the pounds afterwards

Erez: "First of all – yes, exactly [we all laugh together], and second, I'm like . . . I'm very critical of all that hoopla . . . I'm being careful so as not to say that I don't believe those who report it."

Me:	"Do you feel that it's an idealization?"
Erez:	"I'm almost sure of it. It's an invention. It's very . . . It's extremely strong, and it has infinite power – to produce reality and to assign significance, but it's an invention."

Erez's rejection of the possibility that pregnancy could be a constitutive experience that fosters the forging of a deep bond with the infant in the fetal stage is an example of the way some fathers cope in order to relieve themselves of maternal debt, and thus to eliminate feelings of envy and inferiority vis-à-vis women in regard to their parenting. While Erez attempted to eradicate the differences between his parental experience and that of the birth mother, Maoz and Ofir embraced a defensive attitude leading to the devaluation of mothers and motherhood:

Ofir:	"I think that over time we learned and acknowledged that we were no worse than any other mom. Not to mention that there are mothers who are so terrible that they make us feel really good about ourselves. When I see mothers, I say to myself, 'OMG, they really suck'." [Laughs.]
Maoz:	"You can say for sure that we don't have an inferiority complex."

Another way that gay fathers may cope with feelings of self-doubt about the legitimacy of their parenthood is through denial of their very affiliation with the class of gay fathers, and by ridding themselves of internalized homophobia by projecting it onto other gay fathers. This came to light in the following dialogue between the gay couple of Amir and Tommy:

Tommy:	"Look, in the situation that we were in, and the age that we were at, kids was something that we really, really wanted. I don't feel that everyone needs to do it."
Amir:	"Yeah, there's a bit too much of it, and I don't think it should be allowed for gays to be parents . . . [Laughs] Tommy claims that I'm a homophobe and I assume there's something to that. In my phantasy, we are a regular family, not necessarily a gay family. Even though I know . . ."
Tommy:	"No, Amir has exceptional powers of denial."

Amir:	"I don't like to include myself, I admit, with a lot of gay couples that look . . . when I see it on others, it looks odd to me, the gay parenting . . ."
Me:	[astonished] "Really?"
Amir:	"Yes, I'm a homophobe."
Tommy:	"He's a homophobe. Look, I'm telling you – a homophobe!'

I have outlined several spheres of coping that are liable to confront the same-sex parent with feelings of doubt, guilt, and anxiety. Without sufficient working through, these feelings may infiltrate the parental position, especially the parents' relations with children of the same sex: ranging from the social taboo on homosexuality to the internalization of homophobic perceptions of homosexuality as a perversion or a communicable disease; from the reenactment of painful memories rooted in traumatic Oedipal experiences in childhood to experiences of outsiderness and alienation during adolescence or at the coming out stage.

In view of the fact that the taboo on male homosexuality is more severe than the taboo on lesbian relations, these spheres tend to be more fraught for the gay father. What's more, gay fatherhood also entails the transgression of the binary gender system in which the role of childrearing is allocated to women. This transgression may confront the gay father with self-doubts regarding his parental competency and provoke a dimension of profound and agonizing guilt toward the internalized mother figure. This differs markedly from lesbian parenting, which, according to the mothers who participated in the research, may even reinforce the sense of identification and belonging to the community of women.

The research evidence indicates that same-sex parents carry a burden of guilt and anxiety regarding the possibility of seducing the child; subconsciously, a parent may believe in the possibility of altering their child's "natural" heterosexual orientation to a homosexual one. I will now proceed to the characterization of the alternatives to the classic Oedipal configuration (which I have designated the full-blown Oedipal configuration) as defensive infantile solutions that emerge in reaction to parental guilt and anxiety.

Alternative relational configurations as defensive organizations

The full-blown Oedipal configuration – i.e., the classic Oedipal configuration – is characteristic of sons of lesbian mothers and daughters of gay fathers. In other words, to the extent that the family configuration included a parent of the opposite sex, the child's Oedipal configuration tended to include a direct expression of romantic aspirations toward one of the parents. However, children whose parents were of the same sex as them did not manifest such expressions: daughters of lesbian mothers tended to organize the relations according to a Platonic or alternating Oedipal configurations, whereas sons of gay fathers tended not to manifest any Oedipal patterns at all. Earlier I argued that each of the alternative configurations to the full-blown Oedipal configuration offers a defensive strategy in service of coping with the problem of the taboo on homosexuality. I will now proceed to elucidate the unique solution provided by each configuration.

The Platonic Oedipal configuration preserves the Oedipal dynamic in its entirety, absent the romantic coloring. One can therefore regard it as the appropriate solution for children who are denied the possibility of expressing sexual desire or romantic aspirations toward the beloved parent – and indeed this is the most common solution (nine children manifested a Platonic configuration, of which seven had parents of the same sex). Nonetheless, this defense is a subtle one, since – as Avner's descriptions as well as Corbett's case study revealed – the boundary between effusive affection and erotic expression can be quite elusive. In light of the fact that bodily care of the child typically arouses sexual feelings in the parent, and that affection between a child and parent is usually also expressed physically, a parent with intense ambivalence about their own sexuality may need to employ a more forceful denial of the erotic dimension of the relations.

A child's organization of their relations with their parents in an alternating Oedipal configuration – i.e., a situation in which the child switches back and forth between the parents – may primarily provide the child with an outlet from the tension and guilt involved in the continuous rejection of one of the parents; however, it simultaneously offers a systemic solution for the problem of parental guilt over the potential seduction of the child. When the child's preference constantly oscillates between one parent and the other, even when this preference is unmistakably erotic, the very fluctuation of the pattern offers the parent some relief from their concern that their own sexuality might be exerting an influence on the child's homosexual attraction. When the child's attraction is directed toward both parents, it is easier to accept that the source of the attraction is in the child, that such an attraction is "natural," as opposed to a situation in which, in the parent's phantasy, they bear sole responsibility for the child's desire. Three children fell into this category – two girls and one boy, all of them children of lesbian mothers.

Hence, these two alternative Oedipal configurations appear to mitigate parental guilt: the first one, by Platonizing desire, or by displacing it beyond the child-parent relations (Platonic configuration), and the second one, by decentralizing it (alternating configuration). In contrast, the two non-Oedipal configurations – the anti-competitive and the multiple configurations – are more far-reaching; here the child exhibits avoidance of any preference for one parent, or refrains from the very recognition of the exclusive sexual nature of the parental relationship. Non-Oedipal configurations therefore involve a more profound denial of the romantic or erotic element of the relationship. All six children that were classified under non-Oedipal configurations were children of gay fathers, five of whom were boys of gay fathers. The seeming conclusion is that relations between sons and fathers do indeed occasion a more significant denial of the erotic dimension. I venture the possibility that the various spheres of guilt and anxiety with which gay fathers are obliged to cope in the context of both gender and sexuality may in some cases converge, thus contributing to a defensive stance. This defensive position, supported by denial mechanisms, restricts the playful transitional space that is required to constitute an Oedipal situation.

An additional factor that may shed light on the fact that non-Oedipal configurations only appeared among children of gay fathers, derives from the different division of roles typical to lesbian mothers as opposed to gay fathers. Non-Oedipal configurations may be less typical of families of lesbians because the asymmetry between the mothers – with one carrying the fetus in her womb, giving birth, and perhaps nursing the infant – interfere with the possibility of denying the differences between the parental figures, both from the mother's viewpoint and that of the children. This issue will be elaborated further in Part II, which deals with genetics and kinship.

Has sexuality anything to do with psychoanalysis?

The shift of focus from the original sexual element in Freud's Oedipus complex to triangulation processes that stress the transition from dyadic to triadic relations, including the narcissistic injury entailed by this, can be read as part of an overall reorientation that has taken place in psychoanalysis in recent decades with the shift from drive theories to theories that emphasize object relations (Aron, 1996).

As Andre Green (1995) has cautioned, contemporary case studies shy away from sexual issues, from drives, from the body – the very elements that Freud had made central to his theory. Current-day therapists, Green argued, tend to treat sexual materials as if they were merely a defensive sexualization of deeper issues related to object relations and pre-genital fixations. They thus obscure the place of sexuality in the creation of phantasmatic and mythical constructions in society and in the individual. In this vein, one can say that theories that emphasize triangulation processes do indeed offer an efficient conceptual scheme for examining differences between Oedipal and non-Oedipal configurations and even successfully explain the basic split structure that most children manifested in the organization of their relations with their parents, independent of questions of sex and gender. However, they lack the power to explain the differences that emerged between children with parents of the same sex as their own and children with parents of the other sex, as well as the differences between the daughters of lesbian mothers to sons of gay fathers. It follows that relinquishing the role of sexuality in Oedipal constructions and the investigation thereof would be a premature move.

The various theoretical propositions describe a valid yet partial picture of the Oedipal developmental process, which is affected by the child's inclinations, their parents' unconscious messages, as well as the social demands to which both child and parents are exposed. This process consists of erotic elements, triangulation processes, the transition to a depressive position, as well as an inherent narcissistic injury. Throughout this part of the book, I have attempted to lay out the various parts of the puzzle, side by side, and to draw out the interrelations between the various elements, with the hope of providing a comprehensive picture of the Oedipal situation in the context of same-sex families and perhaps even beyond it.

References

Aron, L. (1996). *A meeting of minds: Mutuality in psychoanalysis*. Analytic Press, Inc.

Benjamin, J. (1988). *The bonds of love: Psychoanalysis, feminism, and the problem of domination*. Pantheon Books.

Berkovitch, N. (1997). Motherhood as a national mission: The construction of womanhood in the legal discourse in Israel. *Women's Studies International Forum*, *20*(5–6), 605–619.

Boyarin, D. (1995). Rabbis and their pals; or, are there any Jews in 'the history of sexuality'? *Zemanim: A Historical Quarterly, 52* [Hebrew], 50–66.

Britton, R. (1998). *Belief and imagination: Explorations in psychoanalysis.* Routledge.

Butler, J. (1995). Melancholy gender – refused identification. *Psychoanalytic Dialogues, 5*, 165–180.

Chodorow, N. (1978). *The reproduction of mothering: Psychoanalysis and the sociology of gender.* University of California Press.]

Corbett, K. (2009). Nontraditional family reverie: Masculinity unfolds. In *Boyhoods: Rethinking masculinities.* Yale University Press.

Davies, J. M. (2003). Falling in love with love: Oedipal and Postoedipal manifestations of idealization, mourning, and erotic masochism. *Psychoanalytic Dialogues, 13*(1), 1–27.

Davies, J. M. (2015). From Oedipus complex to Oedipal complexity: Reconfiguring (pardon the expression) the negative Oedipus complex and the disowned erotics of disowned sexualities. *Psychoanalytic Dialogues, 25*(3), 265–283.

Eitan-Persico, Y. (2020). *Oedipus in same-sex families* [PhD dissertation, Ben-Gurion University].

Freud, S. (1910). The future prospects of psycho-analytic therapy. In *The standard edition of the complete psychological works of Sigmund Freud 11* (pp. 139–152). Hogarth Press.

Freud, S. (1923). The ego and the id. In *The standard edition of the complete psychological works of Sigmund Freud 19* (pp. 1–66). Hogarth Press.

Green, A. (1995). Has sexuality anything to do with psychoanalysis? *International Journal of Psychoanalysis, 76*, 871–883.

Heineman, T. V. (2004). A boy and two mothers: New variations on an old theme or a new story of triangulation? Beginning thoughts on psychosexual development of children in non-traditional families. *Psychoanalytic Psychology, 21*(1), 99–115.

Horney, K. (1926). The flight from womanhood: The masculinity-complex in women, as viewed by men and by women. *International Journal of Psychoanalysis, 7*, 324–339.

Laplanche, J. (1987). *New foundations for psychoanalysis.* Blackwell.

Laur, L. (2011). On performative mothering [Hebrew]. *Hamishpat, 27*, 411–440.

Levi-Hazan, Y. (2020). "Not confusing the kids": Queer parenthood and the double demand for heteronormativity [Hebrew]. *Mafte'akh, 15*, 35–44.

Loewald, H. W. (1979). The waning of the Oedipus complex. *Journal of the American Psychoanalytic Association, 27*(4), 751–775.

Maurer, O. (2007, July). Can anyone love me at all: Some thoughts on the fate of homosexual love. Paper presented at *the annual conference of the international association for relational psychoanalysis and psychotherapy in Athens.* Greece.

McDougall, J. (1995). *The many faces of Eros: A psychoanalytic exploration of human sexuality.* W W Norton & Co.

Mitchell, J. (1974). *Psychoanalysis and feminism: Freud, Reich, Laing, and women*. Pantheon.

Ogden, T. H. (2005). *This art of psychoanalysis: Dreaming undreamt dreams and interrupted cries*. Routledge/Taylor & Francis Group.

Palgi-Hecker, A. (2005). *Mother in psychoanalysis: A feminist view* [Hebrew]. Am-Oved.

Riviere, J. (1929). Womanliness as a Masquerade. *International Journal of Psychoanalysis, 10*, 303–313.

Searles, H. F. (1959). Oedipal love in the counter transference. *International Journal of Psychoanalysis, 40*, 180–190.

Slavin, J. H. (2002). The innocence of sexuality. *Psychoanalytic Quarterly, 71*(1), 51–80.

Steiner, J. (1993). *Psychic retreats: Pathological organizations in psychotic, neurotic and borderline patients*. Routledge.

Watney, S. (1987). *Policing desire: Pornography, AIDS, and the media*. Cassell.

Winnicott, D. W. (1957). The mother's contribution to society. In *The child and the family: First relationships* (pp. 141–144)Taylor & Francis.

Winnicott, D. W. (1965). *The family and individual development*. Basic Books.

Yonai, Y., & Spivak, D. (1999). Between silence and damnation: The construction of gay identity in the Israeli legal discourse [Hebrew], 1948–1988. *Israeli Sociology, 1*(2).

Part II

What does genetics have to do with kinship, anyway?

Chapter three

On biological affiliation and kinship

Deeply embedded in the Oedipal situation is a recognition of sexual and intergenerational differences. These differences are perceived by psychoanalytic thought as primordial and immutable facts of life, which are posed against our inner wishes as a vexing inevitability (Britton, 1998). In other words, the Oedipal system organizes relations between the generations and between the sexes by means of the incest taboo and a taboo on homosexuality respectively. Both of these cultural taboos are meant to protect the social order, which relies to a great extent on exogamy and the exchange of women (Rubin, 1975),[1] but no less so are these taboos meant to protect the very continuity of the human species – since incest bears the risks of genetic disorders, and homosexuality lacks procreative potential.

In his article "Queer kinship," A. Ziv (2020) writes that the fact that homosexuality cannot result in childbirth constituted the basis of its homophobic identification in Euro-American discourse with "infertility," the interpretation of this concept expanding from the sexual act to encompass the entire homosexual lifestyle. Homosexuality was posited as a threat to the family order, a notion that was articulated in the neo-conservative buzzword "family values" that came to the fore in the final two decades of the 20th century.

---

1 In his study *The Elementary Structures of Kinship*, Levi-Strauss proposed that the kinship phenomenon was based on the principle of exchange of women by men for the purpose of forging social ties. Gayle Rubin (1975) uncovered the assumptions underlying Levi-Strauss' analysis and showed that preconditions of the kinship system he outlined are the sexual division of labor (responsible for the interdependence of men and women, and making the married couple a minimal economic unit), obligatory heterosexuality, and the restriction of female sexuality. Whereas Levi-Strauss explicitly addresses the incest taboo as crucial for the exchange of women, Rubin shows that, logically speaking, this taboo assumes an earlier taboo on homosexuality (see A. Ziv, 2020b).

DOI: 10.4324/9781032663333-6

But the more assisted reproductive technologies (ART) become mainstream,[2] the more homophobic justifications related to the need to preserve the continuity of the human species lose their force. The development of ART, including sperm and egg donations, surrogacy, in vitro fertilization (IVF), and cloning, undermines the assumptions and logic of kinship and challenges the idea of kinship as a domain of natural facts of life that are removed from any social or political context (Carsten, 2004).

In the Jewish-Israeli political context, in which the aspiration to strengthen the "natural" Jewish collective is axiomatic, thereby generating justifications for Zionism's political and territorial claims, gays and lesbians have not only been perceived as negligent in respect to the task of ensuring familial continuity, but were also condemned for shirking their duty to the collective.

Most of the same-sex couples I spoke to were able to clearly articulate that the harshest aspect of their sexual orientation, in their own perception as well as that of their parents, was the expectation that they give up hope of becoming parents, thus accepting, as it were, a life sentence of loneliness in society's margins. Similarly, they tended to describe their transition to parenthood as a sweetening of this sentence, an avenue for healing rifts with their families of origin, and even as an entry ticket into Israeli society.

However, as part of the very same aspiration of strengthening the "natural" Jewish collective, tremendous importance is attributed in Israel not just to kinship ties, but particularly to blood ties (Birenbaum-Carmeli, 2009). The question of the same-sex couple's social integration reemerges, therefore, when the couple become parents, now due to the inherent reality that only one of the parents is genetically related to each of the children. Couples who unconsciously sought to placate their parents and satisfy cultural norms find themselves struggling against the barrage of voices – both external and internal – that would question their status as social parents who are raising non-genetic children and that of their nuclear family as a valid kinship unit, even if it is not based on blood ties or a legally recognized marriage.

The status of the social parent (the non-genetic parent) is also undermined by the powerful effect of the primal scene phantasy, which posits heterosexual coitus, both as a cultural symbol and as an intrapsychic representation, as that which simultaneously generates and defines kinship.

---

2 See *The Handmaid's Tale*, a dystopian novel by Margaret Atwood (1986), which reflects the contemporary cultural anxieties in light of the decreasing rates of heterosexual sexual reproduction, and which has also been adapted as a popular television series.

On biological affiliation and kinship 109

Within the context of this phantasy, parental coitus symbolizes the ultimate creative union between two people from which the social parent who does not participate in biological reproduction is excluded.

Vicky and Nora are raising three children together: seven-year-old Tom, four-and-a-half-year-old Ada, and 12-month-old Yuli. The two mothers describe themselves as having had a powerful yearning for children, but whereas Vicky could envision herself carrying a pregnancy and breastfeeding, and indeed very much enjoyed these experiences, Nora related that she had never desired pregnancy, not even as a child. On the other hand, she had always cultivated the phantasy of adopting children. "And so she adopted," Vicky quipped, referring to Nora's choice to be the social mother of all three children.

Vicky described the infancy phase with great longing. She had chosen to nurse all three children for a duration of eight months each: "I really love that stage of infancy, that tight closeness," she said. "I hate it," Nora was quick to add facetiously.

Nora: "when they were really infants, then there's that symbiotic bond of mother and child, where there's nothing for me to do except help Vicky. So it wasn't jealousy, but at first, with Tom, our first child, it was very anxiety provoking. Later I learned that when they grow up there would be a place for me, I will have a role, so I don't worry anymore. When Tom was born I wanted to adopt him right away, so everyone would know this was also my child. I was hysterical. Today, I haven't even bothered to adopt Yuli. I plan to do it really soon, but today it's much less of an issue, and I am really not worried."

While Nora describes with satisfaction her eventual success at finding her place and establishing her unique roles within the family, along with the consequent reduction of her anxiety levels, the question of her legitimacy as a social mother continues to be a source of vulnerability:

Nora: "Ada said to me one day: 'You're not my Mommy, I don't want you!'"

Vicky: "Ada often – on purpose – doesn't want Mommy Nora to bathe or to dress her."

Nora: "Because she knows I'm sensitive to this issue. One time when Tom was really angry with me, he said: 'I don't want you to be my mom.' But he said this to me just once in his whole life. I think that in his heart he sometimes feels it but he doesn't say it out loud. It's very insulting. It also sits squarely on my anxiety about not being the biological mother, anxiety that I might be rejected, that maybe I'm not a real mother."

As Nora so tellingly describes, the moments in which her daughter Ada rejects her by refusing to accept parental care are experienced as a realization of her ultimate fear as a social parent (Cf. Hartman & Peleg, 2019; Tabak-Aviram, 2018). This fear is fed to a large degree by the hegemonic discourse of kinship, which places tremendous weight on genetics as a determinant of kinship relations. Conflicts or resentments that are inherent to parent-child relationships, and are even developmentally crucial, may be interpreted in light of this discourse as a reflection of the missing ingredient in the relationship. The question is, therefore, does genetics really play such an important role in the child's attachment to their parents, or in the parents' bonding with their child?

On biological affiliation and attachment

According to Heineman (2004), lesbian mothers sometimes relate how despite having envisioned egalitarian parenting arrangements, there takes place a kind of physical attachment between the infant and birth mother, which differs in quality from the attachment to the social mother. This difference diminishes as the child matures, and still, Heineman argues, vestiges of it often remain, and the child may come to prefer the birth mother's body or touch as a source of soothing at moments of distress or need.

Nonetheless, Heineman's account of the special attachment between the newborn and the birth mother overlooks an important intervening variable: the overwhelming tendency of birth mothers to serve as primary caregivers during the child's early infancy. Among the family members I interviewed, in eight of nine cases in which one of the mothers had served as a primary caregiver, it was the birth mother who had undertaken this role. In the single case of a family in which the social mother had taken on the role of primary caregiver (because the birth mother was recovering from Caesarean section and later was mourning the death of her mother), the twin children exhibited an infantile preference for the social mother, a preference that later assumed romantic overtones as they entered the Oedipal phase. Thus, in all of the lesbian families in which there occurred a role division between a primary caregiver and a primary breadwinner, the children manifested an infantile preference for the primary caregiver, whether she was the birth mother or the social mother. In most cases, this preference persisted in one way or another even after the unequal parental role distribution had evened out.

In lesbian families in which the role division was described as egalitarian, the mothers' accounts revealed that, in most cases in which the social mother had been more emotionally available for the child, the unique attachment described by Heineman (whose vestiges appear in the choices of a soothing object even after a secure attachment with both mothers had been established) was actually characteristic of the relationship with the social mother (and not the birth mother). This can be seen, for example, in the case of the twins Omer and Eran: although both mothers had taken maternity leave jointly to take care of the twins, Rona, the social mother with the gentler and more patient disposition of the two, had an easier time responding to the children's primary needs, thereby establishing her status as the primary object. Over the years, the boys' birth mother, Esty, with the more adventurous temperament, assumed her position as the Oedipal love object; however, in moments of physical and emotional distress, the social mother Rona continues to act as the boys' preferred source of soothing and comforting.

Unlike lesbian mothers – for whom the initial role division might be informed by the different physical and emotional experiences each mother undergoes during pregnancy, birth, and sometimes breastfeeding, including the cultural entailments thereof – among gay fathers the division of roles tends not to be dictated by biological affiliation. It should be mentioned that the preferred model among gay fathers in Israel is that of producing twins, where each child is genetically related to one of the fathers. Due to the challenging nature of twin rearing, some couples took simultaneous paternity leave and became jointly immersed in parenting. In other cases, where a role division between primary caregiver and primary breadwinner did exist, this popular twin model resulted in an arrangement whereby the primary caregiver cared simultaneously for both his genetic and non-genetic children. Even in cases of a single child, the choice of primary caregiver seemed to be determined chiefly by circumstances of employment, finances, as well as by the fathers' individual dispositions and heart's wishes, rather than by biological affiliation.

An overview of all the families with role division between a primary caregiver and a primary breadwinner (lesbian and gay couples alike) shows that when such a role division existed, an infantile preference for the parent who had served as the primary caregiver was almost always established – this occurred in 17 out of 18 families. For most of the children, this preference did not change even with the transition to the Oedipal stage. At that point, 13 of 18 children exhibited a preference for the parent who had acted as primary caregiver, and five showed a preference for the parent who was the main breadwinner.

These findings validate Chodorow's (1978) critical argument that the focus in psychoanalytical thinking on mother-infant relations creates a systematic confusion between the importance of permanency in early caregiving and the erroneous assumption about the exclusive or inevitable role of the birth mother as the child's first attachment object.

Examination of the patterns of preference of all the children I interviewed revealed that, among the 24 children who displayed an infantile preference for one of the parents, 12 preferred the genetic parent and 12 preferred the non-genetic parent. Upon entering the Oedipal phase, 13 of the 24 children who displayed a consistent Oedipal preference for one of the parents – whether in the context of a full-blown or Platonic Oedipal configuration – chose the genetic parent as the beloved object, whereas 11 chose the non-genetic parent. These research findings suggest, therefore, that genetic affiliation does not constitute an advantage in respect to attachment patterns or the child's Oedipal object choice. On the contrary, the findings indicate that it is the intimate relationship forged by the parent's continuous care for the child, and their physical and emotional investment in it, that lays the ground for the child's early preference, as well as for her or his Oedipal object-choice (from among 24 children who exhibited a consistent preference for one of the parents, only among five children did a change of object take place in the Oedipal phase).

Based on these findings, one can conclude that Ada's rejection of Nora, her social mother, which was described earlier, does not reflect an inherent or inevitable difficulty stemming from the absence of a genetic affiliation between them. However, as Nora herself attested, since the social discourse attributes so much importance to genetics as the foundation of kinship relations, it is difficult to escape such an interpretation, to the point that it might become a self-fulfilling prophecy. It is, therefore, the meanings that parents attribute to genetics, and not genetics in and of

On biological affiliation and kinship   113

itself, that are likely to impact family relations. In the following chapters of Part II, I will attempt to examine the meanings that parents and children attribute to genetics. What role do these attributions play in the relational dynamics within the nuclear family and with the extended family?

Having established the argument that the genetic factor per se does not influence the child's attachment processes, we may ask what role it might play in the bonding processes between parent and child. Is it necessarily easier for the genetic parent to bond with the child? And how do the parents' bonding processes impact the child's preference patterns?

Does genetics necessarily produce a sense of closeness?

The notion of "natural" kinship contains an unquestioned assumption that the genetic affiliation between a parent and offspring is a vital ingredient for the development of emotional closeness, identification, and commitment. One of the most common and pleasurable family games is "spotting resemblances" – the recognition of the child's genetic traits and association of such traits with their parents or relatives. This family practice plays a central role in creating connection and a sense of belonging among family members (Mason, 2008; Becker et al., 2005; Nordqvist, 2010, 2017). In psychological terms, one can explain the power of this practice as stemming from the pleasurable narcissistic mirroring it provides, or from its capacity to evoke or resonate well-established intimate relationships with beloved family members. But what happens when the similarities are experienced rather as a source of torment, reflecting to the parent parts which invite self-reproach or are reminiscent of family members with which relations are emotionally loaded?

Daniel: "(Naomi's genetic father): "She's such a character, Naomi. I don't know if it's because she's mine, but something about her behavior sometimes annoys me much more than it does Amos (his partner) or pushes my buttons."

Amos: "Because you see yourself in her."

Daniel: "Myself, my mother, yes, absolutely."

Genetics, as Daniel attests, reflects parts that he has difficulty accepting about himself and even conjures up his complicated relationship with his mother, thus importing ready-made ambivalence into the relationship with his daughter Naomi. This example demonstrates that just as genetic affiliation may facilitate the parent's bonding processes, it may also sabotage these processes and overburden them. Daniel's emotional ambivalence toward Naomi in turn mediates her own choice of Oedipal love object; Naomi displays a clear preference of a romantic nature for Amos, her social father. The fathers report a constant courting of Amos, in gestures that include declarations of love, physical touch, and repeated attempts to take Daniel's place in the parents' bed. Her preference for a parent who can love her wholeheartedly, or in a less conflictual way, facilitates Naomi's formation of a positive self-image and simultaneously provides an arena for vengeance, which allows her to reject Daniel just as he rejects aspects of her personality.

A typical difficulty in the genetic parent's bonding processes may arise due to the child's inheritance of a genetic disorder (cf. Tabak-Aviram, 2018). Under such circumstances, the disorder may produce an intolerable reflection of the genetic parents' flaws or arouse feelings of guilt. In these cases, the non-genetic parent, who is released from responsibility or guilt related to the child's difficulties, may be in a better position to offer the child their unreserved love, or more aptly put, intimacy based on separateness and otherness:

Galia: "My resemblance to Ariel – it was like there was something negative about it. It's still difficult, until now. It's as if we are so much alike, it is like 'I can't bear it.' You know, I'm also hyperactive and hyper-sensitive like that. To encounter that was really hard, precisely because of the biological thing, and in some ways Orna was more able to connect."

Orna "I love you, and the same things I find endearing about you, I also find endearing in Ariel, and so it's easier for me to love those things."

In this case, too, the mothers' bonding processes act as a mediating factor in the daughters' object choices: Ariel demonstrates a clear preference for Orna, the social mother, who accepts her in a more whole-hearted way than does Galia, the genetic mother. But Layla, her twin sister who did not inherit the hyperactivity and sensory hypersensitivity from Galia, and therefore presents a more positive reflection to Galia, shows a clear preference for her.

The answer to the question of whether genetic resemblance promotes intimacy versus distance may also shift over the lifecycle, in correspondence with the child's developmental needs. Thirteen-year-old Noam was born into a parenting partnership between Eyal and a female friend of his. Initially, Eyal's partner Ido was not considered a father, but nevertheless functioned as one in practice, and today she relates to him as "Daddy Ido." During her infancy, the fathers recount, Noam developed a symbiotic relationship with Eyal, and he became her primal attachment figure, even surpassing her mother. Nowadays, Noam speaks of her closeness with Ido, with whom her relationship is experienced as less loaded:

Me: "If you need help with anything, or get into trouble, whom do you feel more comfortable approaching?"

Noam: "Daddy Ido mostly. He's the best at helping out."

Me: "Whom do you feel that you resemble most?"

Noam: "Daddy Eyal. Both inside and out. We are both quick to take offense, let's start with that. We have similar tastes, similar views, we're similar in every possible way."

Me: "So does it feel like you understand one another easily?"

Noam: "Not so much anymore. Since we're alike, there are collisions sometimes. For harmony you need to have Ying and Yang, you know."

This brief glimpse of early adolescence reveals that elements that may have inspired closeness and identification during early childhood may become contentious and fraught at a later developmental stage when the child is engaged in the work of separation and the formation of an autonomous identity. During this phase, the non-genetic parent may be in a better position to offer the adolescent child an intimate space that better meets their emergent need for a sense of separateness and individuality.

Whereas the child's genetic affiliation decidedly does not have a deterministic effect on their object choice or attachment matrix, the emotional meanings that the genetic reflection carries for the parent may play a role in shaping the relationship between the parent and child, and thus, indirectly influence the child's object choice. This statement is just as valid in reference to heteronormative families as it is for families assisted by gamete donation. However, as the conversations revealed, when the identity of the genetic partner is obscure, the intensity of the meanings attached to genetics, for better or for worse, may increase. Erez, the genetic father of the twins Gaya and Michael, explained the issue as follows:

> If anything, I consider the genetics to be a burden on me. Not always. There are things that I am proud of, but when problematic traits show up, I feel like I am the only one in the world who carries the genetic responsibility, because the other party is not there to be dumped on. I feel a responsibility, as if I were guilty of something. And another thing: there are times where I can see myself in them, in their reactions, or in their problems, and I truly feel a very heavy burden of responsibility, as if I am the only one who can thoroughly understand it. It's like, I'm the only responsible party, and the sole savior as well.

Erez describes an experience of bearing exclusive responsibility, stemming from the mere fact that "the other party," i.e., the genetic partner in the child's creation is "not there." As a consequence, when he sees both his positive and negative parts reflected in his children, this arouses powerful feelings, whether of guilt or pride. All of this is pervaded by a sense of loneliness.

The structural genetic asymmetry has divergent implications for families of lesbian mothers versus those of gay fathers. Firstly, as mentioned earlier, in families of lesbian mothers, the asymmetry encompasses the experiences of pregnancy, birth, and sometimes breastfeeding – as well as the cultural entailments and impositions related to these experiences – and therefore its implications may be more far-reaching compared to the asymmetry that characterizes the families of gay fathers, which is restricted to the genetic element alone. Secondly, among lesbian mothers, the child's genetic affiliation to its mother is publicly visible throughout the pregnancy, whereas gay fathers exercise more choice about whether and with whom to share this information, a choice that often results in practice in concealment. Because of these structural differences, the next two chapters will be devoted to a separate examination of the respective implications of genetic asymmetry for families of lesbian mothers versus those of gay fathers.

References

Atwood, M. (1986). *The handmaid's tale*. Random House.

Becker, G., Butler, A., & Nachtigall, R. D. (2005). Resemblance talk: A challenge for parents whose children were conceived with donor gametes in the US. *Social Science & Medicine*, *61*(6), 1300–1309.

Birenbaum-Carmeli, D. (2009). The politics of 'The Natural Family' in Israel: State policy and kinship ideologies [Hebrew]. *Social Science and Medicine, 69*, 1018–1024.

Britton, R. (1998). *Belief and imagination: Explorations in psychoanalysis*. Routledge.

Carsten, J. (2004). *After kinship*. Cambridge University Press.

Chodorow, N. (1978). *The reproduction of mothering: Psychoanalysis and the sociology of gender*. University of California Press.

Hartman, T., & Peleg, A. (2019). Minority stress in an improved social environment: Lesbian mothers and the burden of proof. *Journal of GLBT Family Studies, 15*(5), 442–460.

Heineman, T. V. (2004). A boy and two mothers: New variations on an old theme or a new story of triangulation? Beginning thoughts on psychosexual development of children in non-traditional families. *Psychoanalytic Psychology, 21*(1), 99–115.

Mason, J. (2008). Tangible affinities and the real life fascination of kinship. *Sociology, 42*(1), 29–45.

Nordqvist, P. (2010). Out of sight, out of mind: Family resemblances in lesbian donor conception. *Sociology, 44*(6), 1128–1144.

Nordqvist, P. (2017). Genetic thinking and everyday living: On family practices and family imaginaries. *The Sociological Review, 65*(4), 865–881.

Rubin, G. (1975). The traffic in women: Notes on the political economy of sex. In R. R. Reiter (Ed.), *Toward an anthropology of women* (pp. 157–210). Monthly Review Press.

Tabak-Aviram, I. (2018). A question of genetics: The meanings of genetic affiliation in LGBT families [Hebrew]. *Psichoaktualia*, 41–47.

Ziv, A. (2020). Queer kinship [Hebrew]. *Mafte'akh, 15*, 135–154.

Chapter four

A new hierarchy

Asymmetry between the birth mother and social mother in lesbian couples

In her essay "Compulsory heterosexuality and lesbian existence," Adrienne Rich (1980) posits lesbianism as an actual oppositional force vis-à-vis the problematic power relations between the sexes. In this vein, feminist critics view lesbian motherhood as representing a first-of-its-kind historical opportunity for the raising of children by two parents possessed of potentially equal power, which is not derived from the structurally determined gender hierarchy in which subjects are positioned in accordance with their anatomical sex. However, the possibility of creating an egalitarian family structure is fractured when the structural asymmetry between men and women within the heteronormative system is replaced by a new hierarchy: one that divides the birth mother from the social mother. Alongside the disparities in the legal and cultural status of the two mothers, dissimilarities between each mother's physical and emotional experiences may produce tensions and difficulties, thus undermining the egalitarian vision that they had embraced during the family planning stage.

A. Ziv (2020) argues that non-biological lesbian parenthood is *acquired* and *delegated*: parental status is acquired through parental functioning, and in a complementary fashion also by means of repeated acts in which the biological mother affirms the parental status of her partner vis-à-vis the social environment. The daily performance of various parental and familial practices, together with the explicit and implicit acts of parental validation on the part of the birth mother produce the very essence of the social mother's parenthood.

The position of the birth mother, which accords her the right to delegate parental status to the social mother, is reflected, for example, in the practice of choosing the child's surname. One study that documented these practices in families of lesbian mothers found that, in most families, the birth mother

DOI: 10.4324/9781032663333-7

chose to give her surname to her child, based on a sense of entitlement. Even in cases where it was decided that the child would take the social mother's surname, this choice was described in terms of the birth mother's generosity toward the social mother, or as a desire to underscore the social mother's connection to the child in order to minimize her inferior position (Almack, 2005).

This hierarchy between the birth mother and the social mother may come as an unsettling surprise to the mothers, in light of the fact that, usually, during the family planning phase, lesbians associate motherhood with the intention of raising children with little regard for the biological aspect. The womb of the lesbian partner is perceived at this stage as an instrument of reproduction which belongs to them both – a narrative that subverts the essentialist perception of motherhood. Subsequent to the birth, feelings of competition and jealousy often arise between the mothers, even intensifying in the case of long-term breastfeeding (Corem, 2015).

The breastfeeding issue among lesbian mothers

Breastfeeding is possibly the most emblematic cultural symbol pertaining to motherhood. In object-relation theory, the breast symbolizes the infant's first partial object representation, the first realization of pre-conception, the first link to reality – upon which all future links will be built. To no less degree, breastfeeding symbolizes the ultimate symbiotic connection between the mother and the child, the epitome of a union of two, which does not allow for the entry of a third subject. The topic of breastfeeding is liable to emerge as an arena of conflict among lesbian couples, as an issue that brings to the surface questions regarding the degree of equality between the two mothers, jealousy and competition over the mother role, as well as fear that the symbiosis between the nursing mother and the infant could undermine the intimacy between the mothers. In comparison with heterosexual women who often choose to continue breastfeeding despite the high physical and emotional costs, the toll on their relationship, and sometimes even the detrimental impact on the emotional bond between the mother and infant (Bar Emet Gradman, 2019), the lesbian mothers that I interviewed usually demonstrated a higher capacity to negotiate both at the personal level and with their partners, and to examine to what extent breastfeeding was indeed a suitable choice for them.

Esty and Rona are raising three children together: the four-year-old twins, Omer and Eran, who were born to Esty, and a baby named Nur, whose birth mother is Rona. Esty chose not to breastfeed the twins: "Nursing seems simply like a kind of enslavement," she said. "I preferred to enroll in a carpentry course during my maternal leave. I built them bunk beds." But her choice not to breastfeed was not only a matter of her dynamic temperament but was also motivated, she explained, by her desire that the parental responsibilities would be divided equally. Unlike Esty, when Rona gave birth to Nur, she was surprised to find out how much pleasure she derived from devoting herself to nursing. Rona's choice to breastfeed Nur disrupted the harmonious role distribution that the couple had enjoyed while raising the twins. Esty reported that she began to feel excluded from the dyadic bond that was developing between Rona and Nur, and had trouble finding her place within it. The crisis led to a renewed definition of the role distribution, accompanied by a shared working through of emotions:

Rona: "First of all, I told Esty that if she feels that way, then I'll stop."

Esty: "But I didn't want her to stop – I knew that she was enjoying it, and I also understood that this was good for Nur. We tried having me get up at night, but each time I woke up, she woke up too, she couldn't help it. We understood something after Nur's birth. We grasped that there was some kind of method in the way our family and relationship work. Rona really loved this infancy stage, needing to take care of her, and Nur being dependent on her. She was the same way with the twins. As for me, I'm not crazy about that age, because there isn't much to do: I've gazed at her, kissed her, what next? Nothing happens. In short, we concluded that until the age of 12 months or so, Rona is all the way in. After the age of three, I'm all in. And in the middle, we're both into it. And it's like, we just let go of that place of feeling like we're out of order."

Rona and Esty's need to distribute roles according to some kind of governing logic may reflect a desire to ease feelings of chaos, competitiveness, and jealousy, and perhaps even attenuate the confrontation with the differences between them. The couple's open communication led them to achieve "mutual recognition" (Benjamin, 1988) of each other's needs. This position helped Rona continue to nurse guilt-free, and allowed Esty, on her part, to work through the sense of exclusion and manage to find her comfort zone within the family configuration.

In cases where the social mother harbors harsh feelings about the birth mother's devotion to breastfeeding but these are not worked through, they may be enacted by the social mother applying pressure on the birth mother to stop nursing the infant. For example, while Rina used phrases such as "I enjoyed every minute of it" to describe her breastfeeding experience, her partner Mali, recited her ideological objections to the practice: "I oppose breastfeeding, absolutely. If you want to, pump your milk and give it to him . . . if a child nurses, after two hours or so they need more, it doesn't sustain them." When I asked Mali how she felt when Rina was nursing their child, she replied: "It was difficult for me. Eventually, I told her: 'This is where you stop,' when she was injured and bleeding."

Some birth mothers give up nursing on their own initiative, driven by feelings of guilt toward their partners, or by the desire to protect them from experiencing exclusion. Maya, for instance, suggested to her partner Rotem: "I think that at some level both times that Rotem gave up nursing had something to do with me, whether consciously or not."

Studies of breastfeeding indicate that, in heterosexual families, the desire to involve the father in the infant's feeding correlates with justifications for combining breastfeeding with formula feeding, but not with the choice *not* to breastfeed (Bar Emet Gradman, 2019). Why then, do lesbian mothers choose not to breastfeed, or to stop nursing in response to their partners' distress, and do not resolve the issue as heterosexual women who aspire to egalitarian parenting do, by combining breastfeeding with formula feeding? It is hard to escape the thought that something about the birth mother's use of her physical "advantage" may arouse the social mother's envy, or shatter the illusion of identity between the mothers, an illusion that is precluded in the case of heterosexual couples.

Nevertheless, another factor must be considered. Most of the women I interviewed reported that they had never phantasized about breastfeeding. Many of the lesbian mothers had initially regarded pregnancy and breastfeeding as a deviation from their gender identity (cf. Corem, 2015). In fact, of the 22 lesbian mothers I interviewed, only one described her pregnancy and breastfeeding as a celebration of her femininity: "It's simply a marvelous thing. It's inconceivable that this is happening in my own body – 'Blessed are you God who has made me a woman'."[1] Those were the words of Ayala, a Reform rabbi who chose to nurse her son David for two years, a duration unparalleled by any of the other research participants who had breastfed. When I asked Michelle, Ayala's partner, if she had any difficulties with Ayala's decision to nurse for so long, her reply was:

> Me? No. Why should I? Let her breastfeed. The more the better. If it weren't so difficult for me, I would like to breastfeed Hodaya as well. I told Ayala she should nurse her. It's a waste not to, eh? From the child's perspective, it's wonderful. No, let her breastfeed – sure, why not?! I'm down for it.

Michelle used no less than ten consecutive statements to affirm the legitimacy of Ayala's extended breastfeeding period. Her constant negations of the possibility that her partner's choice might make her uncomfortable suggest a need to deny any reservations she might have had. Any feelings of envy and jealousy she might have had seem to have been superseded by a heightened idealization of Ayala's maternal capacities. Michelle declared:

> There was child abuse in the family I grew up with, extremely strict discipline, with the Holocaust always hovering overhead, and a half-mental grandmother . . . to say "half" is a compliment (laughs) . . . but really, my parenting capacities are inferior, let's put it that way, and Ayala is the warmer parent.

Through her encounter with Ayala, who grew up in a warm and functioning family, Michelle learned that family relationships can be rewarding:

> If you had asked me two years before I met Ayala, I would have told you I wasn't going to have any children. When David was born that was a real apprenticeship for me – I was just an observer – but later I fell in

---

1 Ayala here reverses the wording of the ancient Jewish blessing from the Talmud – "who has not made me a woman" – part of a series of benedictions recited by Orthodox Jews to this day during the traditional morning prayers. Reform Judaism has altered the wording of the traditional blessing to reflect a feminist outlook.

love with the job of being a parent, and by the time Hodaya was born both of us were very much "there." With the next child, I won't let Ayala near him.

Michelle derives great satisfaction from her identification with their children and appreciates her ability – through Ayala – to provide them with the kind of beneficial parenting that she never had the chance to enjoy as a child. This may explain why she is prone to feeling guilty and to delegitimize jealous feelings, as revealed by her facetious comment: "With the next child, I won't let Ayala near him."

When Michelle initially responded to the question of whether Ayala's extended nursing period had caused her any distress, a brief mention was made of the possibility that given Michelle's difficulty adapting to breastfeeding and her decision to give it up early on, Ayala might be able to nurse Michelle's biological daughter, Hodaya, alongside David, her biological son. This notion so starkly violates the social perception that "there is only one mother," and that breastfeeding is the channel for the ultimate bonding between the birth mother and her infant, helping to establish a crucial symbiotic developmental phase, that even Michelle herself did not consider it seriously as a viable possibility.

Corem (2015) describes similar cases in which lesbian partners avoid simultaneous breastfeeding – i.e., each nursing the biological child of their partner – or having one partner nurse the child they gave birth to as well as the child their partner gave birth to, due to a sense of physical discomfort or "bizarreness" vis-à-vis the social environment which may disapprove of this practice. In one case described by Corem, a lesbian couple had consulted with a psychologist about the possibility of simultaneous breastfeeding, and the therapist, espousing a conservative theoretical standpoint that privileges the importance of symbiosis between the birth mother and infant, advised them to avoid such an arrangement. In retrospect, each of the mothers felt that they had paid a heavy price in terms of their primary bond with the infant to which their partner had given birth and regretted their choice to adhere to exclusive breastfeeding of their biological child.

In this context, it should be noted that, since antiquity and until the invention of infant formula in the 20th century, breastfeeding by a wet nurse was a common and accepted practice, in particular among the upper classes. In many developing countries, this reality persists until this very day. In certain cultures, for example among Vietnamese families, and within Sunni Islam, the wet nurse is even perceived as part of the child's kinship group (see, e.g., AlHreashy, 2018; Stevens et al., 2009). Joint nursing by lesbian mothers may be an opportunity for solidarity and equality between mothers, and for breaking down barriers between biology and kinship. As for the concern about disrupting the mother-infant symbiosis, it should be noted that Bowlby, the father of attachment theory, argued (Bowlby, 1969) that a child's attachment is likely to be safer and stronger when they possess more than one early attachment figure.

Corem (2015) notes that extended breastfeeding (longer than a year) frequently exacts a high price from the relationship between the social mother and the child. Michelle and Ayala's descriptions suggest that the prolonged symbiosis between Ayala and David – the extended maternity leave that Ayala took while Michelle worked full time, the protracted period of exclusive breastfeeding, but no less so, Michelle's initial emotional ambivalence in regard to motherhood, as well as the self-doubts in regard to her parenting competencies – took a toll on the connection between Michelle and David. For example, in this exchange:

Michelle: "The connection between David and Ayala is very different from my connection with David."

Ayala: "It's hard to separate it from the biological dimension. I gave birth to David and breastfed him for two years."

Michelle: "The connection between them is very, very strong. He is much more physically connected to Ayala. And I'm, like, the fun one. When it's time for horsing around and playing with swords. And for building stuff."

According to the mothers, the introduction of Hodaya, Michelle's biological daughter, into the family, was received by David, Ayala's biological son, without any signs of difficulty or expressions of jealousy. Now that Ayala was pregnant again, the mothers were concerned things might be more difficult for him. They did not mention being concerned about how the addition of an infant to the family might potentially impact Hodaya: "We're concerned with how he will react now that *I* am giving birth," Ayala recounted.

Because of his attachment to me, because I will be performing for the baby what I did for him, that is, beyond growing him in here (points to her belly) – breastfeeding him; how will he cope with seeing someone else being breastfed? We anticipate that jealousy will arise here because of competition over a resource called *Mom*. Over me.

The expressions of concern for David's feelings reveal an implicit assumption that "There is only one mom," and that she is unquestionably the biological mother. David's lack of jealousy toward Hodaya was interpreted by the mothers as a result of the fact that Michelle is not his biological mother, or may not even be "his mother" at all.

Ayala and Michelle chose to present David with different designations for each of them – "Mommy" and "Mama" respectively – in order to distinguish between the roles that each fulfills in his life. Michelle explained this decision as follows: "Ayala is 'Mommy,' I am 'Mama'." Ayala grew up in an Israeli family; my family's background is Russian, and I called my mother 'Mama,' so we said that we wanted to create some kind of dichotomy . . . in the use of names."

While the choice of different names does indeed reflect each of the mother's intimate relationship with her own mother, it plays no less a role in fixing the unspoken assumption that "there is only one mother." This point of view is also reflected in Michelle's apprehensions about the moment in which David understood that not only did she not carry him in her body, but that he is not her genetic child:

Eventually David will understand that we are not genetically related. That's like on top of everything else that's going on, you know? A kind of dissonance between us. So there's something here that is going to pull him away, that's clear to me, yes?

Although Michelle had described herself as unprepared for parenthood and as assuming more of an observer role rather than that of a bona fide mother during David's early life (and perhaps even because of this), she is anxious that the discovery of their genetic unrelatedness will push David away even more.

The various situations presented illustrate the couple's coping with feelings of competition, jealousy, exclusion, and even disappointment from the way in which biology sabotages the utopia of egalitarian parenting, at least during the child's early years, and as long as the biological mother chooses to breastfeed. These descriptions also shed light on the experiences of contemporary heterosexual couples, who aspire to egalitarian parenting. The mother may sense disappointment in her partner's functioning, perceiving him as less committed than she had imagined during the family planning phase, and the father may sense that the physical connection between the mother and the child or the way in which the mother uses her bond with the child is a usurpation of his own place. Nonetheless, it seems that these tensions, which are organized by means of the Oedipal system and are culturally explicable as a product of sexual difference, are exacerbated among lesbian couples for whom the division of roles is less structurally predetermined, and hence the choice of who will use her body to bear a child may be perceived as more arbitrary. In this respect, the asymmetry between gay fathers, which is reduced to the genetic aspect only, also reduces the competitive feelings and jealousy between the partners and appears to be a-priori more conducive to the possibility of egalitarian parenting from the outset.

Consistent role distribution between the birth mother and the social mother

The previous chapter offered a brief glimpse into the potential dynamics in a family in which there is a consistent distribution of roles between the birth mother and the social mother. This was the case of Vicky and Nora, who are raising three children together: seven-year-old Tom, four-and-a-half-year-old Ada, and Yuli, their 12-month-old. Vicky gave birth to all three children and breastfed them, whereas Nora, who had always phantasized about adoption and did not desire pregnancy for herself, "adopted" the children. Nora related that, with time, she was able to find her own unique parental roles and her anxiety subsided, but the question of her belonging to the family and her legitimacy as a social mother remained a source of vulnerability. Her account broke off abruptly at a point in which Nora shared a painful moment in which her daughter Ada had rudely affronted her: "You're not my Mommy, I don't want you!" Both women attested that this was not a single occurrence but rather a consistent pattern of Ada's brazen rejection of Nora's parental care. In Vicky's words: "Ada often – on purpose – doesn't want Mommy Nora to dress her."

By her own admission, Nora interprets this kind of rejection as stemming directly from the fact that she did not give birth to her children and is not genetically related to them: "It sits squarely on my anxiety about not being the biological mother, anxiety that I might be rejected, that maybe I'm not a real mother." Vicky offered an alternative explanation:

Vicky: "You do this to yourself quite a lot. You place yourself on the sidelines."

Nora: "Um, that's the kind of person I am, I'm never in the center."

Vicky: [addressing me] "It's not just a question of personality; here too, just for example, this business with her studies [Nora has been a student for some 10 years, and during exam periods she secludes herself to immerse herself in her studies], so she doesn't go places.

Nora: "Ok, but I don't do it intentionally."

Vicky: "When we take a photo, she doesn't want to be in it."

Nora: "I don't like being in photos!"

Vicky: "But it's important."

Nora: "Too bad."

Vicky: "But it's important."

Nora: "I admit I do have an issue with the meals."

Vicky: "Yes. So, we sit down to eat, like today we had lunch together and everyone ate the same thing except for Nora."

Nora: "Because I don't like to eat fried chicken and French fries. So, what should I do? I don't eat that junk."

Me: "So you're into health food?"

Nora: "Not necessarily health food, but I don't like to eat the food they eat, so I eat whatever I feel like. It's true that it's difficult for me to be a part of something, even at times within my own family, it's hard to actually be a part. I'm always a kind of joiner. So, let's say when we're eating, it's really tough for me to remain seated until the end of the meal, I always have to get up and clear the table, and this is problematic, I understand that, so I try to remain seated at the table, but at some point I really just can't sit any longer. It's very, very hard for me."

It could be that these self-alienating gestures by which Nora distances herself from family life are related to her ambivalence about mothering and her fear of being swallowed up by it and losing her individuality (which may be fragile and diffuse, according to her own account); they may be related to the difficulty she has identifying with her own mother; they may be part of a defensive pattern whose purpose is to protect her from potential rejection (i.e., to be the one who rejects rather than be rejected), a threat perhaps inflated by feelings of guilt about deciding not to carry her children in her body or by feelings of envy about the symbiotic connection that Vicky was able to develop with their children. Whatever the reason, the children clearly respond to the impermanence of her presence with an unconscious choice to alienate themselves from her as a mother, and to depend mostly on Vicky. If we examine this in light of the Oedipal issue, Nora's self-positioning chiefly as their mother's partner sets her up as a convenient Oedipal rival, almost like the stepmother archetype of folklore and fairy tales. My observations in their home revealed that the two children did indeed exhibit a preference for Vicky. With Ada, as the mothers had also reported, the preference for Vicky was often coupled with an outspoken rejection of Nora, whereas Tom's preference was more muted but no less consistent. It was clear that Vicky is Tom's first port of call whenever he needs something, that he identifies with Vicky, enjoys spending time with her, and that when he says "Mommy" with no name attached, he invariably means Vicky.

But the picture is more complex than that, nonetheless. While is it clear that Vicky sees herself in Tom, enjoys his company, and feels that she understands him deeply and tacitly (an experience that she also described in relation to Yuli, the baby), her perception of Ada is somewhat grounded on projection of rejected parts of herself. Even though she admits to having been a "hot-headed" child just like Ada, she often "forgets" it:

Vicky: "Sometimes I look at Ada and say, 'How on earth did Ada come out of me?'"

Nora: "And I say, I'm lucky that it wasn't I who gave birth to her because then Vicky would have said, 'You with your temperament, with your character'."

Vicky: "Ada is proof that nurture trumps nature . . . (laughs) with me there's just one or two buttons to press, that's it – no need for a manual. But with Ada no manual could cover it all – it's truly exhausting, you always have to sense what kind of mood she's in. Sometimes you can't help but tell her, 'Ada, come on, cut it out, really.' I'm very comfortable with Tom, I love being with him. I really love doing stuff that he likes to do. But Ada, I absolutely do not understand what she wants to do at any given moment."

Nora: "That's true, but I don't get worked up about it as much with Ada when this happens. She and I are similar in that way. I think Ada still hasn't figured out what she likes to do, and that's why she always demands that we engage her and guide her. She flourishes in settings that provide both guidance and space, and I'm a lot like that. I really hope she forms her own identity, not when she's 20-something, but earlier, because I do feel that she's a bit lost. Because with Tom, it's quite clear to him what his interests are, and she is in his shadow."

Although Nora may find it difficult to be consistently present in the family's day-to-day life, it is clear that she senses her children deeply and can provide the appropriate emotional resonance, a skill that may be missing from Vicky's maternal toolbox. This is particularly true in regard to the parents' challenges in containing Ada's stormy temperament. Although her daughter is hardly easy on her, Nora still manages to mobilize from within herself a profound identification and compassion for Ada. Despite the rage and rejection she expresses toward Nora, in a family picture that Ada drew in kindergarten and chose to show me, she and Mommy Nora appear side by side, both sporting heads of curly green hair, a testament of sorts to an unconscious identification with her.

Similar to Vicky and Nora's account of their experience, for Ossi and Iggy, the role distribution between the birth mother and social mother was practically self-evident: while Ossi included pregnancy in her vision of parenthood, Iggy's parenting aspirations developed over time, but were unrelated to carrying a pregnancy, an experience which she considered alien to her gender identity.

Following complications of her pregnancy, Ossi was rushed into emergency Caesarean section in the 35th week of her pregnancy, resulting in the twins Ella and Nadav spending their first month of life in a neonatal intensive care unit (NICU), during which time Ossi recovered from surgery. When Iggy reminisced about the birth, she spoke of her immediate bond with the children, whereas Ossi looked back at those days with a sense of regret and loss:

I didn't really experience it. Iggy would bring my milk to the children in the NICU. . . . Also, the fact that I was under general anesthesia – they were born and I felt nothing. It was Iggy in fact who experienced the entire birth. I learned over time to love them. It wasn't like a bombshell, not a bit.

Close to the time of Ella and Nadav's release from the NICU, Ossi's mother died of cancer. Due to these unfortunate circumstances, Iggy continued to function as the children's main caregiver during their early infancy. Ossi recalled:

[During the pregnancy] Iggy was fearful: "Maybe they won't love me? Maybe I'll be less attached to them? How will I feel them?", but everything turned upside down. There were times when I said to Iggy, "What is this? It's like I'm nobody in the family, they want only you."

Iggy: "The surrogate." [Laughs.]
Ossi: "Exactly. They were really attached to Iggy. It has balanced out a little. I've found my place with them, they found their place. We became a family. It takes time."

Five and a half years later, the children were visibly attached to both mothers, but no less apparent was the fact that Iggy, the social mother, remains the preferred parent for both children: both her son and her daughter "court" her incessantly, battle for her attention, and, according to the mothers' reports, also propose marriage to her.

But even taking into account these background conditions – the fact that Iggy's choice to be the social mother was consolidated and in conformance with her identity; as well as the fact that due to life circumstances, she became the children's unmistakable primary attachment figure as well as their Oedipal love object – none of these facts proved sufficient to quell anxieties about her parental status being compromised by the lack of genetic affiliation with her children. This was evidenced by the intense distress with which she reacted to the family picture that Ella had drawn, in which all the family members, except for Iggy, are holding a balloon.

Iggy: "Why don't I have a balloon?"
Ossi: "Why doesn't Iggy have a balloon?"
Ella: "I'll make one."
Iggy: [in a whining tone] "Why don't I have a balloon?"
Ella: "I'll make you one, Iggy Wiggy!"

Iggy:	[in the third person] "Her balloon burst. What happened to Mommy Iggy?"
Ella:	"I'll make you a balloon that won't burst."
Ossi:	"Oy, oy, oy, Ella."
Iggy:	"I don't have a balloon! Ella, were you in a rush? Wait a minute, maybe my balloon just flew up into the air. Did it fly up?"

Drawing 7 "The family goes on a trip": Ella's family drawing.
(From right to left: Nadav, Ella, Mommy Ossi, and Mommy Iggy.)

The moment Iggy laid eyes on her balloon-less figure, her peace of mind gave way to persecutory disruptive thoughts about the drawing's possible meanings. She had a hard time letting go of the matter and focusing on the couple's interview, and repeatedly asked me to clarify how I would interpret such a representation:

Iggy:	"I want to know your interpretation of my no-balloon. What does it mean?"
Me:	"How did *you* interpret it?"
Iggy:	"I don't know. Something is lacking. I'm lacking something, no? Lack is always negative. Ella didn't answer my question, she

said she was going to add it later . . . unless maybe she was in a hurry or something. Maybe she didn't finish the drawing?"

Iggy panicked at the sight of a possible representation of lack. The potential space for imagination, associative play, and thinking collapsed into a narrow one-dimensional reality: if indeed some kind of lack was there, Iggy immediately associated it with the missing genetic element in her kinship relations with Ella. Iggy asked Ella repeatedly why she had drawn her without a balloon, but her question did not sound like an invitation for open, curious exploration, but rather demanded either negation ("It's not that she has no balloon, it simply burst or flew up into the air"), instant soothing (an alternative explanation, for example, that Ella was in a rush to finish and didn't have time to draw in Iggy's balloon), or a magical reparation (Ella would add another balloon that doesn't burst). The latter solution is magical reparation because the addition of a balloon to Iggy's image would not affect the actual sense of lack, if such a sense existed.

Indeed, the opposite is true here: if the drawing did in fact represent an experience of lack associated with the genetic aspect, instead of this becoming a shared opportunity to work through emotions, the situation resulted in pressure being placed on five-and-a-half-year-old Ella to deny her feelings. Ossi, who was activated by Iggy's distress, joined her expectation that Ella would provide Iggy with the soothing she needed. Nadav was also mobilized to action: when he later heard Iggy continuing to agonize over the missing balloon, he yelled over to us: "Ossi, you're fatter, so that's why we love Iggy more."

As I studied the picture myself, another interpretation – different from Iggy's – came to mind: I saw a representation of a family whose members are all in love with Iggy, courting her and presenting her with tribute. Exactly as in the picture, Ossi, Ella, and Nadav had each in their turn offered Iggy a "balloon," attempting to cheer her up and gratify her when she was in distress. Among the numerous factors that shape the children's Oedipal choice, one can perhaps point out the early attachment to Iggy as the primary caregiver, but also significant is her need for courting by her children in order to assuage her anxieties about the lack of genetic affiliation. This lack, which continues to torment her at an unconscious level, also vexes her children, as part of the enigmatic messages that are transmitted to them in the context of their relationship with her (see Laplanche, 1987).

To paraphrase Freud, this context enables us to declare that biology is not destiny. Having chosen not to give birth herself, Iggy took care of her children almost exclusively during their early infancy, thus establishing her status as the primary attachment figure of both her children and later as their Oedipal object of desire. Nora, differently, positioned herself from the outset as the partner of Vicky, the birth mother, and felt that her place was threatened as Vicky devoted herself to the long and pleasureful symbiotic connection with the children. However, beyond these differences in circumstances, personality differences play a part: whereas Iggy's self-doubts and lack of confidence in regard to her position within the family led her to mobilize the other family members to actively court and assuage her fears, Nora's sensitivity to experiences of exclusion and jealousy enhanced tactics of seclusion and self-distancing, and ultimately exacerbated her experience of alienation. To some measure, each of the mothers chose a coping strategy that was in keeping with her psychological makeup. While Nora tends to elevate the levels of conflict, she is also capable ultimately of containing feelings of non-belonging and alienation in a manner that surpasses Iggy's capacities.

A family configuration in which one of the mothers assumes the role of birth mother for all the children creates a unique vulnerability for the social mother, who is liable to experience anxiety and a sense of threat regarding her place in the family configuration. Conflicts or anger that are inherent to relations between parents and children, and even necessary for the child's development, may be automatically interpreted as a reflection of the missing biological component of the relationship. How the social mother copes with the sense of threat depends on her personality structure, the couple's relationship, and circumstances; but it will nevertheless have an effect on family dynamics, as children find themselves reacting to the social mother's unconscious message, whether by gestures of courtship, or by demonstrations of rage and attempts at exclusion. In this manner, emotions associated with the issue of genetic affiliation are channeled into the child's Oedipal structuration.

From birth mother to social mother and vice versa: on families in which each mother fulfills both roles

One of the ways to trace the differences between the experience of the social mother and that of the biological mother is by attending to the descriptions of lesbian mothers who have experienced both roles, and the transition from one position to the other.

Efrat: "It was very difficult, the reversal of roles. I kind of say to myself, half-joking, but also very seriously, that I was actually a dad before I gave birth. *I went from being a dad to being a mom.*"

Me: "What does that mean to you?"

Efrat: "I was working long hours, and that was enough for me. There was something about it that was detached . . . [clears her throat], not detached, because of course I was very attached to Ruth and loved her a lot, but the way I view it today, once the hormones start to produce stuff, I don't know how to explain it, something happens with all that. It didn't happen to me in the biological sense just in relation to Danny, it happened in relation to them both. Something inside me opened up. It literally turned me from a father into a mother."

The change Efrat describes taking place in her upset the harmonious role division that the couple had enjoyed while raising Ruth.

Efrat: "I think it was hard for Sandra to switch from the role of the unambiguous mom into. . . of course, not into a dad, right? Because a mother can probably never go back to being a father, but to take a step back and let me be in the center, let me be the mother now, that was very, very hard for her. It really made things rocky for us as a couple, this thing. Suddenly the fact that I have an opinion on stuff is annoying. Since when? A dad has no opinion."

Sandra: "Suddenly she's a pain in the neck."

Me: [laughing] "Wow, listening to you two is like watching the gender revolution in fast-forward . . ."

Sandra: "That's right, it's mind blowing. The most difficult crisis I ever experienced was when Efrat gave birth, and I simply went to work two weeks later. I fell into a real depression. I didn't really understand how this was happening, that my baby was just born and I'm going to work, and I'm not staying with him, building my intimacy with him. I was in shock."

Efrat: "It began right at the birth. In my opinion, it was there that Sandra experienced . . ."

Sandra:	"I felt as though my baby was just born but someone had taken him away from me. Just like that."
Efrat:	"She was also very angry at me over this."
Sandra:	"I was really angry. I didn't know how to process all of this. It was really hard."
Me:	"But wasn't this an issue throughout the entire pregnancy? Didn't it feel outside of your control and inside her body?"
Efrat:	"Look, I have to say that Sandra has this ability that maybe not a lot of people share, of, like, truly phantasizing. I think that she was really *certain that she was pregnant*. Like, she actually went through this pregnancy. I'm telling you that as I was giving birth and the baby came out, it's like she didn't understand why they didn't place the baby on her."
Sandra:	"I stood there and for me, it was as though they had taken him out – the experience was one of . . . the way I see it, it's harder for the person who supports the birth than for the person giving birth. That's clear to me today, and I think that the partners of the person giving birth are being wronged. Utterly wronged. He had just come out of the womb, and I just stood there. It was like a kind of abandonment or something. There's one moment there that I think back on for years now and it still makes me cry. I can actually remember the moment when they took him and placed him on Efrat and I stood there all *alone*, and that, that, that was horrible. So you see, this emotional experience has nothing to do with reality. Nothing! She gave birth. The newborn she gave birth to should be placed on her, she's the one who needs to breastfeed. I was totally cut off, self-absorbed. I had no ability to observe, it's like I was inside of some kind of a bubble. An absolute bubble. And that bubble persisted for many months."
Efrat:	"There is a very egocentric flavor to it, but your egocentricity comes from a place that is self-aware. Other women might experience the same thing, but they repress it, they push it off to the side and don't make any room for it. And you made room for it."
Me:	"I understand the problematic aspects here. But there is also an element that is . . . in other words, both for better and for worse, there is also your ability to experience it as though he was inside your

own body. In any case, in terms of parental bonding, that is also
something."

Efrat: "Amazing. Yes, it's amazing."

Beyond her explanation of how difficult it was to share with Efrat a position that had been exclusively hers before, and beyond her confusion about her loss of autonomy in regard to numerous parenting responsibilities, Sandra describes the birth event as a traumatic experience. One of the traumatic elements appears in the way she speaks about the experience in terms of abandonment (perhaps kidnapping), when she is denied the physical possibility of connecting symbiotically with the infant and is instead forced to observe his physical connection with Efrat from the sidelines. This description echoes the primal scene phantasy, which certainly played an active role, even if an unconscious one, in the emotional reactions to the events.

The experience of exclusion from the mother-child dyad, which can be described in terms of Oedipal jealousy, also corresponds to the experience of many heterosexual men in the transition from being a couple to being a triad, as Sandra herself noted. However, Sandra's account suggests that the most traumatic element in Efrat's birth experience relates to her sudden disillusionment – her painful realization that she was simply accompanying Efrat's pregnancy, but wasn't actually carrying it in her body.

> "There is a very egocentric flavor to it," as Efrat suggested, "but your egocentricity comes from a place that is self-aware. Other women might experience the same thing, but they repress it, they push it off to the side and don't make any room for it. And you made room for it."

Efrat's conclusion is convincing; Sandra's overpowering experience can teach us something about the nuances of the experience of other social mothers, who may not allow themselves to recognize their emotional experience in full.

The intensity of the shock and of feelings such as jealousy, or abandonment can be explained by the intensity of Sandra's identification with Efrat, an identification made possible by Sandra's earlier experience as a birth mother, and the feelings of affinity and resemblance that women share in a way perhaps unparalleled in relations between a man and a woman. While this level of identification made it more difficult to reconcile herself to the differences that separated her from Efrat, it remained available for building a connection with her non-biological child. After the initial upheavals had subsided, attachments between the children and their mothers developed in a crisscross pattern: each of the two children displayed a consistent preference for their social mother rather than their birth mother – Danny for Sandra and Ruth for Efrat.

Sandra's lucid account of her emotional experience might shed light on Shir's experience, another mother who described the fierce anxieties that gripped her during her transition from the role of birth mother to that of social mother:

Shir: "When Moran was pregnant, her pregnancy was very, very rough, and I was extremely anxious . . . how the birth would go and stuff like that."

Me: "You were worried for her, for her wellbeing?"

Shir: "I was worried for her, but, pardon me sweetie (laughs), I was more worried about myself. I had this nightmare where something happened during the birth, and the child was taken from me. Actually, two to three weeks before his birth, I had an anxiety attack, we had an ambulance actually come here, and everybody thought it was for Moran, but I was simply experiencing a full-blown panic attack: that something might happen during the birth and the baby would be taken away from me, I have no legal rights over him."

The knowledge that once the baby arrived, Shir would have no legal rights over him, aroused anxiety and a sense of injustice. Sandra's intense experience may illuminate other, less conscious elements in Shir's story, ones associated with her deep identification with Moran, as well as feelings of jealousy and competition over the mother's place. Shir's anxiety about the child being taken away also stems from her recognition of the fact that the moment he is born, Shir will be demoted to second place, while the emergent dyad between the infant and Moran takes the lead. This can also be interpreted as a wish to eliminate Moran and enjoy an exclusive bond with the baby. Shir's feelings of jealousy toward Moran, her competitiveness, as well as the intensity of her identification, are enacted concretely when she ordered an ambulance for herself, while everyone else was sure that it must be Moran on the way to hospital to give birth. The long months of looking after Moran during her difficult pregnancy might have also aroused envy and a need to remind Moran that she also needs looking after.

Sandra and Shir's somatic identification with their pregnant partners can also be seen as a version of couvade – a term coined by the anthropologist Edward Tylor to describe rituals performed in pre-modern societies. In these rituals, the father lies down on a bed in a separate hut from that of the birth mother and mimics the birth contractions, with the aim of warding off spirits and protecting the mother and fetus, while simultaneously solidifying his social identity as the father, in an environment that, according to Tylor's view, did not recognize the direct connection between sexual intercourse and childbirth.

Nowadays, "couvade syndrome" is used as a medical term equivalent to "sympathetic pregnancy." The symptoms include, among others, weight gain, nausea, sleep disturbances, heartburn, breast fullness, or nipple pain, and in rarer cases men experience labor-like pains, and even post-partum depression. Among men who were examined some ten weeks from the start of their partner's pregnancy until a month after it ended, hormonal changes were observed, including lower levels of testosterone and higher levels of prolactin, the hormone responsible for post-partum lactation. Psychological theory regards this phenomenon as psychosomatic and points to the way in which modernization processes have led to a higher incidence of the syndrome and an intensification of its symptoms: men today are more active in the process of pregnancy and in preparing for it, and there is greater identification with the woman as well as a desire on the part of the father for closer proximity and larger involvement in the primary care of the child. Based on the two examples of Sandra and Shir, one can estimate that the social mother's identification with her partner, as well as her desire for closer proximity and sharing in the primary care of the infant, are of a greater magnitude than those of the heterosexual father. This identification, along with its somatic expressions, is even more pronounced in cases like those of Sandra and Shir, in which the social mother has experienced pregnancy and childbirth in the past.

Another possible explanation for the crisis that Sandra and Shir experienced in their transition to the role of social mother is the fact that both mothers had been symbiotic with their first child: they had breastfed exclusively and dedicated themselves to the mother-infant dyad in a way that initially allowed no room for a second parent. Perhaps they feared they would not be able to endure the kind of exclusion that they had previously expected their partners to contain. Unlike Sandra's partner Efrat, who had described herself as having earlier felt comfortable with the role of "father," Moran, Shir's partner, described her traumatic experience in terms of her son Adam being snatched away from her right after his birth, due to tragic circumstances.

"Shir gave birth and her father passed away one month later, and in fact, from the moment she gave birth he began to slowly decline," Moran related.

We were living in the middle of nowhere, and this was the first time I was having a child, I have no institutional recognition of this thing, it has zero validity, and I have to keep on going to work. And Shir traveled to the south of the country to be with her family. Things were really difficult between us. I kept on wanting him to come back, I felt that *she was taking away my child*, I felt like: 'Wait, wait, give me a moment to hold him, to get a sense that it is actually real.' And it created immense hardship for us. And lots of lasting hurt, since I didn't really give her the opportunity to be completely present with her father as he was dying, and for me, truly it was a horrible, horrible, horrible, time, as though my own child, a child was born to me – he's mine, he isn't mine – he is taken away.

The psychological quandary that Moran describes is the outcome of institutional discrimination, but perhaps no less so of discrimination within the relationship. A slip of the tongue by Shir, Moran's partner, later during the couple's interview, brought to the surface her implicit belief that the birth mother is the child's "real" mother:

Shir: "I had a fear about how my mother would accept Eden, because, like, *he's not my son*."
Moran: "What do you mean 'not my son?', Sweetie!"
Shir: "Because he's not my biological son [laughs]. Because I didn't give birth to him."

Shir's belief about Eden, Moran's biological son, was probably also in the air during those moments when Moran's place in Adam's life was being negotiated, when circumstances obliged Shir to be away from their shared home environment.

Shir and Moran's fears, each in her own turn that the baby would be snatched away at birth, materialized to a certain degree as their life played out, when each of the children exhibited a pronounced and enduring

140 What does genetics have to do with kinship, anyway?

preference for their birth mother, a preference that involved rejection of the social mother. Following a deliberate effort to create quality time for each mother with her non-biological child, within two to three years each mother began to find her place in her relationship with each child. After a certain balance was achieved in the relationship of each mother with Adam, their eldest son, during the Oedipal stage his clear preference for Shir reemerged, this time in the form of romantic courting and repeated marriage proposals, which were not manifested toward Moran in any shape or form.

Like two basketball teams: competition between two sub-families

Another phenomenon that can be observed in lesbian families in which each mother gave birth to one of the children is the experience of two sub-families coexisting within the nuclear family. This was most pronounced in Talia and Dahlia's family, in which the mothers had selected a different sperm donor for each of the children, only to later regret having done so. As they attested, they felt that had they chosen to use the same donor, perhaps some kind of connecting thread would have bound the children together. However, as their narrative revealed, the mothers did in fact relate to each of their sons as a clone of his genetic mother, in a way that implied erasure of the sperm donor's genetic contribution.

Dahlia: "The way the children differ from each other corresponds *exactly* to the ways in which we are different from each other. I sometimes look at them and am so aware of the differences that I feel as though this picture was photoshopped – as if two pictures were put together."

Talia: "Like they were pasted into the same frame. It's pretty funny because the whole nature vs. nurture thing really sticks out. Lior resembles Dahlia's family so much – personality-wise and also in his facial features, it's hilarious. Dahlia and her father and Lior look like a coordinated set. But Lior, since he's already a big kid and has his own entire personality, you can see how much the environment has influenced him: what kind of baby he was, what kind of toddler he was, and now that he's a kid, it's like he's beginning to lean a bit toward the side of my family, which is more like – Aah! [being goofy]."

Dahlia: "In short, if we could have mixed up our genes, we would have been happy people. Because sometimes I feel like there's an actual wall. Like there is Lior and there is Yoav. There is Cohen and there is Strauss."

Talia: "So, so true. I often feel this with Lior. That he is a very emotionally complex child, and I am *not*. When he was four he sometimes behaved in ways that were beyond my comprehension. Like, I could watch from the side and hear Dahlia verbalizing his feelings, but didn't have the tools, I am not equipped with that. *They* [the Cohen family] are intellectuals. *We* [the Strauss family] are nature lovers and outdoorsy types. *They* are homebodies. *They* are also more introspective, they're a really introspective family, all with some kind of very high level of self-awareness. With us, it's more like Aah! [waves her hands goofily] a bird! We're all like that, the entire family, like, without exception. Yoav is really like the Strauss family, and Lior is a complete Cohen."

The division into two genetic subgroups within the nuclear family, "us" and "them," naturally pervades the children's experience of the family. In the family drawing assignment, their six-year-old chose to draw "two basketball teams."

Drawing 8 "Two basketball teams": Lior's family drawing.

142   What does genetics have to do with kinship, anyway?

Lior: "I'm making two families – that's the most fun! Basketball hoops, let's make . . . a closed arena, a closed arena [sings to himself as he draws a brown frame around the picture], here's a mother, a father, and brother who's really tall and *huge* because he's 11 years old – that's the family of LA Lakers. And let's make another team: the Lakers are in yellow and their greatest rival is wearing red! I'm drawing the Chicago Bulls like babies because the parents in the Bulls are not allowed to play."

When asked to draw a picture of a family, Lior chose to draw a "closed arena," in which two families co-exist. One of the families is in yellow and the other is in red – two basic colors that share no common element – a choice that echoes the mothers' feelings: "I feel as though this picture was photoshopped"; "Like they were pasted into the same frame."

But the two families are not only radically different, they are also sworn rivals. The rival team is diminished and belittled: they are defined as the babies' team, perhaps the most deprecatory label one child can use against another, indicating how easy it is to defeat them in competition, and the competition, as his description suggests, is over parental resources: whereas the Lakers team has two parents and a child, the children from the Bulls are denied access to parental assistance; furthermore, according to the universal tendency to attribute more complex human traits and feelings to the "in-group," together with the de-humanization of the "out-group" (Haslam, 2006), Lior gave his team members human facial features, while the members of the rival team remain faceless.

The lesbian feminist vision of families free of a predetermined hierarchical structure based on gendered role division encounters various difficulties in light of the structural asymmetry of a family with two mothers: choosing a family configuration in which one of the mothers gives birth to all of the children exposes the social mother to existential vulnerability in regard to her place in the family. She thus becomes susceptible to fears that her children might reject her and is prone to jealousy of the relationship between the biological mother and the children. On the other hand, choosing a family configuration in which each mother gives birth to one of the children often precipitates a crisis of adaptation of each mother to her new role, and may underscore issues of jealousy and competition between the mothers, enhance each child's sense of belonging to their genetic family of origin, and as a result diminish the sense of family belonging and even exacerbate feelings of competition among the children. Nevertheless, even when one of the mothers serves as a dominant attachment figure for the child during early infancy, over time the division of roles between the mothers balances out, and in most cases one observes a recalibration which enables each mother to find her place. The illustrations presented suggest that genetic affiliation means little per se, but the meanings attributed to it – and the emotional responses attached to such attributions – do in turn affect the emotional climate and the matrix of relationships within the family.

Whereas the differences between the birth mother and the social mother involve not only genetic affiliation to the child, but also the experiences of pregnancy, childbirth, and sometimes breastfeeding – which oftentimes affects early parental role division – among gay fathers, the question of biological affinity plays a less significant role in terms of actual parental functioning. This is not to say that the issue of biological affiliation does not induce conflictual feelings among gay couples, or that it does not create an arena of competition, jealousy, anxiety, and loss; but it appears that these phenomena occur with less intensity than in lesbian families, and that the anxieties of the social father in regard to his parental status are often displaced onto the social sphere and are less pertinent to his relationship with his children.

References

AlHreashy, F. A. (2018). Non-maternal nursing in the muslim community: A health perspective review. *Journal of Clinical Neonatology*, 7(4), 191–197.

Almack, K. (2005). What's in a name? The significance of the choice of surnames given to children born within lesbian-parent families. *Sexualities*, 8(2), 239–254.

Bar Emet Gradman, S. (2019). *What nourishes the mother-infant relationship? On breastfeeding, feeding experience, parental embodied mentalizing and mother-infant bonding [Hebrew]*. University of Haifa (Israel) ProQuest Dissertations Publishing.

Benjamin, J. (1988). *The bonds of love: Psychoanalysis, feminism, and the problem of domination*. Pantheon Books.

Bowlby, J. (1969). *Attachment and loss*. Basic Books.

Corem, O. (2015). *"Mama – heart, mama – belly": Maternal identity of Israeli raising (non-biological) lesbian mothers* [Hebrew] [PhD dissertation, The Hebrew University of Jerusalem].

Haslam, N. (2006). Dehumanization: An integrative review. *Personality and Social Psychology Review*, 10(3), 252–264.

Laplanche, J. (1987). *New foundations for psychoanalysis*. Blackwell.

Rich, A. C. (1980). *Compulsory heterosexuality and lesbian existence* (1st ed.). Antelope Publications.

Stevens, E. E., Patrick, T. E., & Pickler, R. (2009). A history of infant feeding, *Journal of Perinatal Education, 18*(2), 32–39.

Ziv, A. (2020). Querying lesbian fatherhood. In H. W. Henriksson & K. Goedecke (Eds.), *Close relations: Critical studies of family and kinship* (pp. 21–36). Springer.

Chapter five

Back to the closet
The issue of the child's genetic origin among gay fathers

Avi and Nathan are jointly raising the twins Noah and Gili, Avi's genetic children. Throughout my interview with them, I sensed a gap between Nathan's explicit ideology, which regards genetics as a trivial and unimportant matter, and feelings of discomfort, shame, and inferiority that he appears to actively disavow.

When I asked how they decided which of them would provide the sperm to create embryos, they answered as follows:

Avi: "It wasn't important at first for Nathan, so the decision was easy." [Laughs.]

Nathan: "To this day, I firmly believe that a child is formed through education and values. As for genetics, like, *givin' the sperm*, well, I don't place too much importance on the whole issue of one's genes. On the contrary, there are often disadvantages to genetic affiliation in terms of being a carrier of disease and stuff like that."

Nathan's emotional need to diminish the importance of genetics was reflected in his use of the belittling expression (*givin' the sperm*) and was made even more apparent by the logical contradiction in his argument. His first point – that genetics has only a marginal influence – is unwittingly undermined by his second statement which attributes immense influence (albeit mostly of a negative sort) to genetics ("There are often disadvantages in terms of being a carrier of disease and stuff like that") – as something that one is better off relinquishing. In his distress, Nathan appears to grasp for straws, as a defense against feelings of lack or inferiority. Later, Nathan related that, although he did not view genetics as

DOI: 10.4324/9781032663333-8

important, ultimately he also provided his own sperm, in order to gratify his mother.

Nathan: "So after we went through the whole process, it turned out I'm more or less shooting blanks. Like, we don't know whether it would have worked out if I had undergone treatments, but the fact is that my sperm did not make the 'Passage to India'."

Me: "Did that affect you in any way?"

Nathan: "Yes, I went through a teeny-tiny crisis. Mostly it was about 'now, that I was ready to go through this thing.' You sort of, you start to imagine stuff. Even though I sincerely didn't think it was important, it's more like I felt I was pushed into a corner that I didn't want to go into, and it kind of made me want to . . ."

Me: "Ah . . . so what is it that you begin to imagine when you suddenly open up this door? What were you able to imagine?"

Nathan: "Truthfully? The answer is Noah and Gili. I think we prove exactly what I've been arguing all the time, that genetics is very marginal. I think that Noah and Gili prove this. From day one, everyone has been telling me that Noah is me; everyone is absolutely certain. By the way, we don't tell people who is who, but they're utterly certain that Noah is from me and that Gili is from Avi."

Nathan's shift to narrating himself in the second person ("*you* start to imagine") exposed how painful it was to stay with his subjective experience and reflected his vulnerability. His need to minimize the crisis around the discovery of his infertility is conspicuous in his addition of the qualifier "teeny-tiny." Any negative feelings that may have arisen were at once translated into anger toward the environment that had cornered him against his will, perhaps also due to some "unthought known" (Bollas, 1987) – some unformulated knowledge relating to his infertility. The door that Nathan had opened just a crack wide was quickly shut during the interview; Nathan went back to denying the feelings that came up when thinking about genetic parenting, choosing instead to defend an ideology that privileges nurture over nature. The repetition of the word "prove" indicates the defensiveness of his position, as though the burden of proof were on him.

When I asked whether their choice not to reveal to their social circle the fact that both children are genetically related to Avi could indicate anxiety or discomfort provoked by the issue, both fathers denied this possibility.

Nathan explained that he had simply acquiesced to his mother's request that he not share this fact with the environment. I later asked what might have motivated his mother to request this. Nathan replied:

Nathan: "I didn't go into it; I respected her request."
Avi: "I assume that had it been your children, there would have been no such request." [Laughs.]
Nathan: [laughing] "Correct."

Nathan accepted Avi's phrasing – "If it had been *your children*" – without any visible sign of protest. This revealed the unconscious belief held by both fathers that their genetic affiliation meant the children were more Avi's than they were Nathan's. The number of times in which Avi repeated formulations of this kind during the interview ("We knew *they were mine* at the outset because Nathan is infertile"; "I think that the fact that *they're mine* made things easier for my father") throws into relief Nathan's experience of feeling inferior, as well as his need to enlist some ideology to combat these feelings. This conflict took place at an unconscious or preconscious level, while at the same time the couple's shared parenting practices tended toward an egalitarian model, in which, however, Nathan takes a more central role in caring for the home and for the children. During the observation, as in the projective tasks that the children performed, no evidence was apparent of any advantage that Avi had over Nathan. Even the feelings of inferiority that he displayed were related more to aspects of his masculine identity, his physical competence, as well as feelings of unworthiness, especially in a social or cultural context, and less in respect to his functioning as a father, his connection or bond with his sons, his understanding of them or their degree of attachment to him – areas that among social mothers could become fertile ground for feelings of inferiority or anxiety.

Inferiority or anxiety about the quality of the social father's bonding with the child may manifest at a low level of intensity when a child is expected and during the first months of their life. At this time, the difficulties of the transition into parenthood and establishing the relationship with the infant may be interpreted by the social father in terms of a lack related to the absence of a genetic affiliation with the child:

Daniel: "We both produced embryos, and two embryos were transferred, one of each. Only one embryo implanted, and so, throughout the

148   What does genetics have to do with kinship, anyway?

	pregnancy, we didn't know which one implanted until we did a paternity test."
Me:	"What did this bring up for you?"
Amos:	"I think that the excitement and the intense activity around the culmination of the pregnancy and the actual birth overshadowed that bit, right? Only later does one think about whose the child is, and why, and what it all means."
Daniel:	"Not true. I remember it being hard for me."
Me:	"Were you disappointed?"
Daniel:	"Of course. And I was jealous. And frightened. I was really frightened about not bonding with Itamar because, like, he's not mine. I was afraid that I wouldn't love him. I think that every new parent might have these thoughts, like, that thing where you don't fall in love with the infant immediately, and it's something that takes time; so because of this situation I thought that this might be happening because . . . because he's *not mine*."

The gap between the experiences of Amos, Itamar's genetic father, and Daniel, his social father, is apparent. Although both experienced difficulty bonding at first with the infant, Daniel overlayed the initial difficulty with additional meanings related to the lack of a genetic affiliation between him and his child. However, Daniel's initial difficulties stemmed not only from the meanings he attached to genetics but also from a sense of loss that his biological embryo did not survive (cf. Tabak-Aviram, 2011).

Daniel's difficulty was exacerbated by the couple's choice not to share the facts about their son Itamar's genetic affiliation with their larger circle. This choice deprived Daniel of the possibility of sharing his feelings and of using the environment for emotional support at a time when he needed it.

Daniel continued to share his experience:

We decided not to tell people and our families because we didn't want it to be like from the very start he is someone's – and then you might have one of the families that feels more attached or less attached. In fact, I kind of had the feeling that I was *lying* to my family. That was very hard for me. That's something that I had nobody to talk to about, because actually nobody else goes through this, at least not in my circles, dealing with a child that you have to start to raise as if he's yours and you *know that he's not yours.* That was an issue in which I felt a bit alone and lacking in support.

Daniel's words embody an implicit assumption that he is concealing the "fact" that the child that he is raising is not actually his, as if the thing requiring concealment is not the information about genetic affiliation but rather the "truth" deriving from it – i.e., that a non-genetic father is not a "real father."

A central concern voiced by gay couples during the interviews was how to handle the fraught question of the child's genetic affiliation. Contradictory strategies of concealment versus disclosure often give rise to a troubling dynamic, which echoes, sometimes unconsciously, the experience of being "in the closet," or coming out of it.

Back to the closet: between concealment and confession

In her highly influential book *The Epistemology of the Closet*, gender theorist Eve Kosofsky Sedgwick (1990) points to the central place of the "closet" in homosexual identity. Her persuasive arguments are significant for analyzing modes of coping with the genetic issue, as manifested in same-sex families generally, and in families of gay fathers in particular.

Sedgwick argues that the "closet" is symptomatic of homophobia, in a sense that has no parallel in other contexts of oppression, except perhaps in the case of religious or cultural oppression. This is because gender, age, or skin color, as examples of other identities that are the object of oppression, are incapable a-priori of concealment. She mentions antisemitism as a reasonable point of comparison:

> Ethnic/ cultural/ religious oppressions such as anti-Semitism are more analogous in that the stigmatized individual has at least notionally some discretion – although, importantly, it is never to be taken for granted how much – over other people's knowledge of her or his membership in the group.

> (p. 75)

Unlike lesbian mothers, for whom pregnancy discloses the identity of the genetic mother, a-priori, gay fathers face a spectrum of choices ("at least notionally," in Kosofsky-Sedgwick's words): whether to speak publicly about their child's genetic affiliation or to conceal it, whether to tell the children themselves, and when, and even whether to find out their child's genetic affiliation themselves. Cumulative research findings about the rates of concealment of genetic affiliation among heterosexual, lesbian, and gay couples who are assisted by gamete donation, reveals that the more the circumstances allow for concealment, the greater the chance that concealment will take place in practice; it follows that these various configurations do not diverge in terms of the degree to which parents experience difficulty in regard to their need of gamete donation, or to the very fact that one of the parents is not genetically affiliated with the child, as much as they differ in the degree to which these elements can be obscured or concealed (Jadva et al., 2012; MacCallum & Keeley, 2012; Freeman et al., 2009; Blake et al., 2016).

Among other matters, Kosofsky-Sedgwick discusses situations in which homosexual identity constitutes an "open secret" and asks how a person's homosexuality can exist in the space between knowing and not knowing. At what moment does it become possible to speak about it? To what extent does the axis of homosexuality/heterosexuality parallel the axes of secrecy/disclosure; knowledge/ignorance; private/public, etc. (Ziv & Gross, 2010)? Inspired by Sedgwick's analysis, I will seek to position the dichotomy of genetic/non-genetic parent as that which implies and generates all the other axes, in families of gay fathers.

After posting a parallel between homophobia and antisemitism, Kosofsky-Sedgwick offers an analysis of the scene in the Book of Esther in which Queen Esther comes out as a Jew to her husband King Ahasuerus, as it is referenced in Proust's citation of the play *Esther* by Racine. She characterizes Esther's story as a simplistic yet powerful coming-out phantasy, with all its transformative potential: "In concealing her Judaism from her husband, King Assuérus (Ahasuerus), Esther the Queen feels she is concealing, simply, her identity: 'The King is to this day unaware who I am'" (p. 75).

A parallel can be found between the terminology used by Nathan, Avi's partner, and the social father of the twins Noah and Gili, to describe the closet of genetic affiliation, and the text concerning Esther's closeted Jewish identity:

From day one, everyone's been telling me that Noah is me, everyone is absolutely certain. By the way, we don't tell people *who is who*, but they're utterly certain that Noah is from me and that Gili is from Avi.

Back to the closet 151

This statement implies that genetic affiliation is perceived in terms of identity: parental identity, the child's identity, and especially the phantasized identity between parent and child which is a product of genetics. The phantasmatic dimension is implied by the notion of an exact genetic copy, which is a more fitting description of cloning than of fertilization.

Later, during the conversation about Avi and Nathan's choice to conceal the children's genetic affiliation, the couple expressed the following:

Nathan: "By the way, there are some people who know *the truth*. People who are very, very close know the truth; it's not that I'm living a secret life."

Avi: "It's not a *kept secret*."

These statements help us begin to understand the double role of the closet, as described by Kosofsky-Sedgwick. The practices of concealment, the obfuscation, and the keeping under wraps – which partition the world into those who know and those who do not know, into private and public – endow genetic affiliation with the status of a "truth," and perhaps even "the truth" (with the definite article): a fundamental truth concerning identity, similar in kind to the identity value that is ascribed to homosexuality.

Some of the couples I interviewed were able to explicitly relate the two experiences: the experience of hiding their sexual identity and the experience of concealing the genetic affiliation of the children. Zohar, Erez's partner and the social father of Gaya and Michael, phrased it as follows:

"Going back to what we discussed earlier," Zohar said, "about whether we told that they are his genetically; I said right from the very start that we should open everything up. I have no interest in all these concealments. Like, enough already, *I've had that my entire life*. Put it out in the open, like, go ahead and tell – it's obvious anyhow that it's one of ours. So, if we don't tell, they'll say it behind our backs. So I say, just put it in the open – open it up."

Zohar's comments clearly raise the issue of choice with which Kosofsky-Sedgwick is concerned in her book. The choice that Zohar described is between concealment and preemptive confession – before the secret is inadvertently revealed. In other words, the social reality in which non-genetic parenthood is regarded as inferior and thus induces embarrassment or shame is one that the fathers are powerless to change. They are left with nothing but a degree of choice about how to position themselves within this reality, and as Zohar's words suggest, their degree of control in this matter is also doubtful. Erez and Zohar also spoke about the tactlessness shown by some people who ask them directly about their children's genetic affiliation, or even engage in guesswork out loud:

> There's a lot of people out there who don't have much tact. They don't just ask, they say at once: "Wow, they're a spitting image of Erez!"; and those who have a bit more tact, you can see in their facial expressions that they think exactly the same.

However, Kosofsky-Sedgwick's analysis reveals the problematic aspect of the operative social assumptions in such interactions – first, in regard to a person's location in the closet as long as they have not explicitly declared their sexual orientation, and second, in regard to the social code that forbids publicizing anything about a person's sexual orientation without their consent, because "a person's sexual orientation is their private matter." Both these assumptions mask the fact that, in effect, only one kind of sexual orientation is considered private (Ziv & Gross, 2010). Similarly, the environment's avoidance of touching on the topic of genetic affiliation, out of "respect" and "sensitivity" to the matter, may to no less degree reflect, and perhaps perpetuate, the shame that is associated with non-genetic parenthood.

Moreover, as Kosofsky-Sedgwick argues, a person can never be completely inside the closet or outside the closet, because coming out is a daily, incessant process, and not a one-time action as it was considered to be in the past. A rich cluster of cultural meanings becomes arrayed around the binary opposition of "genetic parent/non-genetic parent" – meanings that undermine the status of the non-genetic parent as a "real" parent. Thus, the non-genetic parent finds themselves caught up with day-to-day calculations about when to disclose and when to conceal. The most insidious catch in this regard relates to the fact that not mentioning the fact that one is a non-genetic parent is automatically equivalent to concealment, fraud, or lying. On the other hand, sharing this information, in order to avoid implications of deceit, accords an air of confession to the act of disclosure, and may even render the parent vulnerable to insulting or belittling remarks.

Back to the closet   153

An innovative way to cope with the inevitable catch of the "genetic closet" was revealed during the interview with Barak and Niv, who decided not to know the genetic affiliation of their son Dori.

Niv: "We left the matter to the attorney. Only if, God forbid [knocks wood] there is some medical incident, then we can pull it up."

The temptation to assume that Dori is Niv's genetic child, because of the fair skin tone they share, which is so different from Barak's darker tone, was great. But Barak and Niv reiterated that not only did they not have any official knowledge of their child's genetic affiliation, they also entertained no gut feelings or educated guesses about it. Unlike their extended families, which, according to their report, are engaged in such guesswork, they assert that they do not have even a shred of curiosity about the matter.

Niv: "We are not in the least interested in whose he is. He is not affiliated to me or to Barak. There is no issue of affiliation here."
Me: "Some couples do describe some kind of tension around this."
Niv: "Not for a moment. Were you tense?"
Barak: "No."
Me: "Curious, perhaps?"
Barak: "No. No . . ."
Me: "And didn't it make a difference for the families?"
Barak: "Of course it did. The curiosity was *theirs*. 'This one was like this as a kid, this one was like that,' there's a kind of competition [laughs] between the families. They're trying to spot the resemblance and figure it out."
Me: "But in the day-to-day... Don't you ever have moments where you wonder, is that like me, what he's doing?"
Niv: "Nope. I told you. The color of his hair, that's me. And Barak's brother is also blond. Personality-wise he's Barak's complete double: the way they walk, sit. Did you see how he sits on half of the chair? Barak sits that way. He's just like Barak in every way."
Me: "And don't you see yourself in anything?"
Niv: "No. His hair color. That's the only thing. Eyes, and hair color. That's it. All the rest is Barak."
Me: "Is that what you felt from the very beginning?"

| *Niv:* | "Yes, it was utterly clear. From the incubator. About seven minutes after he came out of the womb, one could already see the resemblance to Barak." |

The conversation with Barak and Niv became increasingly complicated. On one hand, Niv stated that he recognized Dori as being externally similar to him, and claimed that all the rest – facial expressions, tendencies, and personality features – reminded them of Barak, a distinction that implied that, although the genetic traits were inherited from Niv, the environmental influences from Barak were more dominant. This is one way of subverting the asymmetry of the genetic factor. On the other hand, Niv argued that Barak's brother was blond, meaning he may even have inherited his fair coloring from Barak, adding that the resemblance between Dori and Barak had been apparent from the moment of Dori's birth; hence, there could have been no long-acting environmental influences to speak of at that moment, but rather something more akin to genetic resemblance. If true, the implication was that Barak is Dori's genetic father, despite the considerable dissimilarities in their physical characteristics. If that is the case, why did they claim they have no clue which of them is Dori's genetic father?

Niv's efforts at persuasion, which led to a logical conundrum, suggested the existence of a suspicion that must be shaken off with some effort. On one hand, I admired the clever way in which they chose to resist the dominant narrative that so hermetically binds together genetics and kinship, as well as their insistence on not allowing the genetic asymmetry to produce a hierarchy between the parents, who are in all other respects full partners in the rearing of their child – achieving this through a strategy of obscuring and confounding the distinctions between them. On the other hand, I found it difficult to believe that they could so easily dispense with the internalization of a principle so saturated with profound cultural meanings. And that they were not at all curious to know stretched my credulity. I felt their messages were making me utterly confused: was this merely an external pretense, intended to help them cope with the invasive environment, or did they wholeheartedly believe that they have no way of identifying to whom their son is genetically affiliated? I wondered if my own feelings had something to teach me about the existential confusion that their contradictory messages were sowing in Dori's mind.

Does the attempt to minimize the place of genetics in family life paradoxically produce a sense of an enormous secret concealing a truth one cannot live with, and thus requires the investment of great resources in denial strategies?

My confusion only increased when listening to the fathers speak with great conviction about how easy it was to recognize genetic ties in other people's children. This surfaced as they recalled how they were accommodated by their Israeli surrogacy agency in the same hotel in India with many other gay couples that came for their child's birth. Their agency must have recommended the same egg donor for several couples, they claimed, because there were clearly half-siblings among the newborn babies:

Niv: "In our hotel there were half-brothers, you could see it from the babies' resemblance to one another . . ."

Barak: "Everyone could see it, you could see it at once . . ."

Statements of this kind resonated with the sense of conviction I had had about Dori's resemblance to Niv; a conviction that had been shaken, but resurged now and again, as if to say "Yes, but . . . "

Returning to the question of whether this was merely a façade meant to help them deal with other people's intrusiveness, or whether the couple truly believed they had no way of recognizing their son's genetic affiliation: the answer may have been different for each of the fathers, as suggested by their very different coping strategies as teenagers or young adults, with their homosexual orientation. Niv's strategy involved the activation of a vertical splitting mechanism, whereas Barak made use of a horizontal splitting mechanism. In other words, Niv spoke of himself as being fully aware of his identity ("I knew it from the very beginning"), as being accustomed to keeping things under wraps ("You become an excellent liar . . . you know how to lie and how to pull the wool over everyone's eyes, in a very methodical way"), and as actually living a double life ("I still continued to go out with women. I was supposed to get married, we had booked a wedding hall."). Barak, on the other hand, described tremendous powers of repression, to the point that he himself was out of touch with his attraction to men: "Never in my life did I think about men, I wasn't interested in that, it never even occurred to me."

If we can extrapolate from the experience of being in a double bind that Niv so clearly described in regard to his sexual identity, we might say that in the context of genetic affiliation, he finds himself caught between a rock and a hard place: between a life of secrets and lies and an unavoidable disappointment with his social milieu. The true difficulty that became apparent to me was that even on the intra-psychic plane, the couple vacillated between self-deception and the self-expectation that they counteract any prejudices concerning genetics, and these two options were, in Niv's words: "two phantasies; two things that are not attainable."

Another aspect, which also resonates with the experience of leading a closeted life, relates to the question of visibility. To what extent can the secret be hidden, and do external appearances expose or disclose the secret? The question of whether a subject "passes" as gay, or whether he can "pass" as straight, seemed to resurface in the genetic context: can children "pass" as the children of the social father also, or does their resemblance to the genetic parent (or their difference from the social parent) immediately disclose the truth? Although in many instances it is possible to visually recognize a genetic connection to one of the fathers, some families nevertheless choose officially to conceal the information from others.

Even in families who choose the path of communicating openly with their social environment about the genetic issue, concealment is often practiced in relation to the children. In Zohar and Erez's case, for example, the couple are aware of the children's unmistakable resemblance to Erez and do not conceal the issue of genetic affiliation from the environment; nevertheless, the topic is still not spoken about directly with their six-year-old children. As Erez noted, "There's a lot of people out there who don't have much tact. They don't just ask, they say at once: 'Wow, they're a spitting image of Erez!'" A situation in which the environment is in the know about something that is hidden from the children to some degree or another almost certainly entails moments in which ambiguous talk about these issues takes place "over the children's heads."

Christopher Bollas (1987) coined the term "the unthought known" in respect to impressions of earlier relational experiences that cannot be described verbally but whose presence influences the individual's thinking and behavior. A state of affairs in which children repeatedly encounter the conscious and unconscious reactions of their parent in respect to their genetic affiliation, and are exposed to semi-enigmatic comments from the environment regarding this issue, without being given the tools to arrive at an understanding of the facts concerning their origins, could generate confusion and create a kind of "unthought known" in their psyches.

Although this approach – which characterizes most of the parents I interviewed – is motivated by a desire to wait for the arrival of questions that will be sparked by the children's own curiosity, and although the existing research indicates that children achieve a mature understanding of the full meaning of gamete donations only between the ages of seven to ten (Blake et al., 2013), clinical experience teaches us that it is necessary to sow some narrative seeds that will allow these questions to germinate and take form, and that indicate the parents' readiness to discuss the topic with them. Accordingly, most heterosexual parents who choose to expose to their child the fact of their being a product of gamete donation begin to discuss this with them using age-appropriate imagery or stories even before the age of four or five, in order to preempt a situation in which they will be required to disclose the information in a surprising or dramatic manner later (Blake et al., 2010).

Using clinical illustrations, Ehrensaft (2007) clarifies the importance of sensitive parental mediation on the topic of the child's origins, of the kind that provides sufficient information, but also leaves room for the child's phantasy and subjective interpretation to develop. The explanation, Ehrensaft argues, should be repeated over and over again, adapted to the child's level of maturity. The process begins with the parents' unilateral volunteering of information, but the hope is that an ongoing dialogue will develop, allowing space for the child's entire spectrum of reactions, both positive and negative. Ehrensaft relies here on the work of Corbett (2009), among others, which emphasizes the importance of working through feelings of anxiety and guilt on the part of the parents, and of creating a family reverie,[1] a space in which family members share feelings and phantasies about the child's origins. The family reverie, as Ehrensaft argues, helps reduce feelings of guilt and anxiety that go hand in hand with the child's phantasies. It encourages the building of identity and a sense of belonging. Ehrensaft believes that with the exception of special circumstances, such as a particularly acute family crisis, severe illness, or threat of physical harm from a hostile environment, the child should be told about their origins: it is their right to know, and this knowledge, in her view, is of crucial importance for their psychological development.

---

1 "Reverie" is a central concept in the thought of Wilfred Bion, describing an open and receptive state of mind, which enables the transformation of raw emotional experience into materials that are amenable to mental representation, and thus to carrying psychological meaning.

References

Blake, L., Carone, N., Slutsky, J., Raffanello, E., Ehrhardt, A. A., & Golombok, S. (2016). Gay father surrogacy families: Relationships with surrogates and egg donors and parental disclosure of children's origins. *Fertility and Sterility, 106*(6), 1503–1509.

Blake, L., Casey, P., Jadva., V, & Golombok, S. (2013). "I was quite amazed": Donor conception and parent-child relationships from the child's perspective. *Children & Society, 28*(6), 425–437.

Blake, L., Casey, P., Readings, J., Jadva, V., & Golombok, S. (2010). "Daddy ran out of tadpoles": how parents tell their children that they are donor conceived, and what their 7-year-olds understand. *Human Reproduction, 25*(10), 2527–2534.

Bollas, C. (1987). *The shadow of the object: Psychoanalysis of the unthought known*. Columbia University Press.

Corbett, K. (2009). Nontraditional family reverie: Masculinity unfolds. In *Boyhoods: Rethinking masculinities*. Yale University Press.

Ehrensaft, D. (2007). The stork didn't bring me, I came from a dish: Psychological experiences of children conceived through assisted reproductive technology. *Journal of Infant, Child, and Adolescent Psychotherapy, 6*(2), 124–140.

Freeman, T., Jadva, V., Kramer, W., & Golombok, S. (2009). Gamete donation: Parents' experiences of searching for their child's donor siblings and donor. *Human Reproduction, 24*, 505–516.

Jadva, V., Blake, L., Casey, P., & Golombok, S. (2012). Surrogacy families 10 years on: Relationship with the surrogate, decisions over disclosure and children's understanding of their surrogacy origins. *Human Reproduction, 27*(10), 3008–3014.

MacCallum, F., & Keeley, S. (2012). Disclosure patterns of embryo donation mothers compared with adoption and IVF. *Reproductive BioMedicine Online, 24*(7), 745–748.

Sedgwick, E. K. (1990). *Epistemology of the closet*. University of California Press.

Tabak-Aviram, I. (2011). A new kind of parenthood? On the differences and similarities between same-sex and heterosexual parenthood [Hebrew]. *Hebpsy* [online blog]. www.hebpsy.net/articles.asp?id=2550

Ziv, A., & Gross, A. (2010). Eve Kosofsky Sedgwick's art of queer reading [Hebrew]. *Theory and Criticism, 37*, 15–43.

Chapter six

The dual role of the extended family

"Song for the Whole Family," by Israeli singer-songwriter Meir Ariel, describes how, when a newborn arrives, the relatives swoop down, one by one, to claim a portion of recognition for the genetic resemblances reflected in the infant's features. But what happens when the newborn does not carry on the family's genetic inheritance?

One cannot underestimate the importance of the extended family in Israeli society; this was evidenced in the space the topic took up in the interviews I held with parents, and in the extent of grandparents' involvement in most of the families I interviewed. Similarly, the importance of blood ties or genetic affiliation within the Israeli conception of kinship cannot be overstated. Paradoxically, the principle that legitimates the extensive involvement of extended family in the same-sex nuclear family is the same principle underlying homophobic attitudes, since homophobia is initially motivated by the need to defend the sacrosanct link between sex and procreation.

I wish to argue that the extended family plays a dual role in the same-sex nuclear family: it serves as the conduit of heteronormative cultural expectations, and simultaneously is used as a canvas for projection by couples who wish to be rid of self-doubts – doubts which in themselves are the product of internalization of the very same cultural expectations. This dual role of the extended family resurfaces at every conflict-ridden juncture confronted by same-sex couples.

From biological grandparenting to social grandparenting and vice versa

Sandra and Efrat described an upheaval in their relationship following the birth of their second child, which came hand in hand with the changes in their roles from birth mother to social mother, and vice versa – changes

DOI: 10.4324/9781032663333-9

160   What does genetics have to do with kinship, anyway?

that Efrat described as a shift from the role of "father" to that of "mother" (see Chapter Four, pp. 118). However, they devoted the greater part of the interview to describing the difficulties they experienced with the extended family during this transition.

Efrat: "Our home went through quite a storm during those years. There were all sorts of dramas with our parents that really affected us. I think that because of the crisis we were experiencing at the time, lots of external noises were allowed entry – coming from both families, and it was very confusing. Because when we only had Ruth, we were living in a kind of La-La Land where everything was amazing, we were accepted. When it came to my family, I was having a hard time with them, because they weren't as involved as I thought they should be with Ruth [their non-biological granddaughter], or as I imagined that my parents would be as Grandma and Grandpa. They always had a ton of excuses, but to be honest, I didn't feel I needed them that much. Sandra's family was very central. I was very much the 'Dad.' We were very strong as a couple. We didn't need any help. And then Danny was born, and stuff happened in our families that I didn't foresee. Sandra's father didn't show up for the birth, and he didn't come to the circumcision ceremony, and his response was as if it was unrelated to him, which really, really surprised me, because Sandra's father had a central part in Ruth's life: they would visit once a week, they were really involved in her life, and suddenly he stopped coming over."

Sandra: "So I went and said to him, 'I've got two kids. One I didn't give birth to, and one that I gave birth to: from your perspective, there's no difference. You're either the grandfather of both, or you're no grandfather at all.' And that was it. I made it clear-cut. Cut and dried. Until he came along and said: 'I want to talk,' because he realized that he was losing everyone around him – my sisters stopped coming home to visit. And then I made things explicit. I gave him examples. I said, 'You're walking down the street with Danny and people ask you, 'Who is this?' – that's your grandson. If I ever hear that anything else came out of your mouth, I will shut you right out. You won't see me again.' And he got it. He understood that not only would he lose me, he would

	lose everyone around him. And since then, there's been a kind of status quo."
Efrat:	"Is she amazing, or what? In my family what happened was that Danny was born, and suddenly we found out that my mother was actually the grandmother that I thought she would be. Suddenly, there's an outpouring of love that you can't miss. Suddenly there's no traffic jams in the afternoon . . . the inhibitions fell away."
Sandra:	"Suddenly she was the perfect grandmother. Perfect! So *I* had a really hard time with that."
Efrat:	"It's important for me not to lose my family, and I really work hard at it and make an effort to maintain it. Like, even when stuff happens that if it were up to Sandra, it would be a crossed line, with no way back. Maybe it's also because I was the dad, and not the mom, and when I saw it wasn't just flowing from my mom spontaneously, I didn't know how to say to her – you're going to fake it now, just like Sandra went to her dad and told him."
Sandra:	"It created a lot of difficulties. But I have to say that somehow, against all odds, we got through it. Like, we were able to draw the line where it was acceptable to both of us."

We saw previously that in a family configuration where each mother fulfills both roles – that of birth mother as well as social mother – a crisis of adaptation takes place during the period of transition between the roles, providing the mothers fertile ground for comparisons. Each mother will compare her emotions and functioning with her biological and non-biological child, as well as compare herself with her partner's functioning and emotions with each of them. When this occurs, displacing the conflict and struggle onto the grandparents' generation may help the couple forge a united front. In most of the families, there was no blatant discrimination of the kind that Sandra and Efrat described, but self-doubts and fears about bonding with the non-biological child frequently were expressed as concerns about the acceptance of the child by the extended family.

"Make me a biological grandchild"

Each of the parents who chose to function as social parents for all of their children, without having a biological child of their own, described this choice as a zone of conflict with their family of origin.

Zohar, Michael and Gaya's social father, who chose not to have another child merely for the sake of fathering a genetic offspring, described the situation as follows:

> The reality, to use a euphemism, is challenging, it is difficult. They're twins – two amazing kids. On the other hand, they're intense, and I don't think I can go back again to those moments with the diapers. I like the fact that they're growing up, and they're healthy kids – touch wood – I don't feel the need for them to be mine biologically. My parents told me for a long time that they want me also to have kids, I mean, genetically, kids that are also mine. They would go on saying that until I told them in no uncertain terms that I don't want to. I don't want to. We still have frozen embryos somewhere in India, but I don't want to, I don't want to.

This is a very subtle example of the kind of pressure a parent might feel to live up to the prevailing ideal of genetic kinship. Between the lines, one can hear Zohar's need to protect himself from his parent's wishes. The four-time repeated phrase "I don't want to" renders a combative air to his speech, and may even contain the echoes of childhood arguments that were crucial for asserting his identity. The negative formulation is repeated without being countered, raising the question of whether his argument is with his parents, with the broader cultural messages, or with the internalizations of both, which assault him from within.

A lesbian woman who chooses the role of social mother for all of the couple's children may experience another dimension of conflict, less related to the genetic factor than to the issue of physical childbearing, in other words, to the notion that pregnancy and childbirth are experiences that both reflect and constitute the identification between a mother and her daughter when she herself becomes a mother.

Iggy, the mother of the twins Ella and Nadav (who were conceived and carried by her partner, Ossi), chose not to bear children herself, feeling that pregnancy would be incompatible with her gender identity. During the interview, the couple shared that they were planning to have another child, and Iggy – realizing this would be her last chance to become pregnant – thought it over again but decided to remain with her role as the social mother. Iggy described the pressure to become pregnant coming at her from all sides, and especially from her mother, while weighing her options.

"Everyone has something to say," Iggy protested.

My mom is positively freaked out by the fact that I'm not trying. My mom recently had a dream that Ossi was pregnant, and I was crying in the dream. So that's that, as far as she's concerned. Because it was supposed to be my turn, that's that [claps her hands together to signal the finality of the issue]. Her perception of the whole thing is distorted, like, if I don't experience it, then I have no part in it. It's such a diminishing message. So we have an issue now – I'm not speaking with her.

Me: "Because of that dream?"
Iggy: "Yes. Ossi and I just started talking about expanding the family, and suddenly it appears in her dream, it's like, there you go, you've got your response."
Me: "But you know. I think it's also her way of grieving and saying goodbye to that idea."
Iggy: "Saying goodbye to that phantasy, yes."
Me: "Yes, she also needs to go through some kind of process to come to terms with it, and here, for a moment you said that you might become pregnant after all, and decided not to, so she'll have to go through a similar process. To me, this dream actually sounds as though she's trying to work through it somehow."
Iggy: "But it's unbelievable. Ossi and I hadn't even had the chance to work through the loss, and already she's having a dream. Her emotion is so very . . ."
Me: "Were you very connected?"
Iggy: "Very much so, we were very connected."

Within her close circle, it is her mother who has the hardest time coming to terms with Iggy's relinquishing of the potential to realize motherhood in the bodily sense. This might stem from her closeness to and degree of her involvement in her daughter's life, but the difficulty may also reflect the mother's unconscious realization that her daughter's choice contains an aspect of rejection of physical motherhood, i.e., of her mother's own body. This interpretation resonates with Kristeva's concept of abjection (Kristeva, 1982). The abject is an index of that which has been removed from the body, excreted, and signified as "not me." As such, it confronts the psyche with its earliest attempts to separate itself from the maternal entity. Through care of the child – of his or her body and excrements – the mother becomes one who contains everything that the child has rejected from its own body and thus signifies herself as one who cannot be differentiated for her own sake, as herself. Kristeva describes a process by which the transition to motherhood connects the mother to her own mother through the willingness to contain the filth on her child's behalf (Friedman, 2013). One can thus think about the refusal to become pregnant and give birth as motivated, among other things, by a refusal to identify with the abject, which is related to the representation of the mother. This conflict with the mother may occur somewhat differently among gay fathers.

"A child needs a mother"

The preceding words were used by Maoz to describe the pressure from his mother not to write off the possibility of having a mother figure in his children's lives:

> My mom said to me at first, "But why just the two of you? Why not with a woman?" It seemed strange to her. Okay, you can be gay, but have the kids through a woman. Like, it seemed much more logical to her that way. She really tried to put pressure on us to go that route, and like Ofir said, we were very confident in our choice. I said to her, "Okay, it seems weird to you. Get used to it!" [laughs], and they did.

Just as the question of Iggy's identification with the mother's body, and indeed with her own mother, is implicitly interwoven in her dialogue with her mother, thus the dialogue between Moaz and his mother about whether it is essential for his kids to have a mother in their lives harbors the question of his own mother's importance. By choosing a family configuration with two fathers, Maoz seemingly is not merely forfeiting a mother figure for his children but is also relinquishing his own mother. Alternatively, one could argue that his mother's presence is so essential, and his identification with her is so strong, that he desires her assets and her functions for himself. This interpretation echoes concepts that I treated in Chapter Two, such as womb envy and the debt to the mother. One can also discern that the conflict between Maoz and his mother serves as an arena for the projection of Maoz's own internal conflict, which stems from the internalization of a binary gender system in which the role of childrearing is the preserve of women.

Interpretations aside, the grandparents eventually "got used to it," as Maoz summed up the matter. Indeed, when a conflict erupts in the relations with the extended family, if the couple is relatively self-assured about their choice, and are sufficiently united, the social environment tends to "get used to it," and over time the intensity of the conflict subsides. In most cases, once the non-biological grandchildren arrive, the fears evaporate, and to all appearances, they are embraced unreservedly by the extended family.

Throughout this section of the book, which dealt with biology and kinship, I pointed out the elusive ways in which the social discourse pervades the family's daily existence, as well as parental beliefs and experiences, and how these in turn shape the family relations and the child's object choices. To conclude this theme, I will attempt to situate the families in the discursive context in which they function, and subsequently examine the differences between the concept of kinship as constructed by the parents and the kinship concept that takes shape in the minds of their children.

References

Friedman, L. (2013). *In the footsteps of psychoanalysis: A postmodern gendered criticism of Freud*. Bar-Ilan University Press.

Kristeva, J. (1982). *Powers of horror: An essay on abjection*. Columbia University Press.

Chapter seven

The power of interpellation

Kinship conceptualization among
same-sex parents and their children

All classic definitions of kinship in Western culture, on which the Oedipal model draws but has also reproduced, revolve around sexual reproduction. The anthropologist David Schneider (1968) criticized the exaggerated emphasis placed on blood ties by most of the anthropologists studying kinship and argued that kinship must be understood not in terms of social recognition of the inherent importance of biological ties, but rather as the use of biology to symbolize social bonds of solidarity. Schneider suggested that heterosexual intercourse serves as a central symbol within the Euro-American kinship system because it incorporates two of its core elements: blood and love. Intercourse is an expression of the love between a husband and a wife and creates blood ties between parents and children, as well as between siblings. As a symbol, sexual intercourse has the power to define the members of the family as relatives, to distinguish them from one another, and to order their mutual relations (e.g., which ties contain a sexual component, and which ties forbid it), in addition to defining the family as a cultural unit.

Ziv (2020a) has pointed out the way in which even Schneider's proposal – to view kinship as a symbolic system and not as a natural fact – privileges the heterosexual order for its capacity to conjoin the symbolism of love and that of blood; or, put differently, to transform a love relationship into a biological relationship through the alchemy of sexual intercourse. Further, as in the case of the relationship between sex and gender or between the penis and the phallus, the analytical distinction between biological kinship and social kinship and the recognition of the cultural or symbolic dimensions of the second term do not free the latter from its ontological dependence on the former.

Contemporary theorizations of kinship, which are influenced by Schneider's critique and follow the path that it outlined, offer an understanding of kinship in terms of practice and affect and emphasize its performative

DOI: 10.4324/9781032663333-10

aspect. Thus, for example, Butler (2002) treat kinship as a system of practices that emerge to address fundamental forms of human dependency: birth, childrearing, relations of emotional dependency and support, intergenerational ties, illness, dying, and death. Weston, who conducted a study of practices and discourses of kinship in the lesbian and gay community in the San Francisco Bay Area, found that its members drew an opposition between "blood family" and "chosen family" and favored the latter. The validity of chosen kinship ties and their distinction from other ties that are not considered family ties rests on their permanence and endurance over time. Contrary to the dominant ideology of kinship, this quality was not seen by members of this culture as an inherent characteristic of blood ties, but rather as produced through intentional and sustained effort (Carsten, 2004).

The discursive turn – from an understanding of kinship as rooted in the "enduring" order of nature (Schneider, 1968) to an understanding of it in terms of choice, commitment, and ongoing investment – is reflected in everyday language as well. Consider the pairs of terms, mothering and motherhood, fathering and fatherhood, and parenting and parenthood. The first term in each pair is, in English, the newer term (see Morgan, 2011). Its equivalent does not exist in some other languages, such as Hebrew. However, the emergence of a performative discourse of kinship has not harbingered the demise of the essentialist discourse. In fact, the flourishing of genetic science as a knowledge field in the past decades has led to what may be termed "the geneticization of society" – the tendency of Western societies to explain everything in terms of genetics (Haraway, 1997), oftentimes while translating scientific ideas into everyday language, in such a way that scientific principles are oversimplified and distorted (see Nordqvist & Smart, 2014; Carsten, 2004). However this may be, concepts such as "genes" and "genetics" continue to bear decisive importance in respect to the cultural definition of family relations, and are brought up constantly in everyday discussions of family relations, reproduction, and children (Nordqvist, 2017).

Petra Nordqvist, a contemporary sociologist, studies the place of ideologies in the shaping of family practices. According to her "people deploy, even live, ideas and concepts of what makes a family" (Nordqvist, 2017, p. 886). Thus, inevitably, same-sex parents navigate between these two discursive systems regarding kinship: the normative genetic discourse and the performative – choice-based – discourse. Sociologists and anthropologists have long shown that these two systems are not mutually exclusive; just as the genetic basis of kinship is not a sufficient condition to guarantee relationships of closeness, care, and love, family practices may in themselves engender feelings of security and permanent affiliation between non-genetic kin (see, e.g., Carsten, 2004; Edwards, 2000; Mason & Finch, 1993).

However, in the context of families assisted by gamete donation, these two discursive systems point to, and identify, two different sets of parents: whereas the genetic discourse points to the genitor and genetrix (i.e., the genetic parent and the sperm or egg donor); the performative discourse points to the two actual parents raising the child. In this respect these two discursive systems are indeed mutually exclusive and are therefore bound to conflict.

From the interviews that I conducted with the parents in this study, two central strategies for coping with the structural genetic asymmetry emerged, parallel to the two aforementioned discourses: the first strategy strives to reduce the gap between same-sex kinship and heteronormative kinship, and the second establishes an alternative kinship model based on emotional commitment and investment rather than on genetics.

Since the Israeli gayby boom is closely related to the rise and strengthening of homonormative and homonational trends, it is not surprising that most of the couples who participated in the research were identified with the first strategy, and tended to adopt the genetic kinship discourse. This strategy was premised on the assumption that there is no essential difference between same-sex kinship and heterosexual kinship, and that the current state of affairs is merely a temporary one, necessitating compromise until technological developments enable same-sex couples to create a shared genetic child.[1] From among the 19 couples who were asked about this, 15 expressed a desire for a shared genetic child. The remaining four couples expressed ambivalence about the matter, and more than once it seemed that the question confronted them with an unconscious wish, which was at odds with the agenda that ostensibly guided their actions.

The preceding strategy goes hand in hand with various practices of normalization, which aim to maintain a "genetic equilibrium" between the two

---

1 At the time of writing of this chapter, the possibility of creating a fetus from the genetic material of three partners (two men and a woman, or two woman and a man) does exist, but is not yet in use due to ethical and presumably also political considerations. Promising technological advances make it likely that fertilization based on the genetic material from two ova or two sperm will become available for use some time in the future. If such a future materializes, kinship relations in LGBT families will also be blood-based.

parents and produce genetic ties between siblings. Thus, for example, producing at least one genetic child to each parent while using the same gamete donor to form genetic ties between siblings was highly important to most parents. Among gay fathers, all of the couples that underwent the surrogacy process in a country that permits transferring embryos of disparate genetic origins chose this model, hoping to achieve a twin pregnancy using two embryos, each genetically related to one of the intended fathers. This option was chosen despite the fact that a multifetal pregnancy entails medical and developmental risks. In cases where a symmetrical model was unachievable, a desire arose to select a donor who bears a physical resemblance to the non-genetic parent, aspiring thus toward the genetic reproduction of their external appearance, family likeness, or ethnic origin.[2]

Most of the couples (14 of 18 whom I questioned on the matter) planned to use the same genetic source for each of the planned children in the family and undertook efforts to realize this aspiration even in the face of technical difficulties. The connection between the siblings was described in terms of genetics or blood ties, by employing the terms of a heteronormative kinship discourse. Thus, for example: "They are both biological siblings. They come from the same egg donor, so there is a blood tie." Some of the couples described feeling as though the genetic connection between the children even reinforced their legitimacy as a couple: "One of them is mine and one is yours. But the other half is that they're brothers; it really unites us."

Since the inclusion criterion of the research limited the pool to couples who are raising their children under one roof, having used gamete donation to assist reproduction, it is no wonder that the parents I interviewed nearly all aspired to minimize the differences between their family and the heteronormative model, and attributed a great deal of importance to genetics as the basis of kinship. Those aspiring to build an alternative kinship model might choose paths to parenthood that were not included in the research – such as adoption – a route that excludes the genetic element of kinship a-priori; or to establish family configurations that more radically subvert the Oedipal model of kinship, such as, for example, parenting partnerships

---

2 Hayden (1995) has a different understanding to mine of parents' choice of a single donor as the genetic source for all of the children, or the choice of a donor who resembles the non-genetic parent. In her view, this is a strategic use of genetics as a resource in order to create an effect of resemblance, with physical reproduction acting as a *signifier* of kinship relatedness, but this use does not express a perception of genetics as *establishing* kinship.

among three or four partners. An arrangement that confers equal status on several parental figures complicates the association between genetics and kinship and minimizes the implicit hierarchy that may appear in families in which one parent is a genetic parent and the second is a social parent.

Outside the official research sample, I also met with three families that had children in the framework of parenting partnerships. In two of them, the father avoided significant romantic relationships and developed a Platonic couplehood with the mother of his children. In the third family, the genetic father had a partner who was not defined as a father within the family constellation – nor did he fully participate in the raising of the children. It was my impression that even among parents who choose the path of a parenting partnership, only a minority attempt to establish an alternative organization of kinship ties. parenting partnerships between more than two parents are not recognized by Israeli law (at the time of the writing of this chapter) and, accordingly, are also less common. However, as the example of the gay fathers who avoid romantic relationships while co-parenting with a woman demonstrates, the Oedipalization seen in most of the families is not just the product of the law or of societal demands, it also reflects the unconscious internalizations that impact each and every parent's choice of one or another family model.

Several couples of lesbian mothers took a critical stance toward the discourse of genetic kinship and the uses that LGBT families make of strategies associated with it. Instead, these mothers sought to establish an alternative kinship model, based on choice, commitment, and love. One of the practices reflecting this strategy is the deliberate choice of a different genetic donor for each of the children. Only three couples of lesbian mothers pursued this course of action, one of which later regretted it. Rona and Esty explained the rationale of their choice to me:

> I think that the community communicates a kind of contradictory message. We keep on saying, and rightly so . . . we are quite militant about that fact that she is the mother of the twins in the same way that I am their mother, and I am Nur's mother just as much as she is, but people constantly fail to understand this: "But it's not really yours," and "You'll feel differently when it's yours," and all sorts of stuff like that. We insist on saying that it's exactly the same thing. And then many lesbian mothers come and say, "Yeah, we're exactly the same as mothers, but the kids are truly siblings" – suddenly, biology is significant.

Esty and Rona even went as far as refraining from formally adopting the child birthed by their partner, in order to give no purchase to the state in their kinship arrangements. "We are utterly a family by choice. There is no biological thread connecting us and no seal of approval by the government," said Rona.

Another practice that characterizes the alternative kinship model is a focus on resemblances ascribed to environmental influences rather than genetic heredity. Galia, the birth mother of the twins Layla and Ariel, recounted:

> Layla just went through a period where she kept on – a couple of times she burst into tears because of it – "Why don't I look like you? I don't resemble anyone in the family." But what we did, simply, was to say, "Yes, you do resemble us: you're similar to Mommy Orna because you both like tomatoes, and both Ariel and I don't. You take after me in your creativity." That calmed the whole thing down. And sometimes she goes back to: "I'm white, and you're yellow, and you're red, and I'm pinkish." That's one of her issues.

Orna shed light on this interaction: "It's also a response to Mommy Galia who often says that Ariel is very much like herself . . ."

These examples demonstrate that, even in families that adopt a critical stance toward the genetic discourse, its effects are inescapable and these effects continue to present in the emotional world of parents and children as issues that require working through. Generally speaking, however much the couple's ideology is well-articulated, they are always exposed to the influences of two discursive systems: those who choose an assimilative approach realize at certain moments that their discourse produces a hierarchy between the two parents, and are quick to attenuate it by using ideas derived from the discourse of social kinship; yet couples that seek to create a queer kinship system cannot shake completely free of beliefs and hegemonic social assumptions that they have internalized.

Nonetheless, whereas same-sex parents have largely been raised and educated within heterosexual families and in light of heteronormative values, their children are born into a different family reality. Accordingly, they exhibit a more flexible concept of kinship, which corresponds to a great degree with the discourse of performative kinship.

Staying together for a long time: flexibilization of the concept of kinship among children

In order to assess the internalized representations of family among children, I asked the children I met to draw a picture of any family that came to mind, not necessarily their own particular family. Twenty-one of the 26 children who chose to participate in the family drawing task expressed a need to alter the family composition: to remove or add a figure (for details of the types of modifications made by the children, see Eitan-Persico, 2020). I would like to offer a few observations about the liberty that the children exercised in adding and removing characters, at whim, as evidence for the establishment of a kinship concept of a flexible and playful nature.

This liberty rests on a double foundation: the first is related to the internalization of two different models – that of their concrete family and the heteronormative model – and where two alternatives exist, it is but a short path to finding a third alternative, in other words, to recognizing that no truth is set in stone (Berman, 2003); the second foundation is rooted in the fact that each of the families contains both genetic and non-genetic ties, thus posing an intrinsic challenge to a concept of kinship based on blood. Since the concept of kinship does not derive (at least not exclusively) from immutable blood ties, but rather from family affinity by choice, it follows that families' boundaries are less rigid and can be manipulated and easily played with in phantasy. Thus, for example, upon hearing the instructions for the family drawing task, four-year-old Nina partly asked and partly declared: "To be part of the family, you don't have to be the same animal. Right, Mommy?" She then announced, in amusement, that she was drawing "a snake in the same family as a snail." Like Nina, many of the children amused themselves with family types created through an "unnatural" compounding of its members. Some of the children even included in their family drawing figures from the extended family, or friends.

Evidence of the flexible thinking that characterized the children's kinship concept, was evinced also in the direct definition of the concept of family. For example, when I asked four-year-old Eran what a family was in his opinion, he responded: "A family is being together. That means that *all of the people that call each other family – so they stay together for a long time*." When I asked him whether he knew how he came into the world, Eran replied: "Yes, two babies came out of Mommy Esty's tummy [he and his twin brother] and they called Esty and Rona Mommy Esty and Mommy Rona."

Four-year-old Eran's reply manages to clarify with the utmost simplicity the way interpellation processes work. This term was coined by Althusser (1971) to characterize the way in which ideology hails the subject, offering them an identity that they accept as "natural" or "self-evident." Indeed, as Eran explained, calling an "other" by the name "Mommy" or "son" is a call that establishes one's identity, just as calling a group of people by the name "family" subjects those people to family ideology and obtains their commitment to "stay together for a long time."

To the question, "What is a family, in your opinion?", many of the children gave flexible responses that emphasized the time spent together or the ongoing emotional involvement and commitment. Thus, four-year-old Ori replied:

Ori: "If you don't have a family, you ought to find one."
Me: "To find?"
Ori: "Yes, find."
Me: "Why are families needed?"
Ori: "For looking after, so that nothing happens to their child. Right?"
Me: "Yes. Parents take care of the child?"
Ori: "Yes, but he also takes care of them. Even if they're grown-up."

The notion of finding one's family was also articulated by four-year-old Anna, who, in response to the family task, prompt chose to draw "a princess who found a kangaroo and they ended up being a family"; in other words, a family is something that can be found or chosen, something that takes shape and is emergent, and not an absolute pre-existing fact. Indeed, not one of the children spoke about family in genetic or biological terms, and did not relate the concept of family with reproduction.

As the illustrations suggest, the kinship concepts of most of the children I interviewed emphasized the performative aspect of kinship: a dimension of commitment, mutual care, as well as joint presence in time and space. In most cases, it was apparent that the flexible kinship concept still produces a system of sufficient internal logic, one that allows the child to experience belonging and security, alongside freedom and openness. However, the radical versions of such a concept may be accompanied by an experience of instability. Indicators of such instability appeared only in Ariel's drawings.

174   What does genetics have to do with kinship, anyway?

Drawing 9 "A family flying to a far-away country": Ariel's first family drawing.

(Clockwise from the top right: Ariel; three home-schooled peers; Mommy Orna; and Layla, her twin sister. Mommy Galia was omitted from the drawing.)

The family configuration that Ariel drew presents an amalgam of different figures, without any hierarchy or systematic order. Ariel's need to compartmentalize the figures with rigid and artificial lines attests to difficulties tolerating the level of fluidity that characterizes her experience of family relationships. Ariel chose to draw a second family picture (see Drawing 10), depicting two girls going to a demonstration. They are alone on the roadway, unaccompanied by parent figures. This representation deepens the impression that Ariel lacks the sense of belonging, security, and safety that other children seemed to find in their family environment.

If we consider this finding – that kinship notions of children in same-sex families are based on performative principles, rather than on genetics or procreation – together with the findings presented in Chapter Three, which

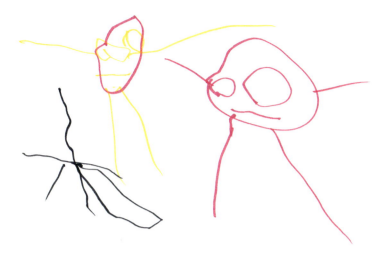

Drawing 10 "Two girls going to a demonstration": Ariel's second family drawing.

showed that genetics, in and of itself, does not play a significant role in the infantile attachment process or in Oedipal object choices, we are faced with a reality in which the genetic discourse of kinship does not merely misrepresent reality but even inflicts damage on families that embody a structural genetic asymmetry.

The destructive potential of the genetic discourse is most sharply illustrated in the cases of the separation of same-sex couples who are raising children together. In a study that documented and analyzed separation processes among eight same-sex couples with children, Daphna Birenbaum-Carmeli (2020) demonstrated the central place of genetic affiliation between parents and children in respect to custody arrangements, at times amounting to complete detachment and formal dissolution of kin relations between non-genetic kin.

With the exception of one couple, all of the couples that Birenbaum-Carmeli describes took for granted that, in the event of separation, each parent would "take" their genetic child; children stopped, or were asked to stop calling their social parent by the designations of "Daddy" or "Mommy"; the part played by the social parent in the child's identity was symbolically erased by excising their name from the child's surname, and members of the extended family, who took part in the day-to-day care of the child, disappeared in one fell swoop.

176   What does genetics have to do with kinship, anyway?

It should be noted that in most of the cases examined by Birenbaum-Carmeli's study, the court's decision prioritized social kinship, and regarded the perseverance of existing kinship ties as being in the child's best interest. This trend has been further reinforced since her study's publication, and in July 2022, Israel's Supreme Court ruled that parenting orders may not be revoked, nor can the rights of non-biological parents be restricted:

> Four pathways lead into the chambers of parenthood [biological parenthood, surrogate-assisted parenthood, adoption, and parenthood based on couplehood with the biological parent], and each of these paths occasions unique challenges and obstacles. However, once a person has passed the gates into the chambers of parenthood, which path was taken loses importance, and all parents bear an identical set of rights and duties toward their children.[3]

Of the eight families described in Birenbaum-Carmeli's study, the only family in which the couple did not only seek to maintain equal parental rights after separating, but also viewed their children as an inseparable sibling unit, was the family of a gay couple who had adopted their children. In other words, this was the only family in which the kinship arrangement relied on the social principle from the outset and did not embody a structural asymmetry. One of the most surprising and thought-provoking facts mentioned in the description of this family is that, despite the lack of genetic affiliation between the parents and children, each father expressed a sense of closer bonding to "his" adopted child. This sense of ownership appears to be based on the circumstances accompanying the adoption process: because gay men were prohibited from adopting in the children's country of origin, each of the fathers officially adopted one of the children as a single father. One can speculate that the personal effort required of each father to prove parental capacity as a single father – by means of a series of emotionally demanding and intrusive tests – served to "mobilize" his emotional involvement and created a sense of ownership of the child, despite the fact that both parents planned to adopt both children together, and shared equal responsibility for raising them. This furnishes overwhelming proof of the power of interpellation (Althusser, 1971). If such a powerful

---

3 From the decision by the Deputy President (Emeritus) of the Supreme Court, Neal Handel.

emotional effect can be produced by institutional intervention, it is difficult to imagine how decisive the role of genetic discourse can be in producing differences between the emotional attitude of the biological parent and that of the social parent.

The four chapters in this part of the book have shown that, although genetic affiliation does not affect the quality of parent-child relationships, the various meanings that parents attribute to genetics significantly influence the patterns of family relations. Children, on their part, tend to display great sensitivity to the parents' emotional states, and to respond to them unconsciously.

The concept of the "unthought known," coined by Bollas (1987) to denote the impressions of early relational experiences that are not amenable to verbal expression, may shed light on the way in which both conscious and unconscious meanings that parents ascribe to genetics permeate relationships and influence the children's positioning within the matrix of family relations. These influences are at work even when the concept of genetic heredity is not yet within the child's cognitive reach and when they are not informed by their parents about their genetic origins. Illustrations of this have been presented throughout the last four chapters, such as the child's preference for the social parent when the genetic parent finds the similarity between him and the child unsettling; the increased need of children to court the social parent, when the latter exhibits a need for assurance in regard to their parental status, or the appearance of expressions of hostility and rivalry toward the social parent, when the latter positions themselves chiefly as the partner of the genetic parent and exhibits ambivalence in regard to their parental role. The importance of the "unthought known" as a concept in the present context stems from its ability to explain the inscrutable ways in which the social discourse infiltrates the emotional experiences in the family's everyday existence. It thus constitutes the missing link in the consideration of the impact of discourse on family practices.

While the genetic discourse does indeed permeate parents' emotional attitudes, and is passed down by them to the children, a more flexible concept of kinship – based on choice and emotional commitment, rather than on genetics – is still capable of taking form in their minds. As Corbett, following Jane Flax, argues, children and families grow within and against the "logic" of the normative social structure. The social structure is reproduced but also leaves room for diversity.

References

Althusser, L. (1971). Ideology and ideological state apparatuses. In L. Althusser (Ed.), *Lenin and philosophy and other essays*. Monthly Review Press.

Berman, E. (2003). Introduction: The other voice and his contribution to psychoanalytic psychotherapy [Hebrew]. In *Sándor Ferenczi, confusion of tongues between adults and the child* (pp. 11–70). Am-Oved.

Birenbaum-Carmeli, D. (2020). Negotiating kinship: On disassembling same-sex families with children. *Journal of GLBT Family Studies*, *16*(4), 385–401.

Bollas, C. (1987). *The shadow of the object: Psychoanalysis of the unthought known*. Columbia University Press.

Butler, J. (2002). Is kinship always already heterosexual? *Differences: A Journal of Feminist Cultural Studies*, *13*(1), 14–44.

Carsten, J. (2004). *After kinship*. Cambridge University Press.

Edwards J. (2000). *Born and bred: Idioms of kinship and new reproductive technologies in England*. Oxford University Press.

Eitan-Persico, Y. (2020). *Oedipus in same-sex families* [PhD dissertation, Ben-Gurion University].

Haraway, D. J. (1997). *Modest_Witness@Second_Millenium.FemaleMan_Meets_OncoMouse: Feminism and technoscience*. Routledge.

Hayden, C. P. (1995). Gender, genetics, and generation: Reformulating biology in lesbian kinship. *Cultural Anthropology*, *10*(1), 41–63.

Mason, J., & Finch, J. (1993). *Negotiating family responsibilities*. Routledge.

Morgan, D. (2011). *Rethinking family practices*. Springer.

Nordqvist, P. (2017). Genetic thinking and everyday living: On family practices and family imaginaries. *The Sociological Review*, *65*(4), 865–881.

Nordqvist, P., & Smart, C. (2014). *Relative strangers: Family life, genes and donor conception*. Palgrave Macmillan.

Schneider, D. M. (1968). *American kinship: A cultural account*. Prentice-Hall.

Ziv, A. (2020a). Queer kinship [Hebrew]. *Mafte'akh*, *15*, 135–154.

Part III

What does procreation have to do with parental coitus, anyway?

Chapter eight

Between longing and dread

Representations of gamete donors and surrogates in the children's inner-worlds

Part II, titled "What does genetics have to do with kinship, anyway?", implicitly addressed the concept of the primal scene as an unconscious phantasy premised on the inter-entailment of heterosexual sexuality and kinship, enabling us thus to explore the implications of the built-in genetic asymmetry that characterizes the same-sex family. The next chapters venture deeper into the concept of the primal scene, this time in order to contend with the question of the child's origins and to explore how this question is represented in the psychic life of same-sex parents and their children.

As recalled, I showed earlier how same-sex families navigate a path between two discursive systems of kinship: the heteronormative genetic discourse and the performative discourse. Contrary to the prevalent view among sociologists and anthropologists, who posit that these discourses are not mutually exclusive (see, e.g., Carsten, 2004, Edwards, 2000; Mason & Finch, 1993), I argued that in the context of families assisted by gamete donation, these two discursive systems point the way to two alternative options of meaning-making, which are translated in practice to a divergent identification of the parental pair: the genetic discourse indexes the two partners in fertilization – the genitor and genetrix – or in other words, the genetic parent and the egg or sperm donor; whereas the performative discourse indexes the two parents who partner in the planning of a pregnancy and raising of a child. Consequently, an inherent contradiction exists between these two discursive systems, which in turn lead, in the context of the same-sex family, to an inevitable clash.

The primal scene refers to the symbolic representation of parental coitus in the child's psychic life (even after the child has become a parent, even a same-sex parent). This representation wraps together the recognition of the parents' exclusive relations, and the concomitant jealousy and sense of inferiority spurred by the mythical dimension attributed to parental sexuality,

DOI: 10.4324/9781032663333-12

with the recognition that the child is ultimately a product of these relations. This latter recognition implies not only that the child's parents share a history of which he or she is not a part, and that there are factors that bind them together besides the child, but also that the bond between the parents may result in the creation of additional offspring. This recognition exacerbates feelings of inferiority and jealousy and, in turn, gives birth to an existential threat.

Because the primal scene – both as a central symbol in the psychological life of the child and their parents and as a theoretical psychoanalytic construction – echoes the broader cultural symbolism of heterosexual coitus as that which generates and defines kinship, within the context of the same-sex family we are confronted with the same inherent contradiction described.

If traditionally the recognition of sexual relations between the parents and recognition of the fact that the child is ultimately the product of these relations were two sides of the same coin, the invention of contraceptives and reproductive technologies has in any event loosened the Gordian knot linking parental coitus with the creation of offspring. In families assisted by gamete donation or surrogacy, not only does parental coitus harbor neither the promise nor the threat of bearing offspring, but the creation of a child indeed necessitates the involvement of a partner or partners who are not considered as parents and do not take part in raising the child. Thus, the two facets of the primal scene – on one hand, the child's phantasmatic engagement with his parents' sexuality along with his or her own implied exclusion from it, and, on the other hand, the phantasmatic dramatization of the moment of their conception and the question of their origins – these two facets relate to different sets of parents: the actual parent couple who raise the child, in the first case, and the genetic parent and birth other in the second case.

The term "birth other" was coined by Dianne Ehrensaft – whose pioneering work focused on the psychological challenges facing children created by gamete donation and their parents (whether in the case of heterosexual, homosexual, or single parenting). This term refers to any partners in the "creation" of the child who do not function as parents, i.e., the sperm or egg donor, or the surrogate. In one of her articles, Ehrensaft (2007) describes the invention of the term as a result of a typing error. She had meant to designate the egg donor as the "birth mother," but missed the "m" key, and was suddenly struck with the idea that the term "birth other" is indeed a more accurate and fitting one for describing the status of those who contributed to the birth but did not plan or were not designated to undertake a parental role at any point in the process. This term is particularly apt because it manages to encompass the ways in which the stranger who is a partner to the fertilization may function as an "other" within the most intimate space, or as I will specify in the next chapter, as "unheimlich" within the home sphere ("heimlich").

The contradiction inherent in the notion of the primal scene, which I indicated earlier, holds far-reaching implications. Psychoanalytic theory, and especially Kleinian theory – which incorporated the primal scene phantasy into the Oedipus complex – may encourage the perception that the Oedipal deep structure of a child growing up in a same-sex family will relate not to their two parents, but to the two participants in their (pro)creation, i.e., their genetic father or mother and the "birth other" (see Ofer, 2014). My findings contravene this possibility: as will be recalled, I showed in Chapter One that most children establish a psychic Oedipal construction in relation to the parents who raise them, whereas in Chapter Three, I showed how genetic affinity does not play a significant role in the children's object choices it follows, then, that there is no reason to assume that a genetic parent would be prioritized within the foundational psychic construction.

As will be recalled, Freud himself viewed the Oedipus complex and the Primal scene as two infantile constructions belonging to what he termed "Primal phantasies": foundational phantasies that aim to respond to the child's curiosity about the questions of origins. The primal scene dramatizes the child's beginning, the moment of their creation, whereas the Oedipal phantasy responds to the emergence of sexuality (Laplanche & Pontalis, 1973). In other words, for Freud, these two phantasies are interrelated, yet still have an autonomous status within the child's psyche.

Ken Corbett (2009) is critical of analytic views of the primal scene that accord the representation of heterosexual parental coitus the status of reality testing in respect to sexual procreation. He argues, correctly, that in realistic terms, reproduction is now open to variance, since there is no longer a need in our technological age for a man and a woman – whole objects – to engage in heterosexual coitus in order to produce a child; consequently, he suggests differentiating between phantasies of parental sexual union and conception phantasies. However, while recommending that these two phantasies be distinguished from one another, Corbett unwittingly merges the two in his coinage of the term "donor-dad."

The task of interpreting children's material not infrequently poses difficulties and requires a cautious approach. One can easily recognize heteronormative representations in the inner world of children raised in same-sex families, but it is more difficult to ascertain their meaning. Is every representation of a heterosexual couple an expression of longing for a different type of family experience? A preoccupation with the birth other as a partner in the child's birth and a carrier of half of their genetic material? Or is it an expression of curiosity or longing for a relationship with a parent of the sex missing from the actual family configuration? Or might it be, as some would argue, evidence of the existence of a deep Oedipal structure in which both the genetic parent and the birth other take part? In order to grapple with this difficulty, I will attempt to present the interpretive process openly, allowing room for the reader's own judgment.

"The tooth fairy, Mommy and Daddy" – how to understand culturally conventional representations?

Children raised in a same-sex family within a heteronormative cultural context are required to perform the work of psychic integration between cultural representations and their actual family experience. On the road to achieving such integration, one comes across fully incorporated representations, lacking accommodation to the family reality (Piaget & Inhelder, 1972). An example of this emerges clearly from my conversation with four-year-old Ori about her relationship with Miri and Yael, her two mothers. In response to my question, "When you fall and get hurt, who helps you most?", Ori replied:

Ori: "Mommy and Daddy."
Me: "Mommy and Daddy?"
Ori: "Yes. Right? Am I right?"

Ori's response implicitly assumes that "rightness" is found within the bounds of the heteronormative. If her encounters with books, teachers, and other children taught her this "truth" – that when a child is hurt, they are helped by their mother and father – here she reproduced the "correct" answer, perhaps even in an attempt to demonstrate that she is a clever child with an understanding of the world. But her way of doing this lacked any sort of integration with her private life and personal experience.

Efrat, the mother of five-year-old Ruth, recounted: "Like all of our friends' kids – the default is Mommy and Daddy. She just lost a tooth, so we gave her a present from the tooth fairy. Then she says, 'Was the tooth fairy really here?,' so I say, 'Yes,' and she says 'No, was it really and truly the tooth fairy or did Mommy and Daddy put the present there?"

This anecdote features two cultural conventions: "the tooth fairy" and "Mommy and Daddy." Ruth has no doubt heard that it is "really" "Mommy and Daddy" who place the gift under a child's pillow when they lose a tooth and has accepted this as a concrete universal truth, without understanding the intention behind this explanation – that, in this context, "Mommy and Daddy" represent a parental couple; translating this into her own life circumstances would mean that it is "Mommy and Mommy" who hide the present.

It would seem therefore that children's minds absorb cultural schemas and these are retrieved automatically, without accommodation to their own life realities and actual experience. The parents I interviewed reported that, when their children play house or show them family drawings, they usually present a mother and a father. Even children who sometimes include alternative family representations in their play tend to do so following their parents' direct encouragement and not spontaneously. Despite this assertion, the children's representations contain another element that cannot be explained except as wishful thinking. We see this, for instance, in the analysis of children's responses to the following image, representing a couple of female parents – two lionesses – and a lion cub.

Only seven of the 27 children who composed a story for this picture identified in it a female parental couple, even though most of the children displayed impressive naming abilities (see Card 2, pp. 52).

Four-year-old Gili, for example, took a look at the picture and declared: "A lioness, and a lion, and a teeny-tiny lion cub" (Hebrew *kfir* – a young lion, in a literary/archaic register). No doubt a child who demonstrates such expertise in naming the various members of a lion clan would also know how to distinguish between the visual characteristics of a male and female lion. It is tempting, therefore, to assume that the attribution of complementary gender roles to the parents – mother and father – is one more example of a knee-jerk evocation of the stereotypical cultural schema. However, the response "Mommy and Daddy" or "lion and lioness" was actually more common among children of lesbian mothers, whom one would expect to identify more easily with the representation of two lionesses and a cub; more than half of the children of lesbian couples produced this response, whereas this response was relatively infrequent among children of gay

186   What does procreation have to do with parental coitus, anyway?

fathers – only three among 11 children. In other words, it was precisely the children who were familiar with the option of two mothers raising a child, based on their own life experience, who refused to identify this as an acceptable option and tended to correct it according to the heteronormative model. This fact may indicate the existence of an emotional conflict and a wish for a family reality that conforms to social expectations.[1]

The only child who performed an active accommodation of the stimulus to her family reality was six-year-old Gaya, the daughter of Erez and Zohar, who recognized the pair of lionesses as "Two leopards, a daddy and a daddy, going for a walk with their baby." Her ability to recognize a same-sex couple in the picture in terms that matched her family experience indicates a capacity for integration that was lacking, for instance, in Ruth's response in the tooth-fairy anecdote recounted earlier. It may be that this ability of Gaya's requires cognitive maturity that was lacking in most of the respondents – six-year-old Gaya was one of the older respondents among the children, thus approaching the concrete operational stage of development (Piaget & Inhelder, 1972). However, as I will show in the next chapter, even among adults the integration is never complete, due to the inherent contradiction I pointed out earlier.

Children's representations of the birth other

Most of the children I interviewed exhibited an undeniable preoccupation with the question of their origins,[2] with phantasies about the birth other, or a longing for a parent of the missing sex in their family configuration. Not infrequently the children's curiosity was accompanied by feelings of anxiety

---

1 This finding is in accord with a classic study in which African American children aged four to seven were asked to choose between a dark-skinned doll and a light-skinned one. The findings indicated that children are fully aware of the social categories that classify them as part of an underprivileged minority and show a preference for an object that matches the hegemonic model (see Clark & Clark, 1947).

2 The analysis of the children's projective material was undertaken in consultation with Avi Saroff, an expert in the field of psychological assessment of children. At first, I asked Saroff to identify a common denominator among the children based on innocent observation, without prior knowledge about the aims for the research or the children themselves, except for their age. Saroff suggested that these children are especially preoccupied with the question of where children come from. I wish to thank Avi for his insightful thinking.

and guilt toward their parents (cf. Ofer, 2014, 2020; Corbett, 2009; Ehrensaft, 2000, 2007, 2008). To illustrate this, I will now present two elaborated examples (Anna's and Omer's), after which I will step back to consider the main themes that recurred in the children's material.

Anna – explicit preoccupation with the birth other

Four-year-old Anna's family comprises her two fathers Ron and Gabriel and her twin sister Libby. The girls' births were assisted by the same egg donor and surrogate; genetically, Anna is Gabriel's child and Libby is Ron's. As I showed in Chapter One, the two girls were engaged in a romantic Oedipal affair with Daddy Ron, who was the girls' main caregiver in their infancy. However, unlike Libby, who was wholly invested in the Oedipal drama, Anna's engagement with Oedipal dynamics was minor and accompanied by intense phantasies expressing a longing for a mother figure.

In the family drawing task, Anna produced two pictures. The first one, "A princess who found a kangaroo and they ended up being a family" describes a family romance: a phantasy about her belonging to a different family, or more precisely, about a symbiotic merger with a mother figure (see Drawing 2, pp. 51). Although the story describes the moment in which she finds the mother kangaroo, the picture locates the mother figure on the left side of the drawing, identified with the phantasy region, outside the princess's field of vision (Urban, 1963). It is unclear whether the infant in the kangaroo's pouch represents Anna herself, or perhaps Libby, her twin sister, who shared the surrogate's womb with her and is a perpetual source of competition over a place in the family.

Anna's second drawing, "The queen of the cats with a baby in her tummy", presents a similar theme: a wish to reenter the womb and reunite with an idealized mother figure (see Drawing 3, pp. 52). The princess-baby looks like a miniature double of her mother-queen. Though she seems to be a fully developed girl, the same age as Anna, she enjoys the sanctuary of her mother's belly. In both drawings, the mother and the daughter have flowing blond hair, whereas in reality, Anna's hair is dark and curly. During my visit with the family, I learned that both fathers incessantly admire the twin sister Libby's straight blond hair, which has never been cut. I also learned that this is a physical feature of the egg donor; Libby, as the fathers like to repeat, inherited her hair and her beauty. This suggests that Anna's drawing does not only express a wish to merge with the mother, but also to resemble her, while also expressing jealousy toward Libby who inherited her looks.

In the apperception task, Anna returned again and again to her preoccupation with the mother figure. For example, in relation to Card 6, a deliberately ambiguous image that allows the child to attribute the hands of the parent holding the infant to either a mother or a father figure, or even to either one or two parent figures, Anna exclaimed:

Anna: "A baby, she was born in Thailand."
Me: And who is holding her?"
Anna: "A woman who gave us, the eggs, to Daddy"
(Anna and Daddy Gabriel laugh.)

Card 6 An infant being held.

The story told by Anna indicates that in her mind the two birth others – the egg donor and the surrogate – are merged into a single figure: the one who held her in her arms when she was born is also the one who gave the eggs (out of which she and her twin sister were created) to her father. In her phantasy, there was a mother figure who held her in her arms as a baby but then gave her and her twin sister up and handed them to her father. The attribution of mother status to the birth other, here merely suggested, is articulated explicitly in response to Card 7:

Between longing and dread   189

Anna; "Like the mother who borned us! Like the mother who borned us!"

In response to this picture, which unlike the previous one is meant to elicit responses related to the birth other, Anna directly and explicitly designates the birth other as "mother." It should be noted here that Anna was the only one of the children who related directly to the birth other in her stories. This could be explained by the fact that Gabriel and Ron conduct a radically open discourse on the topic with their daughters. The daughters have seen pictures of the egg donor and of the surrogate and know them by name. The fathers encourage discussion of the topic, and frequently joke about it in ways that at times seem counter-phobic, in other words as an attempt to deny the anxiety triggered by the topic and to gain a sense of control about it.

Whereas the phantasy of the mother figure, her abandonment, and the hope to reunite with her – phantasies that can be read in terms of a family romance – occupied a central role in Anna's inner world, I did not find evidence of an Oedipal structure that includes the figure of the mother and the genetic father. On the contrary, as Freud argues, it seems that the family romance concerning the mother figure represents a defensive symbiotic escape from the Oedipal situation, which characterizes her relations with the fathers, and results from her twinship relationship with her sister. This interpretation is supported by Anna's reaction to "The Bedroom" image (Card 4, see pp. 56):

Card 7 A woman with blurred features.

Anna:	"A baby's bed. The baby was in her bed, and she was acting wild the whole time, but just because she was having fun."
Me:	Was she alone?"
Anna:	"No. With her mommy. The baby is here [points to the cradle], Mommy is here [points to the parents' bed]".

In this story of Anna's, the mother replaces the two fathers in the parental bed; her figure is mentioned only after the question I posed prevents her from continuing to deny the presence of the parents' bed – i.e., the parental sexual union.

Omer – conception phantasies and the question of origins

Four-year-old Omer's family consists of his mothers, Rona and Esty, his identical twin Eran, and his baby sister Nur. Omer and Eran were born from the same fertilization process that matched the donor's sperm and Mommy Esty's egg, and Rona conceived Nur with the assistance of a different sperm donor. As I showed in Chapter One, during infancy, Rona, the boys' social mother, became their primary attachment figure. At the Oedipal stage, the boys' preference shifted as they both developed an Oedipal romance with Mommy Esty, who to them is the more stimulating and adventurous parent. While Mommy Rona remained a source of holding and containing during times of difficulty or regression, during moments of excitement they seemed to turn away from her. The two boys are preoccupied with the mothers' exclusive relationship and demonstrate signs of jealousy and inferiority in regard to their mothers' sexuality: "They are often extremely embarrassed when we kiss," Esty said, "they kind of just stand there and say, 'I also want . . .'," and Rona added: "One time we were kissing, and Eran said: 'I don't know how to kiss like that'." In addition to the Oedipal dynamic, as I will show presently, Omer is also preoccupied with phantasies surrounding his birth, his origins, and his search for a male identification figure.

Omer started the family drawing task by sketching a father figure. At first, he drew the body while naming the various body parts: "Legs, bottom, bellybutton, and here is where the peepee should pop out." This figure was positioned in the center of the page, taking up most of the space, using an intense color. The other figures in the drawing, made with colored pencils in fainter and more blurred hues, were smaller and were placed in a scattered pattern around the dominant father. If this were not enough, Omer provided the father with a pair of "rear hands," in addition to his "human hands," explaining that the father had lots of other hands in fact: "here, here, here, here, here" – perhaps representing the father's omnipotence in his phantasy. On the right, second, in terms of size, Omer drew the mother, at first devoid of any facial features. He fiercely colored in her belly and chest, explaining: "Here are the breasts, and this is the tummy. Behind the shirt, she has a tummy." Later, Omer also "drew out" the mother's "peepee" from between her legs. On the left, Omer drew two boys, one of which he drew initially without a "peepee," but later added one in black. Finally, he drew an infant between the father and the mother. At first, he similarly forgot to give the baby facial features, and upon realizing this, was momentarily alarmed and hurried to fill in the lacking features in blue and yellow. At this point, he remarked:

Drawing 11 "A family in which everybody's holding a parrot": Omer's family drawing.
(From left to right: Two children; Daddy; a baby; Mommy)

Omer: "This is a baby girl that isn't growing."
Me: "She isn't growing? Why isn't she growing?"
Omer: "Because they only have two children, and they want her to grow and grow and grow, but you need to wait."

Me:	"And the children want her to grow?"
Omer:	"Yes, but they need to wait a bit longer."

After completing the drawing, Omer composed the following narrative: "This story is about a family where everybody holds a parrot." A moment later he changed his mind and pointed to the father: "But only this one here, this is the parrot." Given the contradictory versions, I asked whether the mother also had a parrot, and Omer replied: "Yes, and here too, and he has one too." When asked whether he had ever seen a parrot, he replied that they had visited an animal farm that morning and he had held a yellow parrot.

What is the precise meaning of the parrot? It is difficult to say. It might represent the phallus, or perhaps an offspring; maybe that very morning, when spending time with his family at an animal farm, Omer had observed some father holding a parrot, the same parrot he himself had held – and was deeply impressed by the experience, because it resonated with his phantasy. Whatever the case, the drawing unambiguously shows that the father figure occupies a central role in his emotional life.

Another prominent element in the drawing is Omer's intense preoccupation with the figures' physicality. A drawing of a human figure typically begins with the sketching of the head, the rest of the body following later (Urban, 1963). Omer drew the bodies of the figure first, paying much attention to the details, and only later added their heads while leaving the female figures without facial features. In addition, Omer's drawing emphasized the figures' sexual organs and evinced an anxious preoccupation with the mother's body, particularly in his intense coloring-in of her breasts and belly. Omer is obviously perturbed by whatever it is that goes on, in his understanding, inside the mother's body, underneath her clothes: in her belly, which could have children inside; as well as in her breasts, be they maternal nurturing breasts or sexual ones. It will be recalled that Omer has a baby sister; in the year preceding our encounter, he was witness to Rona's evolving pregnancy, the appearance of his sister Nur, and Rona's nursing breasts.

Freud (1905b, with an addendum from 1915) claims that the threat of the actual or presumed addition of a new sibling to the family is what stimulates the child's exploratory thinking about the question of where children come from. According to Freud, this is also the question, under a different guise, that lies behind the Sphinx's riddle in the *Oedipus Rex*. Omer's case illustrates that the Sphinx's riddle contains additional questions about the course of human development: how does the infant turn into a child? How does the child become a man? And perhaps also, what is old age and what is death? These questions about the nature of the transformation a person undergoes in the course of their life were also sparked in Omer following the birth of his baby sister Nur: he had been promised a sister that he could play with, but realized he has "to wait a bit longer" until she becomes a genuine playmate, and stops stealing such a large portion of his mothers' attention, and especially Rona's. Although Omer was formed inside Esty's womb, Rona is the mother who serves as his primary attachment figure, and it is toward her that Omer directs his primary needs.

During early childhood, children lack cognitive abilities such as "conservation" and "reversibility" (Piaget & Inhelder, 1972), and therefore the category of "children" is perceived as separate from the category of "babies." Omer, who is just beginning to acquire and establish these abilities, already understands that these are not separate categories, but parts of a continuum: every infant is destined to become a child and then an adult, and every adult was previously a child and prior to that an infant. Omer is obviously engaged in making sense of this developmental trajectory, and repeatedly returns to the topic, sometimes folding in knowledge that he has picked up about the theory of evolution. For example, when I asked him how Nur came into the world, his reply was: "First she was inside a monkey's tummy, and after that she was inside her Mommy, a human being mommy, Mommy Rona, and after that she was a baby, and in the end she'll be a girl, and then, at the very-very end – she's going to be a woman!"

Freud (ibid.) argued that the riddle of where children come from precedes the distinction between the sexes. According to Freud, a boy will adhere to the assumption that everyone possesses a sexual organ like his own and will defend this assumption from the evidence to the contrary that arises from his observation of the surrounding world. Only after fierce internal struggles does he relinquish this belief. In his family drawing, Omer is concerned with the question of who is and who isn't holding a parrot, who has a "peepee" dangling between their legs, and who lacks one. He is certain that the father has one; in respect to his mothers, he evidently has doubts, but is not yet ready to reconcile himself to the realization that has begun to take hold in his mind. The questions that preoccupy Omer – where do children come from, how are they created, and how do they grow? – in turn provoke his curiosity, perhaps more intensively so due to his family circumstances, about the differences between the sexes.

Card 8 Silhouette of a man.

In response to card 8, intended to elicit representations of the birth other, Omer said:

Omer: "This is a funny man."
Me: "Why is he funny? What's funny about this man?"
Omer: "This man . . . what? What is that number?"
Me: "That's a question mark. Do you know what a question mark is?"
Omer: "What is it?"
Me: "It's when you ask a question. Do you want to make up a question?"
Omer: "My question is [thinks for a moment] where do all the mulberries come from?"

The question that occurs to him at the sight of the mysterious silhouette of a male figure – "Where do all the mulberries come from?" – is undoubtedly a displacement of the question that is troubling him: where do all the children come from?

Later in the interview I realize that Omer is quite engaged in exploring the possibility that the mulberry tree in their back yard might bear fruit. When I asked him what he likes to do with his Mommy Esty (his Oedipal love object), Omer replied:

Omer: "I love everything we do together! Sliding with her, going to the playground, and also water sliding, and going to the pool with her, and also practicing diving underwater."

Me:	"Wow! What adventures you have together!"
Omer:	"But there's one adventure that I'm excited about the most."
Me:	"What's that?"
Omer:	"Seeing mulberries come out on our tree."
Me:	"Mulberries on your tree? That's the most exciting thing for you?"
Omer:	"Yup. That is a mulberry tree [points to the large tree in their back yard]. A mulberry is about to come out. And there's a lot there too, a lot of mulberries."

I was subsequently extremely surprised, after describing to Rona and Esty Omer's excitement and curiosity about the mulberry tree in their yard, when they informed me that it was not a mulberry tree, but rather a "a non-fruit-bearing tree." The mothers were reminded that "two days ago the boys planted popcorn seeds so that a popcorn tree would come out. And now, they're waiting. Checking on it, etc."

Many children conduct scientific experiments of this type – planting a seed with the hope of sprouting a sapling – perhaps as part of an exploration aimed at uncovering the mystery of birth. It is only to be expected that when children whose births were assisted by gamete donation conduct such experiments, the exploration will bear unique nuances and meanings.

Ofer (2014) describes a case of a child, the daughter of a lesbian couple, busying herself with planting apple seeds and following their germination and growth as a central part of the therapeutic process that enabled her to work through issues concerning her origins as the offspring of a sperm donation. If we attempt to analyze the nuances of Omer's case, something about the sharp contrast between his vitality and enthusiasm when describing the fruit-laden tree, and the recognition that the tree is actually barren, brought to mind his primal scene phantasy, and what it might mean for him to recognize that the sexual union between his mothers – a source of curiosity as well as threat, as his mothers' reports make clear – is not a fruit-bearing union. Another thought that came to mind, in view of his shift from describing his joint adventures with Mommy Esty, to describing his excitement about the ultimate adventure – "seeing mulberries come out of the tree" – was that in his phantasy, perhaps, the advantage he holds over his Oedipal rival (Mommy Rona) is the fact that unlike the connection between the mothers, his connection to Mommy Esty has the potential to produce children.

A merging wish with an idealized parent figure

In their family drawings, children typically draw themselves as the main figure (Urban, 1963). In Omer's case, the father figure is granted this status. This could suggest a kind of merging between his own figure and that of the absent father figure. This possibility is also suggested by his response to card 9, which is intended to elicit representations of the birth other.

Card 9 A man carrying suitcases.

Omer: "Someone who's too tall. Look, you can't see him. Mens are first of all babies. After that they start to be big, big, big until they're mens."
Me: "So are you going to be a man some day?"
Omer: "Yes. I'm starting to be a kid that isn't a kid anymore; he's already a man."
Me: "And what will you be like when you become a man?"
Omer: You know what I'll be? You know what kind of driver I'll be?"
Me: "What kind of driver?"
Omer: An airplane driver!"
Me: "Oh, really? A pilot?"
Omer: "Yes, and on the airplane I'll bring everyone ice-cream and we'll fly, fly, fly, fly, fly . . . would you like to?"
Me: "Of course. If you become a pilot and bring everyone ice-cream, just pass by my house and bring me some too."
Omer: "Okay, I'll bring you some. But you have to get on the plane. Because I'll have really fast jets! Like this [makes a jet sound], you've got to see it flying fast [the excitement is followed by a thoughtful tone], I hope it happens."

In his response, Omer interprets the partial nature of the object as evidence of its greatness. He is so high up that he cannot be seen. Omer's interpretation suggests that when circumstances rule out an encounter with the actual object and recognition of its limitations, idealization may flourish. His associative stream of thought led us from the idealized representation of the birth other to thoughts about his own development from a child into a man, culminating in grandiose phantasies of power and glamor, which are associated in his mind with adult manliness. In Omer's phantasy, when he grows up to be a man, he will be a pilot dispensing ice-cream up in the sky. Like his reference to the birth other as someone "too tall," so much so that "you can't see him," he has also placed the adult version of himself way up in the sky, beyond the scope of vision. He'll have loads of ice-cream to give away generously on demand – this, too, possibly echoes a phantasy about the generous man who donated his sperm, who may also have provided a thrilling moment to each beneficiary (a ride on his swift aircraft), before moving on and disappearing out of sight at jet-speed.

I should, however, qualify my reliance on this associative chain of thought, because of the leading nature of my own interventions in the conversation. To enhance the reliability of the inferred information, I now present another response to the same image of a partial male figure carrying suitcases, this one from Nadav, the five-and-a-half-year-old son of Mommy Iggy and Mommy Ossi:

Nadav: "I don't see anything that you can make up here!"
Me: "What do you see?"
Nadav: "Nothing!"
Me: "Nothing? You don't see anything here?"
Nadav: All you can see is hands with suitcases."
Me: "So you can't make anything up about it?"
Nadav: "Just a man walking."
Me: "Ok. Do you feel like trying to make something up, or should I show you another picture?"
Nadav: "Um . . . I'll make something up!'
Me: "You'll make something up? Let's see . . ."
Nadav: "Ah. Once a man was walking with suitcases and a camera saw him and took a photo of him. That I can see here [pointing to the focus frame in the center of the image]. That's a superpower camera!"
Me: "A superpower camera? What does it take photos of?"
Nadav: "Special people."

Me:	"And what's special about this person?"
Nadav:	"That . . . no! They didn't know that he was special, but they wanted to check."
Me:	"They wanted to check? And what do you think they found out? Is he special or not?"
Nadav:	[Nods.]
Me:	"Yes, and what do you think is special about him?"
Nadav:	"That he can fly!"
Me:	"He can fly? Wow. And where does he fly to?"
Nadav:	"Wherever he wants. And he saves everyone that's in danger."
Me:	"Oh. Wow! A special person indeed!"

This vignette nicely illustrates the psychological dynamics involved in the creation of a whole phantasized object out of a partial one. Nadav initially reacted to the picture with inhibition and withdrawal, indications of anxiety. He clung to the object's partiality, defensively claiming that it prevented him from inventing a narrative ("I don't see anything that you can make up here!"). A defensive assertion parallel to this one can be found in the claim often voiced by parents who have been assisted by gamete donation, that they don't think about the donor because they do not know him or her as a person, and the partial information they do possess about the donor is insufficient for constructing a mental representation (Vanfraussen et al., 2001). Only after I helped him create a transitional space, in which he had explicit permission to phantasize, along with the freedom to refuse and continue instead with the task, was he able to meet his own curiosity about the birth other. Soon after there appeared a grandiose phantasy about a flying superhero capable of saving anyone in need. This narrative of a superhero who might have appeared out of the blue to save his mothers (who wanted a child) and then taken off (to assist other women in need) – like the figure of the ice-cream dispensing pilot – encapsulates the image of a beneficent hero together with an explanation of his disappearance and of the mystery surrounding his character.

This theme of an idealized parent figure recurred in the cases of seven children: four boys of lesbian couples and three girls of gay couples, with the superhero figure replaced in girls' case by a beautiful and powerful queen. The daughters of lesbians and the sons of gay men exhibited no such preoccupation with queens or superheroes. Why, then, does this theme appear only among children whose parents are of the opposite sex? I venture that the phantasies about an idealized parent who is of the same sex as the child arise as a developmental need for a positive identification figure, for the sake of consolidating their gender identity. Indeed, children who live with a parent of the same sex will also create an idealized representation of their parent, but will also inevitably encounter their limitations. The mystery surrounding the birth other, as well as the child's sense of lack or absence, serve together to intensify the phantasy.

The difference between children with parents of the same sex and those with parents of the opposite sex did not manifest itself only within the narrow context of the idealized parent theme discussed. I found that these two groups of children were clearly differentiated by several other important parameters: the degree of preoccupation with the birth other, the quality of their phantasies surrounding the birth other, as well as the degree to which they manifest day-to-day curiosity and seek proximity to actual parental figures of the sex missing from their family life. Before turning to examine these differences – between children raised by parents of the same sex as their own as opposed to those raised by parents of the opposite sex – I will digress momentarily from the progression of the argument just outlined in order to discuss a phenomenon that is relevant to this theme.

Gender solitary

During my encounters with the different families, I noted that some children were not only of a different sex than their parents but also than that of the rest of their family – a novel phenomenon that can occur either in single-parent families or in families where parents of the same sex are raising children. Children raised in these circumstances, whom I choose to call "gender solitary," in the absence of an existing designation in the literature, tended to refer to this aspect as a meaningful element of their identity.

In the interview with Rani and Freddy, fathers to six-year-old Alma, who has younger twin brothers, the couple spoke about Alma's remarkable development, resilience, and wellbeing, yet noted that there was one aspect of their family configuration that perpetually upsets her:

Freddy: "The only thing bothering her is the fact that she's the only girl in the family. She keeps on saying this."

Me: "That's something I noticed too. There might be something about children that do not share their gender with anyone else in their family, a kind of minor melancholy, a kind of loneliness."

Freddy: "True. That's something Alma does have. And she's always saying, 'I'm the only girl in the family and I want a sister'."

Rani: "During the pregnancy with the twins, she really wanted girls, and she walked out of the sonogram very dramatically when she realized it was two boys. Crying and all. She was four years old. She said, 'I'm sure it's going to change. They made a mistake!'"

Recurring motifs that came up in my meetings with each of the ten *gender solitary* children suggested that this circumstance may carry two opposite meanings: a deep-seated sense of outsiderness, accompanied by jealousy toward the gender coalition that they perceive to exist among the rest of the family members, and a longing for a sibling of the same gender; or alternatively, a sense of uniqueness and sexual power. In an Oedipal context, the latter experience may inspire a belief that they have the power to provide the beloved parent with what he or she lacks in order to beget a child, or a wish to embody the parent of the missing sex in their own person. These motifs occurred also among children whose parents belonged to the opposite sex (e.g., in the case of Omer). It follows that gender solitariness may be regarded as a particular, distilled instance of the broader category of children to parents of the opposite sex.

Drawing 12 "An African family that saw a monkey": Tom's Family drawing. (From left to right: a monkey; a girl; Mommy; Daddy.)

Like Alma, seven-year-old Tom, the son of Vicky and Nora, and brother to two sisters – four-and-a-half-year-old Ada and 12-month-old Yuli – was very preoccupied with his being the only boy in the family. When I asked Tom if he could tell me a bit about his family, the first thing he chose to share was: "I'm the only boy here, and everyone else is a girl." In his family drawing he chose to draw "an African family that saw a monkey." To my question of whether he had ever seen an African family, he replied that he had once seen "brown people" in his hometown.

Tom: "An African family – Daddy, Mommy, and a girl – who saw a monkey! And the girl said, 'What's a monkey doing here?!'"

Tom's family drawing reflects the experience of being the odd one out. This is evident primarily in his choice of an African family representation, linked with a memory of his encounter with a family of "brown people," whose appearance immediately disclosed their outsider status in the context of the conservative, ethnically homogeneous social environment in which he lives. The sense of outsiderness is further accentuated by the figure of the monkey, whose different color and distinctive attitude – approaching the family by surprise, not an integral part of it – set him apart from the rest of the family. The encounter with the monkey, according to Tom, draws an outspoken, puzzled reaction from the girl: "What's a monkey doing here!?" The significant weight that Tom's family drawing accords the element of outsiderness may reflect the family's out-of-place status in the heteronormative social landscape typical of his residential environment – an issue that came up in conversations with Tom and his mothers as a source of distress. However, based on the findings, I propose that children who live a gender solitary existence within their family may be more sensitive to other elements of discrepancy in their lives as well, and may sometimes even interpret other contexts of difference in terms of gender. Thus, for example, 13-year-old Noam, who was born in the context of a parenting partnership and spends half of the week at her mother's home and half with her father and his partner, employed the terms of gender difference to explain to herself the experience of exclusion and jealousy vis-à-vis her six-year-old brother Judah, who was born through a surrogacy process and spends every day at his fathers' home. In her phantasy, she is sent off to her mother and does not belong fully to her brother and pair of fathers' family only because she is a girl.

Tom's experience of outsiderness arouses in him a fierce longing for similarity and identification, a longing that can be described in terms of twinship needs (Kohut, 1984). When I asked him if he thinks he'll want kids of his own when he's grown up, he replied: "I'd prefer twins." When asked what he likes about twins, he replied: "They like almost the same things."

Vicky and Nora, Tom's mothers, described him as intensely curious about father figures in his social environment – a curiosity unparalleled in intensity, in their estimation, by that of his four-and-a-half-year-old sister Ada.

Nora: "Take Dan's Dad – when Tom goes over to his best friend Dan's, he talks to Dan's dad sometimes, asks him questions about how to build stuff and Dan's dad willingly shows him. Tom is curious about him."

Vicky: "Um, male figures are quite intriguing to Tom. You can suddenly see him standing at the playground and staring at an interaction between a father and a son. Sometimes he asks to join in. Dads usually really like him."

In the apperception task, Tom displayed a repeated preoccupation with phantasies of adoption by a male figure. For example, while looking at a picture of a chick hatching out of an egg (card 10), he said: "There once was a chick that lost its parents and didn't know what to do. He waited and waited and then found a man who raised him, his owner."

Card 10 A chick hatching from an egg.

In response to (card 11), depicting a toddler inside a suitcase, he said: "A baby inside a suitcase who was looking for his owner."

Card 11 A boy in a suitcase.³

At times, Tom replaced the expression "his owner" (Hebrew: *be'alim*, plural of *ba'al*) with the expression "his husband" (*ba'al*). Given his Platonic Oedipal style, which indicates that he is preoccupied with Oedipal dynamics but does not direct romantic feelings toward his chosen maternal Oedipal object, and taking into account the mothers' reports, which attribute to Tom a homosexual preference, the possibility occurred to me that in his phantasy the longing for a father figure is conflated with romantic longings, or in other words, that Tom's romantic Oedipal libido is invested in phantasies of uniting with a father figure.

Conflation between a male love object to whom romantic aspirations are directed (*husband*) and a phantasy about being adopted by a father figure (*owner*) can be seen in the following narrative, composed in response to the picture of the sitting hen (Card 12): "There once was a hen who laid golden eggs, and her husband, her owner, was rich."

---

3 The figures appearing in the book are for illustration only. In the original photo shown to Tom, the child in the suitcase appears younger, and fits the description of a "toddler" or "young child," unlike the child depicted in Card 11.

Card 12 A hen sitting on eggs.

As in dreamwork, the conciseness of this story is achieved through condensation. In addition to the representation of a "husband/owner," it also contains a representation of an idealized object to which are attributed both riches and hyper-fertility. The hen may be a representation of himself as the only child in his family who has "eggs" (in Hebrew also "balls," or testicles), as well as a representation of his mother Vicky, who has already produced two babies from her body during his lifetime; and at the same time an expression of a family romance that deals with his own origination from a rich and fertile object.

In addition to these possible meanings, Tom's story also alludes to a well-known Aesopian fable, which tells of a poor farmer with a hen who laid a single golden egg every day. The farmer believed that inside the hen lay a stash of gold and hence decided to cut her belly open. But upon doing so, he discovered that her insides were the same as those of any other hen, and thus by imagining that he could become instantly rich, the poor farmer denied himself the opportunity of earning a handsome profit, one day at a time.

From a Kleinian perspective, the fable can be read as dealing with curiosity about exploring the mother's body from within and seeking the treasures that lie therein: the birth-giving potential, and the father. The fable's moral points toward the guilt associated with Tom's curiosity about his origins and about a possible father figure – a curiosity that is very much present in his stories and in his obvious attraction to the father figures around him but is entirely absent from his explicit discourse with his mothers. As Nora explains, "I think that he often refrains from telling us things like this, because he is protecting us." Tom's avoidance may be motivated by anxiety that seeking a father will destroy the mother and leave him orphaned. He is better off, so it seems, not being greedy and making do with the handsome daily profits of his relations with his mothers.

Unlike Tom, the gender solitariness of five-year-old Nadav is primarily interpreted in terms of uniqueness and sexual power.

Drawing 13 "I am showing the egg": Nadav's family drawing.

Nadav's family drawing describes a moment during a family trip in which Nadav – the oversize figure depicted on the left – shows the female members of his family an egg that he found inside a cave. From left to right, in miniature and awestruck, are his sister Ella, Mommy Ossi, and Mommy Iggy. At first Nadav only drew hands for himself. Upon completing the task, he saw that the other figures lacked hands and added them in.

Nadav's self-presentation as the only figure in the family with agency, and his exhibitionist position, as the one who is showing the girls his "egg," resonate with his idealized representation of the birth other. As will be recalled, Nadav described the birth other as a flying superhero who helps everyone in danger. Based on the assumption that the left side of the drawing represents phantasy, one could surmise that, as the only male figure in his family, Nadav unconsciously believes that he himself embodies the idealized father.

However, as every superhero fan knows: "With great power comes great responsibility." For example, in response to Card 13:

Nadav: "A polar bear once was hugging his little boy-bear. And then a wolf came, but the little bear rammed him with his head and the wolf died. The boy killed the wolf to prevent him from eating the mother up because she was asleep and didn't know the wolf was getting close. So the cub protected his mother."

Card 13 Polar bears.

In Nadav's response there is a fluidity in the representation of the object. The bear that is hugging the cub is initially presented as male and later as female, as a mother. Seen from another angle, the male figure is initially presented as an object of longing and merging, and later as a violent intruder from which the mother must be protected. In any case, Nadav attributes to the little cub the ability to batter the wolf to death and save his mother, who is deep in sleep and unaware of the entire drama. Perhaps the thing of which the mother is unaware is the degree of his longing for a father figure, and moreover, of the guilt he carries about having such longings, which are perceived as endangering the mother, requiring him to defend her from potential intrusion. The theme of rivalry between a male parent figure and a female one will be discussed later in the chapter.

Preoccupation with the birth other as part of gender identity formation and as a refuge from the Oedipal situation

All the evidence presented up to this point to support the notion that children in same-sex families are likely to be preoccupied in their phantasy with the figure of the birth other, or with a parent figure of the sex that is missing from their family configuration, was derived from my encounters with four children: Anna, Omer, Tom, and Nadav. All four are children of a different sex than their parents, and the last two are not only different in sex from their parents, but also from the rest of their family members – in other words they are characterized by gender solitariness. This is not a matter of coincidence. Children whose biological sex differs from that of their parents tended to display a greater preoccupation with phantasies about the birth other as well as a day-to-day heightened curiosity about parent figures of their own sex – apparently motivated by an identification wish, as part of the process of gender identity construction.[4] This finding accords well with the findings of a Belgian study, a country in which the law, as in Israel, requires donor anonymity. When children were asked hypothetically whether they would like to meet their sperm donor, it was usually the boys who expressed such a wish. The researchers explained this as the boys' need for a male identification model (Vanfraussen et al., 2001).

---

4 Whereas children to parents of the same sex as their own mostly displayed a slight degree or no curiosity about the issues at hand (12 children compared to three who displayed intense curiosity about these issues), among children to parents of the opposite sex, the exact reverse was true – most of them displayed an intense preoccupation with the issues (only two or three children displayed either no interest or a slight interest in the issues, compared to 14 children who were intensely preoccupied with them). Finally, from among the ten children characterized as gender solitary (and therefore also included in the previous group of children to parents of the opposite sex), nine displayed an intense preoccupation with the issues under discussion, whereas one girl displayed a slight preoccupation. It should be noted that even the girl classified as only slightly preoccupied was placed in this category due to a lack of sufficient evidence of a repetitive engagement with the issue, and this was due to her partial cooperation. The small number of responses she did produce clearly manifested a preoccupation with the experience of outsiderness and with a longing for a mother figure (see Eitan-Persico, 2020).

It is important to point out that at stake is not an actual developmental need, but rather a wish, which one may assume is based to a large degree on the centrality of three different types the gender dichotomy as a culturally determined component of identity. Researchers have found that children of lesbians show similar levels of psychological wellbeing, whether their birth was assisted by a known donor, who played a continuous part in their lives; whether in the case of an open donation (allowing the donor's identity to be revealed to the child at the age of 18); or whether in the context of an anonymous donation. (Bos & Gartrell, 2010). It follows that the child's wellbeing does not necessitate an actual presence of a parent from the child's sex. It is rather sufficient to show empathy toward the child's need to engage in phantasy about such a parental figure. Children are liable to feel guilt and anxiety about their phantasies – as seems to be suggested by Tom's story about the hen who laid golden eggs or Nadav's story about the bear cub who killed the wolf in order to protect his mother – and they need their parents' validation and support in order to explore and work through these issues in their phantasy life.

Powerful phantasies about the birth other were, as mentioned, characteristic of gender solitary children and of children with parents of the opposite sex more generally. In Chapters One and Two, I showed that the full-blown Oedipal configuration was especially characteristic of children whose parents were of the opposite sex. It follows, therefore, that there is an overlap between these two phenomena. In Nadav's case, for instance, the ambivalent narrative reflecting a merging wish with a father figure and a need to defend the mother from his hostile intrusion co-exists with a full-blown Oedipal dynamics in which his two mothers take part: his chosen love object is his social mother – Iggy, while his birth mother Ossi is cast as an Oedipal rival. Therefore, although it is quite tempting to view the narratives in which a rivalry between the father and mother figures plays a central part (as in Nadav's case) as evidence of the existence of an Oedipal configuration in which the biological mother and the birth other take part, the full picture indicates, rather, that the birth other does not play a role within the Oedipal configuration itself, but rather functions as a figure of identification that is external to the Oedipal triangle.

Ofer (2014), a contemporary Kleinian, who assumes that the Oedipal deep structure of a child inevitably refers to his genitor and genetrix, has articulated a similar insight:

> Parallel to the child's experience of growing up with two mothers, in other words, in the presence of an actual triangle, which confronts the

child with the mothers' couplehood and sexuality, the child maintains their own couple relationship with the phantasized father (here the postmodern family produces an innovation: the infidelity is not with one parent versus the other, but with the father who has been "banished" by both mothers.)

In other words, parallel to their relations with their actual parents, on the basis of which the child's Oedipal configuration is formed – and within which they work through the recognition of their parents' couplehood and sexuality, including experiences of exclusion and jealousy induced by this recognition – the child is also invested in phantasmatic relations with the birth other. The birth other does not feature here as a potential partner of the genetic parent, but as a familial alternative to the parental couple. Furthermore, the need for such an external figure may even increase the more dominant the Oedipal preoccupation with the actual parents is. According to Freud (1909), this is precisely the developmental role of the family romance.

The family romance and the birth other

Freud describes the family romance as a broad phantasmatic system at the center of which there is an alternative parental figure or figures that are a figment of the child's imagination. The flexibility of this phantasmatic system allows it to be shaped according to the emotional demands that arise within each and every child. Thus, among children who were created by means of a gamete donation, the representation of the unknown biological source merges with the phantasmatic representation of the alternative parent, on whom the child's innermost wishes are often overlaid (Corbett, 2009; Ehrensaft, 2007, 2008; Warner, 1993).

The family romance spun by children raised by same-sex parents therefore fulfills several functions: as a motivating force in service of the increasing separation from the parents; a need to construct an identity despite lack of access to half of their genetic heritage; a need to identify with a parental figure of the missing sex in the family configuration, especially in the case of children whose parents are of a different sex than their own; a means of coping with the feelings of jealousy and inferiority that arise with the child's recognition that their family is part of a minority group; the imperative to reconcile between two contradictory conceptions of kinship – the one which their family is founded upon, and the other, reflecting the hegemonic social outlook; finally, the family romance offers a defensive refuge from the pain of recognizing one's parents sexuality. This refuge is achieved by representing the male birth other as the Holy Spirit, rather than as an Oedipal sexual rival, or of the female birth other as a symbiotic safe haven, more than as a sexual woman who desires the father for herself.

Freud entreats us not to be alarmed by these phantasies, or from the open hostility toward the parents enacted in them. The child's ingratitude and disloyalty are only apparently so. In fact, under a thin veil, these phantasies safeguard the child's original affection for his parents, since the imaginary parents are usually equipped with the traits that the child derives from their relations with their actual parents. The attempt to replace the actual parent with a more "exalted" one is no more than an expression of the child's yearning and longing for the times when their parents appeared to them strong and perfect, the most decent and precious of human beings.

The family romance: themes of adoption, abandonment, or reunion with a long-lost parent

More than half of the children with whom I met presented phantasized narratives of adoption, abandonment, or kidnapping. Some repeated these motifs over and over again, in various stories or through free play.

When I visited the home of Rani and Freddy for the first time to interview their daughter Alma, her twin brothers, Jeremy and Tzur, were only two years old. I paid a second visit to the family home when they turned five. As I walked in, the twins wanted to show me a mysterious room in the basement level of their home, which contained a single bed. "This is our nanny's room," they explained. Playfully and joyfully, the children began to pull jewelry out of a jewelry box that stood on a shelf, piling necklaces and bracelets on me, as much as I could support. To my surprise, I learned from their fathers that the children don't have a nanny, and that the room they had shown me was simply a guest room. During the first year of their lives, the parents explained, when the family was living abroad, they actually did have a live-in nanny. The jewelry box and its entire contents, it turned out, belonged to Alma, Jeremy and Tzur's older sister.

In Dora's case study, Freud (1905a) writes about the room and the jewelry box as representations that carry a symbolic meaning related to female anatomy. It seems then, the boys' play merges various female figures into a single maternal object; the nanny who was once an inseparable part of the family daily life, and left a void when she disappeared from their lives; the surrogate who bore them in her womb, and is informed now and again about how they are doing, but does not fulfill a mothering role; their older sister, four-and-a-half years their senior, who does serve as a little mother to them; and perhaps even myself, a female authority figure whose sudden appearance in their home aroused the impulse to take me to the empty room and weigh me down with jewelry, as in a secret coronation ceremony.

A Kleinian interpretation of the boys' play would emphasize their wish to penetrate the maternal body, to explore it from within, and to gain control over its assets and treasures. This interpretation is supported by the following occurrence: when I was introduced to Jeremy and Tzur, I took a bag of surprises out of my handbag and pulled out two small gifts for them. Throughout the meeting, the boys continued to search my handbag for the bag of surprises, and to raid its contents.

Another possible reading would identify the mysterious room in the basement as "the other room" (Britton, 1998) – the site where the primal scene transpires. Their preoccupation with a female figure that they associate with this room suggests that they do not imagine it as the site where the sexual union between the fathers occurs, or a sexual union between one of the fathers and a mother figure, but rather as a place where the boys imagine installing a mother figure or their birth other, as part of their family romance. Both Jeremy and Tzur were classified as exhibiting the full-blown Oedipal configuration. Their preoccupation with the mother figure was an accompaniment to the active Oedipal dynamic in relation to their two fathers, not a substitution for it. This evidence reinforces Corbett's claim (Corbett, 2009) that among donor children the primal scene phantasy comprises two different phantasies that exist side by side: the phantasy of parental sexual union and conception phantasies.

An additional illustration of an Oedipal construction relating to two fathers, coexisting side by side with a family romance centered on the wish to reunite with a mother figure, was suggested by Gaya's interview material. In response to the "family hug" image (Card 3, see p. 55), six-year-old Gaya, the daughter of Daddy Erez and Daddy Zohar, and Michael's twin sister related the following story:

Gaya: "There once was an animal that was walking down the street, and then she met two animals who were strange to her, and then she hugged them, and finally they wanted to be kids and their

	mother; and she was looking for children. Do I have some kind of bruise here?"
Me:	"It looks a little red."
Gaya:	"I know. 'Cause I was at the pool."

The image, intended to elicit Oedipal contents of exclusion and jealousy vis-à-vis the parental union, brought to Gaya's mind an association of a mother with two children. Gaya has a twin brother, meaning that even during the uterine stage, her development took place within the context of triangular relations. In her made-up story, Gaya described a female figure who meets two children in the street. The unfamiliarity and strangeness that characterize the moment of encounter are swiftly transformed into an embrace and mutual adoption. When the story ended, Gaya asked me to look at her bruise. Possibly, the phantasmatic representation of adoption by a mother figure aroused some pain. Her association of the hurt with time spent at the pool may be an expression of an inner representation of her time in the womb, in other words, of her birth other.

Because of her gender solitary status, as an only girl in a family of boys, Gaya's phantasies about a mother figure also function as a space for working through questions about the source of her femininity. For example, in response to Card 14:

Card 14 A girl in a suitcase.

Gaya:	"There once was a baby. She stole her mother's necklace and went inside a suitcase. And then her mother searched and searched for her but couldn't find her. She went to a policeman and said, 'Come search with me.' And then she found her."

This time, the female parent figure is not described as an adoptive mother, but as a "real" mother who is searching for her lost baby. The story describes a girl who stole her mother's necklace and hid inside a suitcase. The mother searched for her, and perhaps also for the purloined necklace, finding her eventually, only after involving a policeman in the search. Gaya appears to carry unconscious guilt about the loss of the mother figure, as well as for having stolen something belonging to the mother, something associated perhaps with her femininity, and which therefore could not belong to any of her family members who are all male – except for her.

The family romance narratives presented up till now have emphasized a longing for a union with a parent figure of the sex that is missing from the family configuration. Another variation of the family romance centers the narrative around relations of rivalry between a female parent figure and a male parent figure.

Rivalry between the parents and the birth other

In the course of free play, six-year-old Adam told me the following: "There's a bad guy who captured a kid using his outfit. The bad guys try to steal people and I have two swapping shields. I have two swapping shields and they've got swords inside them."

As a mirror image of the merging wish with a superhero that I presented earlier, Adam describes the birth other in terms of a conniving kidnapper (Cf. Ehrensaft, 2007, 2008). But, fortunately, he has two "swapping shields" – Moran and Shir – his two interchangeable mothers, each of which shields him from traumatic invasiveness by means of her adaptive care (Khan, 1963). However, according to Adam's description, the maternal function is not limited to creating a protective covering, since the shields are depicted as equipped with swords. The swords may represent a phallus attributed to the mothers, the father within the mother, as it were, or the mother's unconscious murderous attitude toward this potential kidnapper – the birth other.

In reference to the image of a hen sitting on eggs (Card 12, see p. 204), many children added an antagonist such as a predator or a potential kidnapper threatening the mother-infant relationship. For example, Nina, the four-year-old daughter of Mommy Tali and Mommy Inbal, said:

A hen who is watching over her birds and sitting on the eggs. And suddenly a crow arrives! And she was so frightened that she got off the nest and then he broke the eggs (laughs). And that's a happy thing, because I don't like hens.

The plot thickened after I presented the next card in the sequence, depicting a chick hatching from an egg (Card 10, see p. 202): "That's when the eggs cracked open and chicks came out, it's because of the crow. The crow actually tried to help the hen (laughs). He went like this with his beak, and that cut [open] the eggs."

The two stories in sequence suggest an ambivalence that Nina holds toward the birth other. Is he a hostile invader who arouses anxiety in the mother and endangers the wellbeing of the offspring, or is he a positive figure to whom one owes a debt of gratitude for his role in fertilizing the eggs? Who does Nina identify with? With the greedy crow who seeks to destroy the mother's offspring (Nina has a baby brother who undoubtedly arouses aggressive phantasies), or with the protective mother, who is herself fearful of the male figure?

The following story was told by five-year-old Tzur, the son of Rani and Freddy, in response to the picture of the sitting hen (Card 12, see p. 204):

> There once was a hen. She didn't know how to build a nest, so she built her nest out of eggs. The truth is that the eggs were a nest inside a nest. And the hen was the egg. Then lions came, but the hen – boom-boom – pecked at them, until the lions ran away.

The motif of rivalry between the mother figure and potential predators, this time in the plural (perhaps representing a pair of fathers), as well as the mother's role as provider of protection, appear in Tzur's story together with other motifs related to the question of the fertility of the father's couple relationship, or to the issue of the parental capacity of the birth other. The hen is described as someone who "doesn't know how to build a nest, so she built her nest out of eggs"; it is unclear whether this is the birth other, who doesn't "know" how to build a family unit, but only how to supply ova ("eggs"), or whether it is actually Rani and Freddy, who didn't "know" how to build a heteronormative nest and therefore built a family unit composed only of "eggs" (in Hebrew also "balls"), without a woman. Rani and Freddy themselves joked about their fertility "setback" when they said: "We weren't all that successful when we tried to have kids together."

The narrative constructed by Tzur takes a philosophical turn: "The truth is that the eggs were a nest inside a nest . . ." – this statement might be related to the phantasmatic relationship with the mother figure Tzur is invested in as part of his family romance, which constitutes a kind of private family within the family, much like the empty room that was intended in his imagination for a female nanny figure. As a paraphrase on the question of which came first, the chicken, or the egg, Tzur stated: "The chicken was the egg." He seems to be pondering the status of the mother figure: is she a hen – a whole object capable of potentially functioning as a parent, or is she no more than an egg – a partial object representing the potential of procreation, her role limited to only this.

Tzur's response to the image of the polar bears (Card 13, pp. 206), designed to elicit symbiotic parent-infant contents, evidenced a claustrophobic fear of the mother's body:

Tzur: "Once there was a snow bear who was playing with its cub, but he drowned, and only the cub was left. And then the snow cub was worried, he wanted to make sure the mother would succeed, but then one day a snow avalanche came down on the igloo and he was trapped there foreveeeer."

Although this terrifying version of the family romance does not feature a description of being snatched from the parent's bosom, it appears that relations with the mother are only permissible with the death of the father. In other words, these are rivalrous relations that are mutually exclusive. Moreover, his description of the father as having drowned while playing with the cub suggests that the child's mere play endangers the father. Earlier, I described the twins Tzur and Jeremy's libidinal play in the "nanny's room," and with the jewelry box, in terms of exploring the maternal figure. If we combine these narratives, they suggest that Tzur holds an unconscious belief that exploring the interior of the mother figure in phantasy, or expressing concern and care for her (as in the current narrative), harbor a danger for the father's wellbeing and for his own sense of wholeness.

The image of the cub trapped forever inside the igloo reflects claustrophobic fears. Klein (1926, 1946) believes that the roots of claustrophobia are to be found in the early fear of being trapped within the mother's dangerous body. This threatening image of the mother's body, according to Klein, derives primary from guilt and fear of the mother's retaliation in response to early sadistic wishes, including the wish to invade the object in order to gain control and a sense of ownership over it.

216 What does procreation have to do with parental coitus, anyway?

As an elaboration of these ideas, Meltzer (1992) describes the typical psychological implications of intrusive projective identification, which is acted out by force or by stealth and is accompanied by phantasies of dwelling inside the body of the internal mother. This leads to an experience of claustrophobic trapping of parts of the self in one of the mother's three compartments – the head-breast, the genital compartment, and the rectal compartment – accompanied by the psychological dynamics characteristic of each. It is hard to say on the basis of the existing material whether Tzur's phantasy is identified with the genital or rectal compartment, but one can assume that the notion of having been inside the surrogate's womb is retroactively constructed (Nachträglichkeit) as a realization of the phantasy of dwelling inside the body of the internal mother, with all the attendant feelings of yearning and dread.

In some of the children's stories, the rivalry between the male and female parental figures was ascribed a murderous quality. Six-year-old Gaya, for example, related the following story about the picture of the hen: "There was once a hen who was sitting on eggs and then when a chick was born, a wolf came by and gobbled up the chicks. And then the hen pecked him, and he ate her."

In Gaya's response one can find a phantasmatic explanation for the mother's disappearance. The chicks, representing Gaya and her twin brother Michael, were snatched away from the birth mother by the father, and when she tried to resist, he swallowed her. In many fairy tales, the wolf is known to swallow up animals or humans whole, but when its belly is opened, the creatures it swallowed are taken out safe and sound[5] – a quite fitting

---

5 For example, in the Grimm Brothers' fairy tales of "Little Red Riding Hood," "Thumbling," and "The Wolf and the Seven Young Goats" (see Hunt, 1944), as well as in the folk tale "Peter and the Wolf" (Prokofiev & Dale, 2011). Similar motifs can be found in "Barmaley" by Korney Chukovsky (2015), in which Barmaley is swallowed by a crocodile and emerges unscathed from his throat; or in *Pinocchio* (Collodi, 1995) where, as in the Biblical story of Jonah, the heroes are swallowed by a whale (or large fish) who later spews them out onto the shore in one piece. In *The Day Louis Got Eaten* by John Fardell (2012), there is a series of swallowings, the first of which is perpetrated by a Gulper. A similar motif, with a strong Oedipal inflection, occurs in the ancient Greek myth of Cronus. Having plotted with his mother Gaia to castrate his father Uranus in order to seize his throne, Cronus hears a prophecy that one day his rule too will be overthrown by his own son. To protect himself from this prophecy of wrath, Cronus devours his children the moment they are born. His consort, Rhea finds this abhorrent and when their sixth child, Zeus, is born, she hands Cronus a wrapped stone, which he swallows thinking it is Zeus. Eventually Zeus returns with a potion that causes Cronus to disgorge all of his sons and daughters, who survive in perfect condition (see Shabtai, 2000).

representation for the perception of impregnation and birth in oral terms, or in other words, as incorporation. The motif of rivalry between the mother and a potential predator, which appeared in other children's stories as well, is articulated in more violent terms here, perhaps reflecting the intensity of Gaya's jealousy of the parent's couplehood, or her envy of the absent mother figure's birth-giving potential. This motif of envy toward the mother's femininity also appeared in the story she made up about the theft of the mother's necklace (Klein, 1937). The image of the hen gobbled up by the wolf could also be interpreted as a representation of the maternal function provided by her fathers: the mother within the father (Ogden, 1989; Laur, 2011, Salman-Sagi, 2019).

In some of Gaya's stories, the predatory wolf was replaced by a poisonous snake whose bite spelled death for the object. For example, "There once was a bear who had a cub, and then a poisonous snake bit him and he died," or, another example, "There once was a giraffe and she ended up fainting and going to the hospital, and then she noticed that she had also been bitten by a poisonous snake and she was dead." The shift from representing the father figure as a beast of prey to representing him as a poisonous snake can be described in terms of a shift from interpreting sexuality in an oral vein to a phallic frame of mind (Freud, 1900).

This theme recurred also in her response to a picture that was intended to elicit a representation of the female birth others (Card 15).

Card 15 A vague female figure carrying a suitcase.

> *Gaya:*   "There was once a woman who took a walk, and suddenly her head broke, and so she stopped on the way and was bitten by three poisonous snakes."

All three members of Gaya's family, besides herself, are males: Erez and Zohar, her fathers, and Michael, her twin brother. In her phantasy, they seem to collude and inject the birth other with their venom, causing her to die. Gaya's sadistic view of sexuality (Freud, 1908) seems here to provide an explanation for the mother figure's disappearance.

The parallel condition, of a lacking father figure, was also interpreted by Ella, the five-year-old daughter of Ossi and Iggy, in terms of murderous rivalry on the part of her mothers. After viewing the picture of a man carrying suitcases (Card 9, see p. 196), she composed the following story:

> *Ella:*   "A man with a suitcase without a head. Where is his head? He is looking behind him and sees a pair of tigers that want to eat him."

Based on a previous response, in which Ella called the pair of lionesses I showed her "tigers" (Card 2, p. 52), one can assume that the phantasy Ella is presenting here is about her mothers' murderous attitude toward the birth other, or perhaps toward male figures generally. Given that the birth other is inevitably of the opposite sex than that of the parents, in cases where intense hostility is manifested by lesbian mothers toward men generally, or by gay fathers toward women generally, the child will be overburdened, struggling in an attempt to consolidate a positive representation of his or her birth other.

It should be noted that a narrative like that of Ella's, attributing a murderous impulse to the mothers, was extremely unusual, representing an exception among the children's responses. Most of the children (children of lesbian mothers and children of gay fathers, boys and girls alike) accorded the role of protagonist to the mother figure, were favorably disposed toward her, and attributed to her a right to her offspring, whereas the father figure was given the role of antagonist, who threatens the mother's wellbeing, the safety of her offspring, or the harmony of mother-infant relations. This formulation of power relations is therefore a reflection of the socially constructed belief that offspring primarily belong to their mother, and that it is she who provides them with protection and devoted care.[6] In addition, this formulation reflects the sadistic view of coitus, which is also derived from social constructions that attribute the sexual and aggressive drives to the male (Freud, 1908). It seems that parental reservations toward the birth other that seep into the child's psyche as part of the enigmatic messages forming their unconscious (Laplanche, 1987) are interpreted by the child in accordance with the sadistic view of coitus, such that the children of lesbian couples will tend to interpret their mothers' reservations about the male birth other in terms of the mothers' fear of him, whereas children of gay couples will tend to interpret their fathers' reservations toward the female birth other as an expression of the fathers' aggression.

Manifestations of inhibited curiosity

Inhibition of curiosity, or of the capacity to think or play, are explained in psychoanalytic theory as products of intense anxiety (Klein, 1930, 1931; Bion, 1967, 1962; Segal, 2001; Winnicott, 1971). Even if difficult feelings or contents may arise in phantasy, the child's very capacity to play, that is to work through psychic material, is an indication that anxiety is benign and is not overwhelming them. Winnicott even formulated a rule of thumb of use to mothers: "If the child is playing there is room for a symptom or two, and if a child is able to enjoy play . . . there is no very serious trouble afoot" (1964, p. 130).

Contemporary psychoanalytic theory assumes that some experiences are not amenable to symbolic representation in thought or in play, and are therefore not amenable to repression either, and thus remain as an "unthought known" (Bollas, 1987) or as "beta elements" (Bion, 1962). Where

---

6 This social perception is reflected, among other things, in the arguments behind the "Early Childhood Presumption," a principle of Israeli family law, which stipulates that in the case of divorce, children under the age of six are considered to be in their mother's custody unless otherwise warranted. Many Western countries have rescinded policies of this kind, and in Israel the first steps toward legal reform have been take, subsequent to the recommendations of the Schnitt Committee, but no statutory changes have yet been made.

no transformation is allowed for, the psyche is burdened with overstimulation that can only be evacuated by means of a somatic, mental, or behavioral symptoms (Bion, 1962; Britton, 1998).

Various manifestations of inhibited curiosity were evidenced among 12 of the children I encountered. In the case of mild inhibition, it was articulated in the context of the narrative itself, for example in the story told by five-and-a-half-year-old Nadav in response to the silhouette of a man (Card 8 , see pp. 194) : "There once was a man "There once was a man who had no ideas, so he couldn't think, and then a good witch fixed it so that he had lots of thoughts. A whole lot. And then he had a clue."

In this story, Nadav expressed a wish to be able to think through and understand ideas that lie beyond his grasp, perhaps the perplexing issues related to his birth, and to his mysterious birth other. He requires a clue, some sort of lead, that will help him think the unthought known. The good witch may represent his mothers, who have the capacity to provide him with the needed clues, as well as the permission to think and explore.

In cases of more intense anxiety than that exhibited by Nadav, a likely outcome is the collapse of the capacity to play. The distinction between the two emotional states could be described as analogous to the differences between nightmares and night terrors (Ogden, 2005). When the child is in a raw emotional state that can be likened to night terrors, the picture presented on the card is experienced as a painful encounter with an actual bad object, indistinguishable from the "thing-in-itself." Unequipped to digest it, the psyche is thus bound to rid itself from pain by retreating from reality (Bion, 1967).

Throughout my time with Ada, the four-and-a-half-year-old daughter of mothers Vicky and Nora, she was wholeheartedly engaged with the research tasks. During the apperception task she generated highly imaginative stories, indicating a rich inner world; however, upon viewing two of the images, she recoiled and attempted to hand me back the cards, and was unable to compose a narrative about them. Both were images designed to elicit representations of the birth other. They were not presented to her in sequence. The first, the silhouette of a man (Card 8, see pp. 194) yielded the following reaction: "Darrrkness. Why is it in black, tell me? And why has he got a question mark?"

After these abrupt questions, Ada hurried to give me back the card. Her response reveals a momentary collapse of the highly developed capacity for play that she exhibited in response to the images on the other cards. Her thoughts and imagination failed her and her questions for me were tinged with suspicion. Her suspiciousness subsided and her playing capacity was restored as we moved on to other images but resurfaced more forcefully in response to the second card dealing with the figure of the birth other. This time around, in view of a man carrying suitcases (Card 9, see pp. 196), she experienced a temporary breakdown that culminated in her inability to persevere with the task:

Ada: "Somebody walking with a suitcase. Tell me, how did you get all these pictures? Why is there a camera sign here?"

Ada knocked the card away to the other side of the room: "Boom! I bounced it all the way to Tom's bed," she said, roaring with laughter. "Now I'm going to have to go get it, Ohhhhh . . . ." At this point Ada was gripped by hysterical laughter. I asked her if she had run out of patience and if maybe she wanted to stop, but she kept laughing and did not reply. Thinking that a neutral stimulus might help her reintegrate and end the task with some sense of control, I offered her the option of either stopping or choosing another card. Ada replied, "I feeeeel like stoppiiiiinnnng!" To relieve her tension, I suggested we go together to show her mothers the family picture she had drawn. Being back with her mothers had a calming effect, and when no longer distressed, she became excited about showing me another family picture she had drawn in kindergarten.

The morbid-suspicious state of mind that came over Ada upon viewing the first image related to the birth other (the silhouette of a man), precipitating what might be called an "attack on linking" (Bion, 1967) – a disturbance in the processes of perception and thought triggered by the urgent need to disengage from a reality that is experienced as an uncontainable, forceful attack. Her second encounter with an image related to the birth other (the man with the suitcases, Card 9) provoked an intensely paranoid suspicion resulting in momentary breakdown: "Tell me, how did you get all these pictures? Why is there a camera sign here?" The paranoid tone of her response brought to mind two possibilities: first, that Ada believed that I was showing her a picture of her actual sperm donor,[7] or, second, that she believed I had infiltrated her private thoughts and made a copy of her secret image of a father figure, shared with no-one, perhaps not even herself. Whichever the case, her extreme alarm indicated that the stimulus reflected an intensely emotionally charged object in her phantasy.

The various illustrations presented throughout this chapter indicate that children whose birth was assisted by gamete donation construct two narratives: the first relates to their recognition of their parents' exclusive couplehood, and the second relates to the riddle of their arrival in the world (see also Corbett, 2009). These two narratives are worked through within two distinct phantasmatic systems co-habiting their psychic lives: the Oedipus complex and the family romance complex, correspondingly. The family romance narrates the child's relationship with his or her birth other, whose phantasmatic representations may oscillate between an idealized parental figure, evoking the child's innermost longings, to terrifying representations, which might be the product of guilt over these longings, perceived as betrayal in his or her beloved parents, and felt as endangering them. Another source for these terrifying representations might be the child's sadistic view of coitus, with its discomforting affect, whether the parent is perceived as a victim or as an aggressor.

For children whose birth was assisted by gamete donation, these two phantasmatic systems, reflecting the two aspects of the primal scene, never achieve full integration, because they derive from two irreconcilable logics of kinship. I now turn to examine how the inherent contradiction between these two systems of logic is manifested in the psychic life of the parents.

References

Bion, W. R. (1962). *Learning from experience*. Karnac Books.
Bion, W. R. (1967). *Second thoughts: Selected papers on psychoanalysis*. Routledge.

---

7 As will be recalled, the figures presented in the book are for the purpose of illustration only; in the research setting, she was shown a photograph of a male figure carrying suitcases, which would have created a more realistic impression.

Bollas, C. (1987). *The shadow of the object: Psychoanalysis of the unthought known*. Columbia University Press.

Bos, H. M. W., & Gartrell, N. K. (2010). Adolescents of the US national longitudinal lesbian family study: The impact of having a known or an unknown donor on the stability of psychological adjustment. *Human Reproduction*, *26*(3), 630–637.

Britton, R. (1998). *Belief and imagination: Explorations in psychoanalysis*. Routledge.

Carsten, J. (2004). *After kinship*. Cambridge University Press.

Chukovsky, K. (2015). *Barmaley* [Hebrew]. Am-Oved.

Clark, K., & Clark, M. (1947). Racial identification and preference in Negro children. In E. E. Maccoby, T. M. Newcomb, & E. L. Hartley (Eds.), *Readings in social psychology* (pp. 169–178). Holt.

Collodi, C. (1995). *Pinocchio*. Wordsworth Editions.

Corbett, K. (2009). Nontraditional family reverie: Masculinity unfolds. In *Boyhoods: Rethinking masculinities*. Yale University Press.

Edwards, J. (2000). *Born and bred: Idioms of kinship and new reproductive technologies in England*. Oxford University Press.

Ehrensaft, D. (2000). Alternatives to the stork: Fatherhood Fantasies in donor insemination families. *Studies in Gender and Sexuality*, *1*(4), 371–397.

Ehrensaft, D. (2007). The stork didn't bring me, I came from a dish: Psychological experiences of children conceived through assisted reproductive technology. *Journal of Infant, Child, and Adolescent Psychotherapy*, *6*(2), 124–140.

Ehrensaft, D. (2008). When baby makes three or four or more. *The Psychoanalytic Study of the Child*, *63*(1), 3–23.

Eitan-Persico, Y. (2020). *Oedipus in same-sex families* [PhD dissertation, Ben-Gurion University].

Fardell, J. (2012). *The day Louis got eaten* (American ed.). Andersen Press.

Freud, S. (1900). The interpretation of dreams. In *The standard edition of the complete psychological works of Sigmund Freud 4* (pp. ix–627). Hogarth Press.

Freud, S. (1905a). Fragment of an analysis of a case of hysteria (1905 [1901]). In *The standard edition of the complete psychological works of Sigmund Freud 7* (pp. 1–122). Hogarth Press.

Freud, S. (1905b). Three essays on the theory of sexuality. In *The standard edition of the complete psychological works of Sigmund Freud 7* (pp. 123–246). Hogarth Press.

Freud, S. (1908). On the sexual theories of children. In *The standard edition of the complete psychological works of Sigmund Freud 9* (pp. 205–226). Hogarth Press.

Freud, S. (1909). Family romances. In *The standard edition of the complete psychological works of Sigmund Freud 9* (pp. 235–242). Hogarth Press.

Hunt, M. (Trans.). (1944). *The complete Grimm's fairy tales*. Pantheon Books.

Khan, M. R. (1963). The concept of cumulative trauma. *Psychoanalytic Study of the Child*, *18*, 286–306.

Klein, M. (1926). The psychological principles of early analysis. In *Love, guilt and reparation and other works 1921–1945 (The Writings of Melanie Klein, Volume 1)*. Hogarth Press.

Klein, M. (1930). The importance of symbol-formation in the development of the ego. In *Love, guilt and reparation and other works 1921–1945 (The Writings of Melanie Klein, Volume 1)*. Hogarth Press.

Klein, M. (1931). A contribution to the theory of intellectual inhibition. In *Love, guilt and reparation and other works 1921–1945 (The Writings of Melanie Klein, Volume 1)*. Hogarth Press.

Klein, M. (1937). Love, guilt and reparation. In *Love, guilt and reparation and other works 1921–1945 (The Writings of Melanie Klein, Volume 1)*. Hogarth Press.

Klein, M. (1946). Notes on some schizoid mechanisms. In *Envy and gratitude and other works 1946–1963 (The Writings of Melanie Klein, Volume 3)*. Hogarth Press.

Kohut, H. (1984). *How does analysis cure?* University of Chicago Press.

Laplanche, J. (1987). *New foundations for psychoanalysis*. Blackwell.

Laplanche, J., & Pontalis, J. B. (1973). *The language of psycho-analysis* (D. Nicholson-Smith, Trans.). W. W. Norton.

Laur, L. (2011). On performative mothering [Hebrew]. *Hamishpat*, *27*, 411–440.

Mason, J., & Finch, J. (1993). *Negotiating family responsibilities*. Routledge.

Meltzer, D. (1992). *The claustrum: An investigation of claustrophobic phenomena*. Karnac.

Ofer, M. (2014, July). "Rumours of the father's death have been greatly exaggerated": Some thoughts on the Oedipal conflict in children conceived through sperm donation [Hebrew]. *A paper presented in the Israel psychoanalytic society conference*.

Ofer, M. (2020). Multifocal – New family structures in the light of psychoanalytic theory. *Jahrbuch der Psychoanalyse*, *81*(Autumn).

Ogden, T. H. (1989). *The primitive edge of experience*. Jason Aronson.

Ogden, T. H. (2005). *This art of psychoanalysis: Dreaming undreamt dreams and interrupted cries*. Routledge/Taylor & Francis Group.

Piaget, J., & Inhelder, B. (1972). *The psychology of the child*. Basic Books.

Prokofiev, S., & Dale, J. (2011). *Peter and the wolf*. Unabridged. Brilliance Audio.

Salman-Sagi, O. (2019, July). *"Daddy is not mommy": Israeli gay fathers cope with a society which sanctifies motherhood* [PhD dissertation, Tel-Aviv University].

Segal, H. (2001). Symbolization. In C. Bronstein (Ed.), *Kleinian theory: A contemporary perspective* (pp. 157–164). Whurr.

Shabtai, A. (2000). *Greek mythology* [Hebrew]. Mapa.

Urban, W. H. (1963). *The draw-a-person catalogue for interpretive analysis*. Western Psychological Services.

Vanfraussen, K., Ponjaert-Kristoffersen, I., & Brewaeys, A. (2001). An attempt to reconstruct children's donor concept: A comparison between children's and lesbian parents' attitudes towards donor anonymity. *Human Reproduction*, *16*(9), 2019–2025.

Warner, L. L. (1993). Family romance fantasy resolution in George Eliot's Daniel Deronda. *The Psychoanalytic Study of the Child, 48*(1), 379–397.

Winnicott, D. W. (1964). *The child, the family, and the outside world*. Penguin.

Winnicott, D. W. (1971). Transitional objects and transitional phenomena. In *Playing and reality* (pp. 1–25). Tavistock Publications; Basic Books.

Chapter nine

Gamete donation in light of the primal scene

The parental challenge of integrating the donor's imago

The cultural assumption linking reproduction and parental coitus is so deeply rooted, that a release from its psychic hold seems doubtful. How, then, do same-sex parents reconcile the discrepancies between this internalized "truth" and their actual experience? Is gamete donation unconsciously understood in terms of the primal scene, that is as a sexual union between the two participants in the fertilization process, from which the social parent is excluded?

Among heterosexual individuals or couples who have been assisted by gamete donation, the event of conception is interpreted in phantasy as an act of coitus. This was demonstrated, for example, in a pioneering study by Judith Modell (1989), which revealed that heterosexual women found adoption to be a more acceptable alternative to sperm donation because they associated sperm donation with adultery and the introduction of a third wheel into their couple relationship.

Based on her clinical experience, Ehrensaft[1] (2008) provided several additional illustrations that support this view: a heterosexual single mother who dreamed during her pregnancy that she was sleeping with the sperm donor; a woman who received an egg donation from an old friend and felt as though she had been sentenced to witness her husband's infidelity with her friend, and even to carry the adulterous fruit in her womb; a nine-year-old who, upon hearing an account of how a couple they were friendly with had a child with the assistance of a surrogate, summed up the explanation by saying: "Aha, so he cheated on his wife!"

---

1 This chapter is based on the pioneering work of Ehrensaft, presenting additional evidence supporting her observations and developing her ideas.

DOI: 10.4324/9781032663333-13

Do same-sex couples attach the same meanings to conception in phantasy? Do they also experience the birth other as an intruder in the parental bedroom who threatens the position of the social parent and confronts both parents with feelings of inferiority and lack associated with the fact that their sexual union is not a procreative one?

Based on a landmark ethnographic study that examined kinship concepts in the first gayby boom era, Kath Weston (1991) argued that, unlike the meanings that heterosexual women attach to sperm donation, most of the lesbians who participated in her study established a non-sexual relationship with the donor. The sperm was not perceived by these women as a substitute for something that they expected to receive from their sexual partners. Instead, lesbians viewed donor insemination as a reproductive technique that obviates the need for heterosexual intercourse or enduring heterosexual relations. Weston showed that in cases where there was no intention of granting the donor an active role in the child's life, many of the mothers treated the donation as if it were no more than semen, a bodily fluid. Such an attitude construes the two participants in fertilization not as two gendered subjects, but as a gendered subject and a gender signifier. In the case of anonymous donation, Weston added, the child was sometimes perceived as the bodily offspring of just one parent, i.e., the biological mother.[2] Following Weston, Corinne Hayden (1995) argued that the construal of semen as an object whose importance is unrelated to the donor's identity allows the lesbian social mother to fulfill a parental role without feeling the need to struggle over this place with a male parent figure.

As a scholar who studies ways of resisting heteronormativity, Weston saw great value in the potential meaning attributed to donor insemination as the product of a connection between a gendered person and a gendered signifier, rather than between two gendered subjects. However, from a psychoanalytic

---

2 Weston's study was carried out during the first gayby boom in the United States. During this era, the most common practice was for lesbian couples to make a private arrangement with a gay man who wanted to serve as the sperm donor, outside of any medical context (whether this involved taking on a parenting role, acting as a "godfather," or having no role at all in the child's life). It is interesting to note that even at this stage some couples preferred not to know the identity of the donor, leading to the development of two different practices: one in which several donors were used in order to obscure the original genetic origin, and the second was the use of a "bumblebee" – an informal go-between who transferred the donation while maintaining the donor's anonymity.

perspective, this line of reasoning can be viewed as a defensive retreat from representing the sperm donor as a whole object to diminishing him to a part object. Similarly, when viewed through a psychoanalytic lens, perceiving the offspring as the product of one biological parent only – which Weston regarded as an achievement – can be interpreted as a defensive parthenogenic (self-fertilization) phantasy. The explanation offered by Hayden, whereby the dissociation of the genetic material from the identity of the person who provided it makes it easier for the social mother to fulfill a parental role without feeling the need to vie over this role with a male parent figure, in fact, points to the very threat that lies at the root of these defensive strategies, that is, the threat provoked by the primal scene phantasy. To place these psychoanalytical arguments on firmer ground, it must be established that, at the unconscious level, same-sex couples also attribute coital meanings to fertilization. Using examples from dreams, free associations, parapraxes, and humor – which Freud recognized as conduits for the expression of unconscious contents – I will attempt to show the way in which the flickering of heteronormative logic, which associates procreation with coitus, appear in the thoughts of same-sex parents and occupy their phantasies, despite being at odds with their conscious assumptions and espoused ideology.

Dreams

Rona, Esty's partner, reported a recurring dream she had after becoming pregnant via donor insemination:

> I recall that, after I got pregnant, after the implantation, I dreamed that I was having sex with, uh . . . I never ever slept with a man and I have no affinity to men, I don't even know what their organs are like. In the community we're known as 'Gold star lesbians.' And I never even phantasized or dreamed at night that I was sleeping with men, but suddenly after the implantation, I had a dream, and it repeated itself a few times, that I was sleeping with a man. I also remember that there was no sense of it being either enjoyable or unenjoyable – it was simply there, and I woke up. It's as though my body was kind of explaining to itself how the sperm got there, my brain was kind of trying to make sense of it all.

On the one hand, Rona's dream attests to the fact that even a lesbian woman who denies any sort of attraction to men may interpret her insemination unconsciously as equivalent to sex with a man, yet on the other hand her description of a physical union with a man did not include the full spectrum of libidinal affect that one would expect to find if a heterosexual woman were having a similar dream. Also interesting is Rona's shift in vocabulary from a term associated with heterosexual relations ("I got pregnant") to one drawn from the medical discourse of reproductive technology ("implantation"). This shift reflects both the defensive need to retreat from any speech with a sexual connotation, to the buffer zone that medical neutrality provides, while also reflecting the inevitable collision between the two logics defining kinship.

Associations

Nora, a femme lesbian, who decided not to carry a pregnancy, explained her choice as follows: "I never wanted to become pregnant. Even as a child, I didn't want to be pregnant or marry a man for that matter, those weren't my phantasies." Regardless of Nora's reservations about becoming pregnant, which might be overdetermined, I wish to point out, in the context of my argument, how the pregnancy phantasy in her mind is inseparable from the phantasy about heterosexuality and marriage to a man. Freud (1908) argued that within infantile phantasy, the notion of a wedding already includes and is wrapped up with the notion of coitus. It appears, therefore, that from Nora's point of view, conception, pregnancy, and giving birth – even if resulting from the anonymous donation of a sperm donor – are invested in phantasy with the meaning of coitus.[3]

Parapraxis

When I asked Maya and Rotem what method they would choose for having a child if any imaginable technological innovation were available and feasible, Rotem described a phantasy about her and Maya having a shared biological child, at which point she inadvertently remarked to Maya that what she would like more than anything would be to use "your sperm and my egg." Both of them immediately recognized the absurd nature of this

---

3 Evidence of the association between marriage and coitus can also be found in four-year-old Ori's answer to my question about things that her mothers like to do alone – just the two of them. To this Ori replied: "They like to get married."

statement and burst into laughter. Here we encounter the flip side of the same logic described earlier: whereas conception by donor sperm had implied sexual union in the phantasies of some women, in Rotem's phantasy, the sexual and romantic union with her partner would lead to the conception of a shared biological child. But even within this phantasy, the latent heteronormative logic or "facts of life" dictate that a child is always the product of the union of a sperm and an egg, and if she has an egg – Maya will provide the sperm.

Humor

Giving free rein to forms of thought that are pervasive in the unconscious, which are inevitably judged by consciousness as "thought errors," is the technique informing a great many jokes – thus argued Freud (Freud, 1905a) in his essay "Jokes and their relation to the unconscious." Freud dwelled on the self-irony and subversiveness typical of Jewish joking culture, as the outcome of external and internal oppression to which it was subject (Benyamini, 2008). Equipped with this insight, I was able to recognize in some of the parents' statements expressions of a subversive self-irony intended to dissipate tension arising from their membership in a minority group subject to constant societal oppression. This pressure is applied from without, by the social environment, and from within, due to the internalization of societal logic.

The unconscious anticipation of same-sex coitus to have procreative potential was humorously expressed by several couples. For example, Tommy's partner Amir, stated ironically – drawing on the terminology of heterosexual infertility – that "Tommy simply didn't implant. We tried everything."

Arthur Koestler (1964) argued that a comic effect is produced by the abrupt collision between two sets of rules that are mutually exclusive. The collision obliges the audience to perceive a situation simultaneously through two frames of reference, each of which is internally consistent, but which when put together are irreconcilable. A Koestlerian reading of Amir's humorous remark would then emphasize the inevitable collision between two different frames of reference in regard to kinship – the traditional frame that places heterosexual coitus at the center as that which both generates and defines kinship, and the alternative frame that is founded on choice and emotional commitment as the basis for creating kinship. Such a reading

The somatic channel

Talya and Dahlia's longing for a joint genetic child led them to entertain the possibility that their brothers act as the sperm donors, in other words, that each of them would be inseminated with the sperm of her brother-in-law. "It would be really cool if we could mix our genes," Talya said.

> We even toyed with the idea, totally theoretically, just as a thought – we both have big brothers. But that's intolerable. Even as we toyed with the idea, while we were amusing ourselves with the thought, we smacked ourselves on the mouth. Like, it's yuck . . . yuck, ugh.

The immediate sensation of disgust that the possibility of using their brothers' semen aroused is probably rooted in the power of the incest taboo and in the transgression involved in generating a double kinship bond (an uncle who is also the father).[4] Implicit in this threat of incest is the ascription of the meaning of coitus to the act of insemination. When Talya described thinking about this possibility, her speech was replete with diminutive expressions, such as "toyed with," "totally theoretical," "just as a thought" – as if to ensure that they were not even for a brief moment close to realizing it.

The illustrations provided indicate that even same-sex parents make an unconscious association in phantasy between fertilization and coitus. But is this sufficient proof of a wish or of the existence of a sense of inferiority around the fact that same-sex sexuality is not procreative?

The idea that the shared offspring of a same-sex couple is not a product of the couple's coital relations, and that they are not genetically related to both parents, repeatedly collides with the fundamental premise of kinship and leads to logical stumbling blocks not only in the parents' minds, but also in those of unbiased adults. Thus, Shir, Moran's partner, related the following:

---

4 Roland Barthes (1989) recognized this taboo in his discussion of the writings of the Marquis de Sade, where Barthes pointed out Sade's enjoyment of the semantic transgressions involved in incestuous scenarios – the fact that incest causes one person to belong to two kinship categories which are meant to be mutually exclusive.

"It's really funny. Because throughout the pregnancy Adam was in the 90th percentile. Now, I'm not tall. And like, when we would tell people about this, everyone would say, 'Yes, but Moran is really tall'."

Ron related a similar anecdote:

I was at a filling station with a male friend of mine, and this woman asks: "Hey you two, is this your girl?" So I answer: "Mine, why do you ask?", and then she says, "Because she looks like you but has his coloring." So I said, "You know, what you just said, like, doesn't make any sense," and then she started to laugh.

The laughter that makes a recurrent appearance in many of these illustrations bespeaks recognition of the logical fallacy that arises from the attempt to reconcile two different systems of logic. Ron's example of the fallacy involving a bystander's sudden recognition illustrates that such logical fallacies are not necessarily motivated by an unconscious wish but emerge ineluctably out of the inherent contradiction.

Chapter Eight illustrated the way in which cultural schemes are internalized by children and sometimes retrieved as is, without accommodation to their life realities and their actual experiences. At the same time, and based on the fact that it was precisely the children of lesbian mothers who failed or refused to identify the image of a pair of lionesses and a cub as an acceptable scenario, but tended to correct it to fit the heteronormative model, I have argued that there is another element to the representations in the psyches' of children which cannot be explained but as a wish for a family configuration that coincides with societal expectations. It appears that the same conclusion should be drawn in respect to the parents' inner representations. The inescapable collision between the two conceptions of kinship does not explain the picture in full. Another element exists that reflects an emotional conflict or wishful thinking. For example, in the interview with Talya and Dahlia, the couple expressed indignation at the fact that, compared to a heterosexual couple, it takes a longer time for lesbians to become pregnant.

Me: "But why do you think it takes lesbians longer than a straight couple?"

Talya: "It's not like you just screw and make kids."

Me: "Right, but it doesn't necessarily take longer."

Dahlia:	"You have one sample [of semen] per month. When you've got a man, you can take lots and lots of samples from him." [Laughs.]
Me:	"Yes, but you've got one egg per month."

Implicit in Talya and dahlia's logical fallacy is an experience of lack. In her imagination, a heterosexual woman enjoys unlimited access to the required resource – semen – whereas they are in need of a donation and are allotted a bare minimum and, therefore, by necessity, will require a longer time to conceive. This assumption ignores the fact that a woman only ovulates once a month and that the insemination of donor sperm is optimally timed to increase chances of success. Dahlia's phrasing – "When you've got a man, you can take lots and lots of samples from him," her choice of vocabulary – "take" rather than "get," along with the accompanying childish laughter, appears to reflect a child-like greediness. An analogous wish common to many children is for their parent to be a shop-owner, granting them unlimited access to candy. It is not difficult to recognize here the early infantile primal scene – an experience of inferiority juxtaposed with the free access each parent has to their partner's sexuality, from which the child is denied. The heterosexual couple's procreative potential receives mythical dimensions in Talya and Dahlia's phantasy. The roots of this mythical representation are most likely to be found both in the cultural symbolic system and in the early childhood idealization of parental sexuality. Be this as it may, their words belie an unconscious experience of sexual inferiority compared to heterosexual sexuality which includes the promise of a child. Another version of this came up earlier in Amir's joke: "Tommy simply didn't implant. We tried everything."

Parents' representations of the birth other

As was illustrated in the previous chapter, children born with the assistance of gamete donation may hold intense phantasies about the birth other. These oscillate between poles: on the one hand, the birth other may be accorded the status of an idealized object, serving as a kind of alter ego and arousing merging wishes, or offering a more desired alternative to the child's relations with their parents. On the other hand, the figure of the birth other may be painted in the tones of a persecutory and threatening object, who endangers the safety of the parents, the offspring, or the relations between parents and offspring. To complete the picture, the status of the birth other in the parents' psyche should be examined. Do they also harbor similar phantasies to those of the children?

Phantasies with positive affect

a **Genetic alter ego**: Many couples described their choice of a gamete donor as an opportunity to correct a trait that they associate with an experience of inferiority. Thus, a person who was overweight as a child emphasized his choice of the egg donor's slim figure, and someone who suffered because of their short stature, deliberately chose a tall egg donor. Iggy and Ossi, a pair of mothers visibly of Middle Eastern ethnic origin, chose a donor of German descent. "The truth is we really wanted a German," Ossi said, laughing. "What determined our choice?" she wondered out loud, and answered: "Green eyes." And Iggy added: "The look that I like. Fair of course."[5]

It is interesting to trace the way in which the emotional import associated with the parental phantasy pervades the relationships with the children, and ultimately their identity. Iggy describes how her bonding with her daughter Ella, who inherited the sperm donor's bright eyes resembled love at first sight, whereas her bonding with Nadav, who inherited Ossi's dark pigmentation took more time: "With Ella, it was all at once. It was love at first sight. We made eye contact and those stunning eyes, I already knew she had beautiful different eyes that were unfamiliar. Meeting her gaze, what I felt was 'I belong to you; you are my world'." During the interview, when five-and-a-half-year-old Ella was asked to distinguish between a male and female, she said in two different contexts: "He looks like a boy. I can tell by his eyes!" This is just a minor example of the "unthought known" (Bollas, 1987). Something about her eyes distinguishes her from her brother, from her mother's perspective, but the complex meanings associated with her eyes are beyond her grasp: neither the part of the sperm donor, and the phantasies attached to his figure, nor the

---

5 The mothers' comments about their preference for a fair complexion should be understood within the context of Israeli society, in which socially constructed ethnic hierarchies between Jews of European and Middle Eastern descent have long been entrenched. While their admission of this preference would seem to betray their own internalized racism, their joking attitude comes across as an ironic, self-reflexive, and perhaps also self-forgiving acknowledgment of it.

mother's experience as a women of Middle Eastern (Mizrahi) ethnic identity in Israel.

This example illustrates that the birth other may serve for the parent as a kind of alter ego, who has the power, according to the parent's view, to endow their children with better genes than the parent's own. Phantasies of this kind correspond with the phantasies of merging with the idealized parent, which were observed in some of the children. This aspect no doubt exists in the choice of a partner, but the choice of a gamete donor, especially when sourced from a private donor bank, allows a greater degree of control, or at least the illusion of control, of the genetic traits of the partner in procreation. If one takes into account the parent's primal scene phantasy, we can assume that, by creating a child together with an idealized partner, the parent unconsciously believes that he or she themselves is taking part in the original primal scene. In other words, through enactment based on projective identification, the parent takes the place of one of their own parents in the primal scene and thus experiences themselves as part of the idealized original couple (Britton, 1998).

b **Falling in love with the gamete donor**: Much like the classic Israeli song by Haim Hefer, in which soldiers fall in love with the figure of Dina Barzilay as she is conjured in their imaginations by the personal stats in her military personnel file, some parents reported a sense of falling in love with the birth other, despite the paucity of information about them (Cf. Corbett, 2009). Zohar, Gaya and Michael's father, for example, reported the following: "There's something about it that is a bit like falling in love. You kind of project all sorts of stuff on the donor. I had only photos. I looked at her photos and felt like, you say, wow, she's so cute, and she looks like such a nice woman, I might even say – maternal, somehow. Yeah, it's totally like concocting a story, some kind of phantasy."

Vicky and Nora chose to use the sperm of the same donor to create all three of their children. This choice harboured a phantasy referring not only to the donor's personal qualities and charm, as reflected in the taped interview attached to his file, but also the perceived degree of fit between him and Vicky; the speed with which Vicky conceived furnished proof of this, they felt:

There's a fit here that goes beyond whether I knew him or not. There's a good physiological fit, and I really believe in this, that if it really works so well from the get-go, then that means it's a good thing, it will last, and it's healthy.

These examples illustrate some of the parents' need to create a phantasmatic figure they can connect to, and sometimes even fall in love with, in order to augment the value of their partnership in the child's creation, and perhaps as a way of overcoming a feeling of alienation and uncertainty.

Sometimes, when one of the partners was preoccupied with phantasies about the donor, the other partner tended to immerse themselves in the concrete realities of the donor process or would adopt a more critical view, rather than developing an emotional attachment to the donor as a person. Theoretical approaches to couples therapy use the term collusion to describe this type of pattern – a process of mutual projective identification, in which each member of the couple splits off part of their unconscious representations and projects it onto their partner, thereby creating a shared unconscious system which helps each of the partners, and the couple as a unit, maintain equilibrium (Bagarozzi, 2011).

From the point of view of many parents, the birth other functions in service of a narcissistic phantasy: their role is to offer superior genes and to assist in the creation of a child, the raising of which will provide reparation to the feelings of inferiority burdening the parent. But what happens when the birth other fails at this designated role?

Phantasies with negative affect

a **Potential disappointment with the chosen gamete donor**: After a series of failed insemination attempts, Zohar and Erez decided to acquiesce to the suggestion of the owner of the surrogacy agency and choose an egg donor whose fertility had been established by the success of earlier donations. This choice did ultimately lead to the birth of twins, but Erez remained disappointed about their failure to realize the potential of their first choice of a physically beautiful egg donor: "The one whose eggs we ended up using is not pretty, in my view. And for me it was . . . I remember seeing her picture and saying: 'She's not pretty.' I'm disturbed, I'm bummed out that we ended up going with, like, we chose someone whose looks I'm not happy about."
Just as Iggy's phantasies about the German sperm donor are evident in the doting way that she gazes at her bright-eyed daughter, one can imagine that something of Erez's disappointment in their choice of a plain-looking donor – certainly not a stunning "looker" like their first choice of donor – is

apparent in the way he gazes at his children. Every parent hopes that their partner's desirable traits will be reflected in their children and is fearful of seeing a reflection of the traits that they dislike and which they recognize in their partner or in their partner's relatives. However, the partial nature of the information about the birth other may intensify both the grandiose phantasies as well as the anxieties that are related to their genetic contribution to the child's creation. This is manifested in the story related by Maoz and Ofir:

Maoz: "She was simply shining. Something about her is radiant and sweet, optimistic, and life-loving. In her pictures too, she was wearing colorful clothing – something that I connected with being happy, a joie-de-vivre. We really liked it. But on the other hand, it actually sounded kind of simplistic. We actually faced a bit of a dilemma choosing between two potential donors. I remember that one sounded more sophisticated but more depressive [laughs] and we chose life!"

Ofir: "I know that she did give off a happy vibe [laughs]. What I remember, tell me if you felt the same, we were always wondering to what extent that happiness was bordering on stupidity."

Maoz: "I told her so"

Ofir: [laughs)] "Really? Okay, I didn't hear that. So, yes, it was in the background. Somebody that cheerful and all [laugh] in our world that isn't so blessed after all."

Maoz: "But that was back then. In retrospect, we saw that she was sweet."

Ofir: "Yes, she seems sweet. We don't know, we've never spoken with her. I hope she's not a dimwit."

Maoz: "She doesn't seem at all like a dimwit to me, she seems like a great young lady."

The dialogue between Maoz and Ofir clearly illustrates how hard it is to establish a whole object based on partial information about a stranger. One may speculate that an in-depth acquaintance with both candidates could have helped the couple perceive them as complex personalities, as whole objects one can identify with, rather than splitting them into a representation of the death instinct ("the depressive") and of the life instinct ("optimistic, life-loving, "we chose life!"). The partialness of the information and lack of personal contact contribute to the construction of a split object, which invites vacillation between grandiose representations ("she's simply shining") to devaluations ("I hope she's not a dimwit"). One may assume that the gaze the fathers train on their children will exhibit similar vacillations and that, during minor and inevitable moments of disappointment from the children's accomplishments, this very same representation of the dimwitted donor will pop up uncontrollably, inducing a sense of panic and guilt about having chosen her. At the same time, one should consider that according to the research literature, the use of gamete donation from a known donor may considerably aggravate the anxieties about their invasion of the family's life and robbing of the child's love (Ehrensaft, 2008).

Ehrensaft (2000, 2007) has claimed that the politics of family life has not yet produced a construction or conceptualization of the birth other as a whole object. This claim remains valid at the time of the writing of this current treatment. However, when it comes to an anonymous donation mediated by the medical and legal establishment, lacking an in-person encounter with the donor, and sometimes with the knowledge of only a smattering of dry information about them, one is obliged to wonder: is there any genuine possibility of representing the birth other except as a partial or phantasmatic object, based to a significant degree on projective elements? As long as the construction of a whole object means integration of the partial details known about the birth other, the positive and negative phantasies and the ambivalent feelings evoked by their representations, as well as acceptance of their partiality and alienation – one cannot underestimate the importance of this psychological process for both the parents and the children.

b **The birth other as potential kidnapper:** Unconscious anxieties that the birth other who facilitated the child's conception might desire the child for themselves intermingle with realistic fears that stem from the structural discrimination, which privileges biological parenthood. For instance, Maoz explained their choice of a closed donation, which obviates the possibility that their children ever find out the identity of the egg donor, as follows: "It was clear we would choose a closed donation. We also didn't want to find ourselves all of a sudden messed up in some kind of a legal situation. But in retrospect, I saw that she got married, and she has a baby, and I was really glad about that. Like, you know, she's doing her thing, we're doing ours. Because when she did it, she was single."

The phantasmatic element folded into Maoz's realistic deliberations relates to the assumption that, if the egg donor did not have children of her own, she might become envious and covetous of the children whose existence would not have been possible without her help. The relief that Maoz felt upon discovering that the donor had married and had children of her own could be tied to an unconscious sense of guilt or a sense of debt that cannot be repaid. This sense is greatly exacerbated by the thought that he is enjoying her children, while she remains childless – a guilt possibly rooted in the debt to the mother, womb envy, and the infantile phantasy of robbing the mother of her inner assets and her potential offspring (Klein, 1945).[6] This unconscious guilt translates in phantasy to the moment in which the donor appears and claims her parental rights. Paradoxically, many sperm donors describe the moment in which they have a child of their own as the moment in which they first understand the meaning of the donation they made at a younger age: a moment in which they began to think about the child produced by their sperm and wonder whether they resemble each other and whether the child is concerned with their existence. In some cases, the donor's moment of transition to parenthood is described precisely as the time in which the desire to get in touch with their offspring is first kindled (Hertz et al., 2015).

Another representation of the birth other came up in a nightmare that upset the slumbers of Niv, Dori's father, at a time when he and his partner Barak were busy planning a surrogacy procedure in order to have a second child. This dream, described in Chapter Two, was related by Niv as follows:

In my dream, we're traveling to Canada, and Dori isn't allowed to enter Canada because in the surrogacy procedure there's a mother registered on the birth certificate. She is eligible. She has to sign waivers. . . But somehow we decide that we are going with Dori, and then we get a baby girl, and we aren't allowed to leave the country with Dori, because the state claims that he is Indian and has to be returned to the mother. So Dori says to me, "It's okay, Dad, I can go back to being Indian" . . . in short, at some point I woke up in a cold sweat.

---

6 Among lesbian mothers, one may observe the appearance of a parallel guilt, rooted in penis envy (Freud, 1905b) or in the phantasmatic possession of the penis (Riviere, 1929).

The terrifying scenario played out in Niv's nightmare was that as they plan for the arrival of their second child, they will be deprived of their parental rights over Dori. The surrogate was presented in the dream as Dori's legal mother, and moreover, Dori himself was identified as Indian in the dream, i.e., as sharing the identity of the birth other who carried him in her womb. It is interesting to ponder the fact that the real-life context that evoked the nightmare – a second surrogacy procedure in order to have another child – did not engender anxiety about legalizing their parental status vis-à-vis the anticipated child, but rather about the risk of having their existing child taken away from them, the child that they have been lovingly raising for the past four years. This anxiety may indicate a sense of guilt, or fear of greediness – as if to say, "A bird in the hand is better than two in the bush." The desire for "more" of this bounty, which again involves dependence on the goodwill of female figures, arouses fear of punishment – the loss of the existing good. Whatever the case, it is clear that the anxiety about losing parental custody lingers in the parent's consciousness long after attachment has been established and the legal status has been sorted out.

Noel Oxenhandler (2001) has associated the universal phenomenon of parental anxiety about kidnapping, the basis of numerous myths, with the emotional complexity that a parent experiences in the wake of their fierce bonding with the child, for such bonding is accompanied by guilt over their inevitable parental failures, the necessity of coming to terms with the child's increasing separateness, and the simple fact of life that this separateness will only increase, culminating eventually in the child's departure. Within the frame of this phantasy, the feelings of guilt and anxiety which are part and parcel of the parenting experience, are projected onto a malicious other who will steal the child – or the child's love.

I propose viewing the parent's phantasy of the conniving kidnapper as a kind of complementary phantasy to the child's family romance. Just as a child who is developing their separateness relies on the parents' actual failures and the increasing recognition of their place in the social hierarchy as motives for attaching themselves in phantasy to other figures (Freud, 1909), thus the parent is anxious that their parental failures will distance their child, and that the child's phantasized or real attachment to other figures signifies the inevitable separation. Just as the family romance phantasies among donor children tend to focus on images of the birth other as a wonderful and generous person who will show up one day to reunite with the child, thus the tendency emerges to cast the birth other in the role of the conniving kidnapper, in the parents' universal kidnapping phantasy (Ehrensaft, 2008). The fact that the birth other shares genetic material with the child, and is therefore culturally identified as a parent figure, and, moreover, the fact that the child may be immersed in a family romance phantasy predicated on the wish to unite with the birth other only add fuel to the fire (ibid.). The phantasy of the conniving kidnapper manifested among a dozen of the children I met. As I proposed earlier, this representation may express guilt borne by a child about their curiosity and desire to unite with the birth other, as well as anxiety that the realization of these wishes might entail hurting their parents or losing them. In addition, this representation may reflect the parent's anxieties that permeate the child's unconscious.

The interpretation of Niv's dream suggests a fear that while expecting his second child, he will lose custody of his eldest. This anxiety is related to universal anxieties that many parents experience in the period preceding the addition of another child to the family: how can I love two children at one and the same time? Will my bonding with the new child cause me to let slip or lose my bond with the existing child? If I am happy at the moment, is it greedy to want more? But when a child is created through sperm donation, or egg donation and surrogacy, these universal fears tend to be projected on the figures of the birth others.

Even if the representation of the birth other as a potential kidnapper reflects nothing more than a discriminatory and threatening social reality, this does not diminish the emotional difficulty that one faces when attempting to constitute a whole object by combining this threatening person, who may be favored by the law, with the generous person who enabled the birth of their child in the first place. The task of psychic integration placed on the parent is far from simple and requires acknowledging that a broad spectrum of feelings – including gratitude, admiration, romantic thrill, sexual threat, envy, hostility, and anxiety – are all associated with a single object, and if this were not enough, with an unknown object, whose very alienness provokes anxiety. This emotional challenge results in the enlistment of various defensive strategies.

Defensive strategies in relation to the birth other

Objectification or reduction of the birth other to genetic material

Ehrensaft (2007) described a defensive strategy that she called "Honey, I shrunk the donor": the reduction of the birth other to mere genetic material, or to a gender signifier, as described by Weston (1991). This reduction, Ehrensaft says, is rooted in the need to protect oneself from the imago of the conniving kidnapper or from the invasion of a third person into the couple's primal scene. Thus, for example, when Yael told me that she and Miri had decided to maintain genetic continuity between their shared children and Miri's children from her previous marriage to another woman, she avoided talking about the sperm donor, and instead talked only about the sperm samples, which she called "squirts."

Ofir and Maoz, too, who emphasized the importance of the genetic affiliation between their children, avoided mentioning the donor who had made this possible. Ofir phrased it as follows: "We wanted the kids to know that they're, like, also biological siblings. Like, from the same..." Ofir paused a moment, hesitating to complete the sentence, and then added, "egg."

Children who are not twins but who were born a few years apart obviously were not created from the same egg. The need to diminish the role of the birth other steered Ofir toward a fallacy, stemming apparently from his attempt to deflect her representation as a mother – a representation fleetingly suggested by the logic of the heteronormative approach to kinship, which he employed to define the sibling relationship between his children. It seems that the panic evoked by this potential representation led him not only to avoid identifying her as a mother but to go so far as denying her personhood as a donor ("egg").

Another reduction strategy, made conspicuous in Moran's account, is the cynical devaluation of the donor, while emphasizing her proprietary rights to his sperm in an objectifying manner:

It's clear that for all intents and purposes the person who masturbated into the cup has no connection to our life, or to my children. But that's important. We bought potential character traits from him. We bought healthy genetic potential from him. We bought a ton of stuff from him, and that's why it's important to me to know what he looks like.

Phantasies of self-conception or cloning – erasure of the birth other

Among a third of the couples interviewed, the creation of the child was described in terms of "cloning," or "genetic copying," denying the involvement of the birth other in their creation. "It's pretty funny because the whole nature vs. nurture thing really sticks out," said Talya.

Lior resembles Dahlia's family so much – personality-wise and also in his facial features, it's hilarious. Dahlia, her father, and Lior look like a coordinated set. But Lior, since he's already a big kid . . . you can see how much the environment has influenced him . . . it's like he's beginning to lean a bit toward the side of my family.

Talya's description suggests that Lior's entire genetic makeup derives from Dahlia and her family, while everything that falls outside the lines was identified as environmental influences from Talya and her family. This erasure of the donor and his part in the creation of the children was also exhibited in their attitude toward Yoav, Talya's biological son:

Dahlia: "I think that Yoav is simply your mother's egg with your mother's sperm."
Talya: "Yup. He's really a lot like my mom. As if they cloned my mom, in miniature."

If at one end of the scale the emotional ambivalence about the birth others encourage defensive strategies such as reducing him or her to a partial object, objectification, devaluation, or denial of their contribution to the child's creation, at the other end the difficulty of tolerating the ambiguity around the donor's anonymity may engender voyeurism and attempts to gain control of the object by accumulating knowledge about them.

Voyeurism and data gathering

Following Bion's line of thought (1967), one may regard voyeurism or the attempt to obtain information about the birth other, without contacting them and getting to know them as a whole person, as a way to unburden oneself of the frustration born of ignorance. Releasing tension in this way may offer temporary relief but does not improve a person's ability to tolerate the recurring feelings of helplessness, anxiety, and doubt. Moaz and Ofir, for example, related the following:

Maoz: "It piqued our curiosity. We were snooping around a bit, searching for some information about her, and succeeded in obtaining some. It happened in retrospect, actually. Retroactively, we started to get all sorts of leads about her."
Me: "After making your choice you continued to try to learn more information about her?"

244 What does procreation have to do with parental coitus, anyway?

Maoz: "Yes, totally. I'm still curious about it."

Ofir: "And over the years we got more. Maoz figured out her Facebook profile."

In his article "On Arrogance," Bion (1967) proposes an innovative reading of the Oedipus myth. Bion replaces the sexual and murderous wishes that Freud emphasized with the curiosity and arrogance that motivate Oedipus' inquiry, in defiance of Tiresias' warnings. Bion reminds us that sexual curiosity is the first concrete expression of the self's curiosity toward the other, and later, toward the world and reality in general. Bion's Oedipus is a tragic figure because he strives to know the truth at all costs, even when it surpasses his emotional ability to contain it. I recognized Oedipal tendencies as described by Bion in Moran's attitude:

Moran: "The genetic issue is so unimportant to me that I don't even mind meeting other children from the same donation. Like, I'm actually curious to know what part of the genetic makeup they got. I tell our friends, 'Use the same donor we used, look how amazing it came out.' It's such a non-issue, that I don't even care."

Shir: "I'm not willing to have them use the same sample, and I also don't want to become part of a sibling group.[7] Moran really wants to. Moran is curious and I'm not."

Bion suggested viewing the dynamics among the characters in the myth as a representation of the inner dynamics among different psychic functions. In Moran one can identify the figure of Oedipus, striving to discover the truth at any cost, while in the dialogue between the couple, Shir represents Tiresias, who, according to Bion fulfills the function of distortion and avoidance, whose role is to protect against anxiety. This division of roles between the two resurfaced in relation to every conflictual issue. For

---

7 Ehrensaft proposes a distinction between collapsing toward the pole of reducing the sperm donor to genetic material, which she claims is characteristic of mothers in lesbian relationships, and collapsing toward the opposite pole of creating a father figure where no one exists, which is more characteristic of single mothers. This idea is reinforced by the phenomenon of searching for siblings online, which is characteristic of single mothers, whatever their sexual orientation, much more than of lesbian couples.

example, when discussing the question of choosing the donor, the dialogue unfolded as follows:

Shir: "Moran said to me at first, 'Maybe we should take black sperm,'[8] I said, 'I'm not taking black sperm'."

Moran: "It was like I wanted something exotic. But in any case, today I would be less inclined to choose a black donor when I understand the meanings. It was easier for me to say that before I understood the meaning of family and children, and the baggage they carry. Today, I'm really glad that we chose a donor who looks like us."

It seems that Shir, who holds the more conservative or anxious position among the two women, was the one to place restraints and raise reservations whose contribution to maintaining her emotional wellbeing Moran could only recognize in retrospect. Just as she stated that her wish to choose a donor of African heritage did not take into account the emotional implications of such a choice, thus, had she acted on her desire to allow her friends to use the same donor, or to enter a sibling group, she would have risked, like Oedipus, the complications of an encounter with overwhelming truth, that she had no capacity to contain.

In some cases, the negative feelings about the birth other are imbued with a sense of threat, which could be described as uncanny ("*unheimlich*"). This

---

8 Bearing in mind that racial categories are socially and culturally constructed, what the category "black" might mean for Moran should be considered within the particular Israeli historical and cultural context, rather than through reference to the connotations of blackness in the US, for example. Up until the 2000s, when about 30,000 non-Jewish asylum seekers from Eritrea and Sudan resided in Tel-Aviv, the only black community in Israel was that of Jewish Ethiopian-Israelis, representing a mere 2% of the population. Because of the centrality of Judaism in Israel and the Zionist demographic effort, this community was regarded as a Jewish ethnic group and was not understood as culturally related to other black communities in the world. It was only in 2015 that protests emerging from the Ethiopian-Israeli community related their oppression to the wider context of the black problem, joining the Black Lives Matter movement. In the formative years of Moran's development, the only available representations of black people stemmed from American popular culture, and involved mainly famous athletes, musicians and so on. In the provincial Israeli eye, black people were associated with the cool African-American and represented the exotic, the un-local, without fully grasping the complexity of their identity and its prolonged history of slavery and oppression.

state of affairs involves a failure of repression and the resurfacing of unconscious material that arouses feelings of dread.

The birth other as uncanny

Das Unheimliche is a common term in the German language, lacking precise parallels in other languages. Linguistically constructed by prefixing the negative 'un' to the term "heimlich" (home-like), it signifies "the sense of strangeness that dwells within the intimate itself, the shudder of discomfort at an encounter with something 'home-like' that is at once mysterious and concealed" (trans. I.G.) (Benyamini, 2012, pp. 7–8).

The first to introduce a psychological thesis about the uncanny was Ernst Jentsch, who explained it as the product of intellectual uncertainty that surfaces especially during an encounter with hybrid forms that combine the living and the inanimate, the human and the animal, and the human and the technological (Benyamini, 2012). Jentsch emphasized the loss of orientation that characterizes the experience of the uncanny, which occurs when an object behaves in a way that diverges from the observer's expectations, which rely on that which is familiar. According to him, "It is an old experience that the traditional, the usual and the hereditary is dear and familiar to most people, and that they incorporate the new and the unusual with mistrust, unease and even hostility (misoneism). This can be explained to a great extent by the difficulty of . . . intellectual mastery of the new thing" (Jentsch, 2008, pp. 3–4).

Eighty years later, these same hybrid forms, which Jentsch identifies with the uncanny, became the focus of Donna Haraway's vision, presented in her influential essay "A Cyborg Manifesto" (1991). Haraway, who did not deny the threatening character of a motif that involves the transgression of boundaries, viewed it as a prime avenue of resistance to the systematic splitting that underlies the social hierarchy responsible for oppression and discrimination.

When combined, Haraway and Jentsch's ideas offer the hypothesis that reproductive technology has the potential to liberate human beings from the limitations of sexual reproduction, with all its entailments; however, this departure from secure and familiar ground, which can be viewed as a hybrid form that obscures the boundaries between the human and the technological, is inevitably accompanied by moments of dread arising from the loss of orientation vis-à-vis the traditional world.

But this alone is an inadequate explanation for the experience of the uncanny associated with the use of gamete donation that emerges from the parents' reports. Firstly, gamete donation does not just involve technological means, but also introduces an utter stranger into one's most intimate space – the nuclear family, and into the most intimate creation – that of an offspring. This situation, by definition, contains an element of the uncanny – the mixture of the home-like and the foreign. To these is added another layer, which Freud identified.

Following Jentsch's inquiry, Freud (1919) proposed the insight that the source of the uncanny feeling is the return of the repressed. In Freud's view, this is not a question of encountering something new or unfamiliar; rather, it is an encounter with something that was previously familiar and trusted, but which the process of repression had rendered strange and alien. Freud spoke not only of the repression of specific contents but also of the apparent surge of infantile animistic, and omnipotent ways of thinking that continue to reside in the psyche, lying in wait, as it were, for realistic stimuli to prove their validity.

When I asked Shir and Moran why they had preferred an agency that provided photos of the sperm donor, Shir replied:

I don't know, it quiets a certain anxiety, I guess. So that you don't feel as though you are buying a cat in the sack. So you can make an educated guess. I kept on saying to myself, it would be really amusing if they got the samples mixed up and suddenly some black kid would come out. Like, there's a kind of anxiety about that.

The phrase "to buy a cat in the sack," known also in Yiddish, German, and French, originated in the sphere of the marketplace in previous centuries, where swindlers might offer to sell customers a piglet in a sack, which then turned out to be merely a cat (Rosenthal, 2005). Shir's account suggests that her need to see a photo of the donor is related to anxiety about his being an utter stranger, and to the disorientation caused by his unknowability. However, her words also disclose that the fear of buying "a cat in the sack," in the original sense of the idiom, persevered even after seeing the donor's photo, and was expressed in the concern that she might end up with "some black kid."

The fear that donor sperm samples might get mixed up could be a contemporary version of the older fear of mixing up children at the hospital. The image of a black child is evoked as a way of concretizing a scenario in which a couple confronts immediately visible evidence that some part of their child's genetic makeup derives neither from them, nor from their chosen donor, and also because the cultural connotations associated with blackness endow the child with aspects of strangerhood, otherness, or even threat. However, there is another layer of meaning here. As will be recalled, in the process of choosing the donor, Moran had toyed with the idea of choosing a black donor, for the exotic appeal, whereas Shir had vetoed this possibility. Had Shir been presented with a black child, this would have served as evidence that Moran's wish had been magically fulfilled, in other words, it would have validated the infantile ways of thinking that Shir had ostensibly outgrown.

The motif of the "cat in the sack" was repeated in the accounts of three mothers. Vicky jokingly linked the metaphor of the "cat in a sack" with a sense of mystery and lack of knowledge about what goes on in the "pregnancy sac." In fact, every pregnancy and birth requires dealing with experiences related to lack of control, lack of knowledge, and the blend of strangeness and familiarity. These experiences persevere into the experience of raising the child, who will always be the parent's flesh and blood, a reflection of themselves, but also other and unknown. Jessica Benjamin beautifully described this duality, as manifested during the first days of motherhood:

> Perhaps never will she feel more strongly, than in those first days of her baby's life, the intense mixture of his being part of herself, utterly familiar and yet utterly new, unknown and other. It may be hard for a mother to accept this paradox, the fact that this baby has come from her and yet is so unknown to her.
>
> (Benjamin, 1988, p. 14)

As mentioned earlier, Ehrensaft hypothesized that the psychic representation of the birth other as a conniving kidnapper echoes universal anxieties about the kidnapping of a child. It may be, then, that the involvement of this foreign partner in conception exacerbates anxieties that arise inevitably in pregnancy and birth situations, or adds a unique uncanny tone to them.

Another uncanny theme that Freud (1919) recognized is the phenomenon of the "double."[9] According to Freud, the strong feeling of something uncanny associated with figures that are considered identical because

---

9 Numerous literary works place the figure of the double at their center. Cf. F.M. Dostoyevsky's *The Double*; Oscar Wilde's *The Picture of Dorian Gray*; R.L. Stevenson's *Dr. Jekyll and Mr. Hyde*, and also *The Double*, a contemporary text by Yoni Raz Portugali (2019) that explores the fiction that genetic affiliation creates kinship ties.

Gamete donation in light of the primal scene 249

they look alike stems from a regression to a time when the ego had not yet marked itself off sharply from the external world and from other people.

Iggy, for example, related that they had chosen to obtain a sperm donation overseas, because "in Israel, every donor produces at least ten children, if not more," adding that: "I simply saw photos of kids that looked the same, and they don't know each other, and I've seen the pictures. I said, no way. Even though biology isn't such an important factor, still."

Ossi: "Our main consideration was minimizing the chance of half-siblings. To be honest, it doesn't really mean that much. When you think about it, it has no meaning. The woman in the Israeli sperm bank told us that each sperm produces ten pregnancies. Come on, that's a ton. A ton. It's too much, too much. It's a ton! I don't know, it's like not the most comfortable feeling that I might suddenly recognize among our friends . . . it's a small community."

Iggy: "It's a matter of privacy. It's a kind of private thing, more discreet rather than public, in my opinion. I don't want to see a whole bunch of other Ellas or Nadavs [laughs] walking around. It's like I want them to be exclusive."

Iggy and Ossi's statement reveals wide gaps between the ideology that minimizes the importance of the genetic factor as the basis of kinship relations and the primitive and uncontrollable feelings of discomfort aroused by the possibility of encountering other children whose birth was assisted by the same sperm donor. A sense of uncanniness is reflected not just in their manner of speaking about children who are merely genetic half-siblings as if they were identical twins or doubles, but also in the shock they express about the large number of conceptions assisted by the same donor. This multiplicity represents the looming persecutory potential of encountering uninvited doubles everywhere and anywhere. Iggy even couches the issue in terms of a distinction between private or discreet space and public space – terms that refer us to the etymological meeting point between the Heimlich and the unheimliche (home-like and uncanny).

In the effort to establish an intimate family unit with clear boundaries, many parents attempt to neutralize the presence of the birth other in everyday family life, using various defensive strategies to accomplish this. Some parents report moments of a sneaking recognition that there is something unfamiliar about the child: some trait they cannot identify with themselves, their partner, or with the family heritage. It may be a bodily gesture or a personality tendency, which resonates with some detail or other known to them about the donor, or whose source is entirely unknown to them; it may induce a sense of discomfort and mystery in the parents. As opposed to these fleeting moments involving no more than a mild uncanny sensation, intense uncanniness entails a severe failure of repression mechanisms, leading to persecutory compulsive repetition, which in turn generates a sense that the threatening material is ubiquitous, and cannot be escaped. These characteristics, undoubtedly also tied to the parent's psychological makeup, appeared in their starkest form in Sandra's accounts. It is beyond the scope of this book to inquire into the issue of the parents' psychic structure. Suffice to mention here the powerful sense of identification that Sandra felt with Efrat's pregnancy, which I associated in Chapter Four with the couvade phenomenon. What these two phenomena – couvade and the uncanny – share in common is perhaps the flourishing of early infantile ways of thinking, which involve projective identification.

Sandra's description of her and Efrat's choice of a sperm bank that discloses very few details about the donor communicated a sense of fierce ambivalence, which manifested in frequent oscillations between an impulse to know and not to know, between attraction and aversion, between utter submission to medical authority and mistrust, "We went to a meeting, we didn't even look," Sandra said, adding:

> I don't know, I see my sister these days looking at lists and at traits. We didn't even concern ourselves with that. I think that we both understood from the get-go that this was nonsense, the choice of the sperm. We asked the doctor whether he knew the donors, not that we even trust him [laughs] but whether there was somebody he could tell was a good person. He said there was, and that was it. It doesn't mean that if *we* met that person, we would even . . . never mind, it doesn't matter, you've got to grasp onto something. We grasped onto something.

In Efrat's case, the couple's attempt to minimize their engagement with questions about the donor's identity, in order to assuage anxieties that the topic aroused, worked well, but in Sandra's case, it resulted in an enduring uncanny experience. Sandra related that after giving birth she had been engaged obsessively in attempts to identify her daughter's sperm donor among random men she saw on the street.

Sandra: "I had some kind of [imaginary] picture of him in my head, so I said, 'Aha, that must be him!' I would call Efrat: 'Efrat, listen . . .'" [Pretending to whisper furtively over the phone.]

Me: "Were these people that you seemed to like? Did you recognize something that you would like to see in your children or anything like that?"

Sandra: "No, no, no. The opposite, precisely the opposite."

When I asked Efrat whether she had experienced anything similar to Sandra, she explained:

Efrat: "No. My entire phantasy world is a bit oppressed, for better or for worse. I'm not preoccupied with this matter, and it doesn't plague my thoughts. There was this guy, in no way relevant to our lives – those kinds of statements bug Sandra, because they're logical."

Sandra: "Look, at first he wasn't relevant *at all*."

Efrat: I think's he very relevant, by the way. Not to me, I think he'll be very relevant for the kids."

Sandra: "He's relevant to you too. He enabled you to do what you did! Let's say that if I saw him, I would hug him and say, 'thank you.' Like, fine, it's not that he did it for some altruistic motive, he got like 400 shekels."

I could sense both partners' mixed feelings toward the donor, and especially Sandra's intense ambivalence, accompanied by emotional vacillations: shifting rapidly from wanting to hug and thank him to devaluing him and denying that his motivation for donating could have been altruistic; from utter negation of his relevance to their lives and insisting on his relevance as the one who enabled them to have children, and back again to being alarmed by the thought that other genetic descendants of his could be considered her children's half-siblings:

Sandra: "When Ruth was two weeks old, I went to sit with her at some café in Tel Aviv, and there's this bozo there who has a company for surrogacy, and there was this other guy and girl sitting next to me and we started to talk, and somehow we got around to the fact that I share my life with a woman and that we used a sperm donation. And then he suddenly said – and he's the owner of a company – I want to say something to him, I feel like calling him up. For real. And then he says to me, 'That girl who's sitting next to him? There, she used sperm donation too. So go ahead, talk about the donor, it might be the same guy.' I wasn't up to it, but she went with the flow. And I think it dawned on me that it was the same donor. Yup."

Me: "What are the odds that some guy is going to say, 'Talk about the donor,' and it'll end up being the same one?"

Sandra: "It was him. I think it was him. I'm telling you, it was also from Ichilov [hospital], I know it. In any case, I looked at the kid, and I was also very hormonal, I had just given birth . . . and I looked at that kid, and I simply felt at that moment some kind of thing for him, I don't know, it's bizarre, I don't know what it was. And that was the first time it really dawned on me that there are more offspring from our donation. I didn't really get it, or I hadn't given it any thought. And that was like, boom! The penny dropped at that moment."

Sandra found herself persecuted by the figure of the donor – as it came to be constructed in her imagination – and by his imagined offspring. According to Freud, the uncanny element of these stories stems from Sandra's unconscious belief in the magical power of thought: if she is curious about the donor, then he is likely to present himself to her in the flesh wherever she turns, and if by chance she happens to meet another child created from his sperm, then the archaic belief that her own curiosity summoned this encounter is lamentably validated by the circumstances. Either way, it is evident that Sandra finds it difficult to integrate the different feelings that the imago of the donor and his potential offspring arouse in her.

Unlike Sandra, Vicky described the choice of the donor as a process that entailed grieving.

Vicky: "That was the most difficult part, from my point of view. Like, suddenly to sit down and choose who the donor will be, that was really hard for me. I remember the day, it was a Saturday."

Gamete donation in light of the primal scene 253

Nora: "Yes, she cried."

Vicky: "Yeah, big time. I really had a hard time with it. I don't think I appreciated the distance between the phantasy of having children and the *how* of having children. Like, the bit about sitting down and taking something that you want so much and means so much from someone that you have no idea who they are – that was really, really, hard."

Vicky's account shed light on the inherent emotional difficulty entailed in the need to co-create one's most intimate and meaningful creation with an unknown partner. It is possible to regard grief work of the kind suggested by Vicky's description as a psychological insurance policy against the experience of the uncanny.

On the importance of the family reverie

The previous chapter presented clear evidence of the way in which children in same-sex families are preoccupied by phantasies related to the birth other. It also described the curiosity they evince about parental figures of the sex missing from their family configuration as well as about how they came into the world. In many of the families I encountered, these contents were scarcely manifested in overt conversation between the child and their parents. This finding conforms with earlier reports in the literature (Vanfraussen et al., 2001; Ehrensaft, 2007, 2008; Corbett, 2009; Hartman & Peleg, 2019; Ofer, 2014, 2020).

Parents, for their part, often find it difficult to achieve psychic integration between the positive and negative aspects of the birth other's imago. Driven by the need to establish the boundaries of the nuclear family – in light of which the birth other may be perceived as an unwanted interloper – defensive strategies are recruited that may exacerbate the difficulty of developing a family discourse on the subject.

Most of the families I encountered expressed complicated and perplexed feelings in regard to informing the child about the birth other: is disclosing the full truth about the child's origins the right thing to do? When should the story be told? And what exactly should be said? Ehrensaft (2007, 2008) has argued that parents who choose not to discuss with their children issues concerning their origin from a gamete donation usually rely on considerations pertaining to the child's welfare but are often unconsciously motivated by their own anxiety. However, the attempts to repress thoughts about the birth other are usually futile, because, as the illustrations in Chapter Eight showed, the children tend to phantasize about the birth other, even if they feel subject to an imposed silence about the topic. A good example of a child whose inner world continued to teem with phantasies about the birth other, despite the imposed silence on the topic is four-year-old Eithan. Mali and Rina, Eithan's moms, as well as 12-year-old twins Lizzie and Lia's mom related: "At his age, the girls already knew that they came from a sperm donation, but he doesn't yet know," Mali recounted, adding that:

> He, unlike the girls, constantly talked about his father: "My Daddy is like this, and my Daddy is like that" . . . "My Daddy has this kind of a house." And he knew he doesn't have a Daddy, he knew he has two mommies. It was entirely made up from his imagination. And then one day, I don't know what he had done, Rina says to him, "I'll tell your Daddy what you did." And then he says to her, "But I don't have a Daddy." And ever since then, he stopped talking about it.

Rina's taunting, perhaps even vindictive response ("I'll tell your Daddy"), exemplifies well how parental expressions of hostility or anxiety about the child's phantasies stifle the possibility of sharing these phantasies with them ("And ever since then he stopped talking about it.") These types of parental reactions are liable even to suffuse the child's private phantasmatic activity with anxiety and guilt, to the point of harming their ability to think or play as a means of emotional processing. Recognition of the child's phantasies about the birth other may be upsetting for the parents because they interpret them against the background of their fears of the conniving kidnapper who threatens to steal the child's love away from them, or as evidence that the existing family unit is inadequate. But this is a mistaken interpretation of the state of affairs. In fact, the child's expression of such phantasies is precisely an indication of secure attachment with their parents, and of normal emotional development.

As mentioned in Chapter Five, Ehrensaft (2007) clarified the importance of sensitive parental mediation in regard to the child's origins, which would provide them with information while also leaving room for the child's phantasy and subjective interpretation to unfold. At first, the child needs to be provided with narrative seeds that rely on imagery belonging to the child's world (such as the watering of seeds or the hatching of eggs), which will allow the child to form their own questions and will indicate that their parents are open to discuss the topic. This explanation should be repeated continuously, each time in a manner appropriate to the child's maturity level, with the hope that what begins as the imparting of information will evolve into an ongoing dialogue that will create space for the child's spectrum of reactions, both positive and negative. Ehrensaft explains that in the absence of special circumstances such as an acute family crisis or the danger of physical harm from a hostile environment, the child has a right to know and be told about their origins. Moreover, the very fact of knowing bears crucial importance for their psychological development.

Ehrensaft's arguments draw here on Corbett's work (Corbett, 2009), which emphasized the importance of the family reverie, and the child's phantasmatic space more generally: both serve as sources of strength for working through the questions and wishes that arise when the child attempts to reconcile the contradictions between their personal family reality and the internalized societal ideal. On this journey, the child needs a playful and containing parental environment that will mediate for him or her a variety of issues that I have discussed throughout the book: the fact of having been born through assisted reproductive technologies, and not through their parents' sexual union; the involvement in their conception of a stranger, a person with no intention of fulfilling a parenting role, but who also has never abandoned or given the child up; lack of access to half of their genealogical heritage; their asymmetrical relations with their parents in respect to genetic kinship, and the associated meanings attached to this fact in the context of the extended family relations; recognition of the fact that there might be other offspring of the same birth others; and in some cases also recognition that the way they came into the world may differ from that of their siblings. These issues do not all necessarily have negative meanings or affect attached to them, but they are apt to bring in their wake a sense of outsiderness that requires processing, all the more so within a culture that continues to grant hegemonic status – as the only realizable birth narrative – to the story of two biological parents in a heterosexual couple relationship. Alongside the space that Corbett affords the child's phantasy, his work emphasizes the importance for the parent of processing feelings of guilt and anxiety and of creating a family reverie – a space in which the family members communicate thoughts and phantasies with each other, whether personal or shared ones. The family reverie, in turn, helps reduce the guilt

256 What does procreation have to do with parental coitus, anyway?

and anxiety that accompany the child's phantasies and helps build identity and a sense of belonging (Ehrensaft, 2007).

References

Bagarozzi, D. A. (2011). A closer look at couple collusion: Protecting the self and preserving the system. *The American Journal of Family Therapy*, *39*, 390–403.

Barthes, R. (1989). *Sade, Fourier, Loyola*. University of California Press.

Benjamin, J. (1988). *The bonds of love: Psychoanalysis, feminism, and the problem of domination*. Pantheon Books.

Benyamini, I. (2008). Introduction [Hebrew]. In S. Freud (Ed.), *Jokes and their relation to the Unconscious*, 1905 (pp. 7–22). Resling.

Benyamini, I. (2012). Introduction [Hebrew]. In S. Freud (Ed.), *The Uncanny*, 1919 (pp. 7–14). Resling.

Bion, W. R. (1967). *Second thoughts: Selected papers on psychoanalysis*. Routledge.

Bollas, C. (1987). *The shadow of the object: Psychoanalysis of the unthought known*. Columbia University Press.

Britton, R. (1998). *Belief and imagination: Explorations in psychoanalysis*. Routledge.

Corbett, K. (2009). Nontraditional family reverie: Masculinity unfolds. In *Boyhoods: Rethinking masculinities*. Yale University Press.

Dostoyevsky, F. (2016). *The double: A Petersburg poem*. CreateSpace Independent Publishing Platform.

Ehrensaft, D. (2000). Alternatives to the stork: Fatherhood Fantasies in donor insemination families. *Studies in Gender and Sexuality*, *1*(4), 371–397.

Ehrensaft, D. (2007). The stork didn't bring me, I came from a dish: Psychological experiences of children conceived through assisted reproductive technology. *Journal of Infant, Child, and Adolescent Psychotherapy*, *6*(2), 124–140.

Ehrensaft, D. (2008). When baby makes three or four or more. *The Psychoanalytic Study of the Child*, *63*(1), 3–23.

Freud, S. (1905a). Jokes and their relation to the unconscious. In *The standard edition of the complete psychological works of Sigmund Freud 8* (pp. 1–247). Hogarth Press.

Freud, S. (1905b). Three essays on the theory of sexuality. In *The standard edition of the complete psychological works of Sigmund Freud 7* (pp. 123–246). Hogarth Press.

Freud, S. (1908). On the sexual theories of children. In *The standard edition of the complete psychological works of Sigmund Freud 9* (pp. 205–226). Hogarth Press.

Freud, S. (1909). Family romances. In *The standard edition of the complete psychological works of Sigmund Freud 9* (pp. 235–242). Hogarth Press.

Freud, S. (1919). The 'Uncanny'. In *The standard edition of the complete psychological works of Sigmund Freud 17* (pp. 217–256). Hogarth Press.

Haraway, D. J. (1991). A cyborg manifesto: Science, technology, and socialist-feminism in the late twentieth century. In *Simians, cyborgs, and women: The reinvention of nature* (pp. 149–181). Routledge.

Hartman, T., & Peleg, A. (2019). Minority stress in an improved social environment: Lesbian mothers and the burden of proof. *Journal of GLBT Family Studies*, *15*(5), 442–460.

Hayden, C. P. (1995). Gender, genetics, and generation: Reformulating biology in lesbian kinship. *Cultural Anthropology*, *10*(1), 41–63.

Hertz, R., Nelson, M. K., & Kramer, W. (2015). Sperm donors describe the experience of contact with their donor-conceived offspring. *Facts, Views & Vision in Obgyn*, *7*(2), 91–100.

Jentsch, E. (2008). *On the psychology of the uncanny. Uncanny modernity: Cultural theories and modern anxieties*. Palgrave.

Klein, M. (1945). The Oedipus complex in the light of early anxieties. In *Love, guilt and reparation and other works 1921–1945 (The Writings of Melanie Klein, Volume 1)*. Hogarth Press.

Koestler, A. (1964). *The act of creation*. Penguin.

Modell, J. (1989). Last chance babies: Interpretations of parenthood in an in vitro fertilization program. *Medical Anthropology Quarterly*, *3*(2), 124–138.

Ofer, M. (2014, July). "Rumours of the father's death have been greatly exaggerated": Some thoughts on the Oedipal conflict in children conceived through sperm donation [Hebrew]. *A paper presented in the Israel psychoanalytic society conference*.

Ofer, M. (2020). Multifocal – New family structures in the light of psychoanalytic theory. *Jahrbuch der Psychoanalyse*, *81*(Autumn).

Oxenhandler, N. (2001). *The eros of parenthood: Explorations in light and dark*. St. Martin's Press.

Raz Portugali, Y. (2019). The double [Hebrew]. *Maayan*, *15*, 9–17.

Riviere, J. (1929). Womanliness as a masquerade. *International Journal of Psychoanalysis*, *10*, 303–313.

Rosenthal, R. (2005, October 21). Hazira Haleshonit: Machbesat Milim [Hebrew]. *Maariv*. www.makorrishon.co.il/nrg/online/1/ART/997/957.html

Stevenson, R. L. (1974). *The strange case of Dr. Jekyll and Mr. Hyde*. New English Library.

Vanfraussen, K., Ponjaert-Kristoffersen, I., & Brewaeys, A. (2001). An attempt to reconstruct children's donor concept: A comparison between children's and lesbian parents' attitudes towards donor anonymity. *Human Reproduction*, *16*(9), 2019–2025.

Weston, K. (1991). *Families we choose: Lesbians, gays, kinship*. Columbia University Press.

Wilde, O. (1854–1900/2003). *The picture of Dorian Gray*. Penguin.

Part IV

Afterword

Chapter ten

Oedipus for everyone?

Biases in the Oedipal model: their
roots and how to overcome them

In the foreword of this book, I argued that Freud left psychoanalysis a two-sided, contradictory legacy. On the one hand, Freud seems to have subverted the discursive traditions of his day and avoided creating a rigid classification of personality structures and sexual patterns; on the other hand, however, he sought to codify a normative developmental trajectory that reproduces the conventional structures of his cultural environment (Corbett, 2002; Harris, 2002; Van Haute & Geyskens, 2012). This internal contradiction is intimately related to the question of psychoanalysis' endeavor: is it sufficient to view it as a method for gaining a profound understanding of psychic life, in order to provide relief from the conflicts and pain that are the lot of every human being, or might it perhaps have other designated purposes? One possible purpose is the formulation of general theories that outline normal development. An outline of this kind inscribes the boundaries between the normal and the pathological and inevitably results in the labeling and exclusion of social groups. Alternatively, psychoanalysis can be viewed as an instrument for critically exposing the social forces that affect the individual psyche, thereby aiding the dismantling of oppressive social structures.

Psychoanalytic theories can be distinguished from each other according to their degree of loyalty to each of these emphases. Thus, ego psychology, which dominated American psychoanalysis during the 1950s and 1960s, and considered itself heir to Freud's method, focused on establishing normative developmental theories and creating systems of classification – a trend that, among other things, led to the pathologization of homosexuality and the flourishing of conversion therapies.[1] However, Freud himself

---

1 Later theoreticians swayed the pendulum back and challenged the distinction between the healthy and the pathological or the illusion of a linear connection between early childhood

DOI: 10.4324/9781032663333-15

never viewed homosexuality as evidence of pathological development. He defended this position in various ways throughout his writings, whether by insisting on the idea of innate bisexuality, or by means of the radical distinction he made between the sexual object, i.e., the person one is attracted to, and the sexual aim, that is the act desired by the drive (Freud, 1905). This distinction unequivocally uncouples the choice of object (whether a homosexual or heterosexual choice) from one's level of emotional maturity. This theoretical position is manifested, inter alia, in Freud's refusal to accept conversion therapies, and in his objections to excluding homosexuals from psychoanalytic training institutes (Freud, 1935 in Grotjahn, 1951).

Many of the critiques leveled at the Oedipal model are concerned with its reductive tendency to conflate the variety of human desires and identifications[2] while marginalizing homosexual desire as well as pre-oedipal forms of identification, such as incorporation (Friedman, 2013). This limited version of the Oedipal idea, a result of reducing the complete Oedipus complex to its positive component and understanding it in genital terms only, brought about binary gendering processes and a split between desire and identification. Under these conditions, the individual is obliged to deny parts of his or her identity and is invited to reunite with them within a heterosexual relationship based on splitting and projective identification. This formula produces and reproduces the gender system as a universal "false self" as well as the heteronormative family[3] as an arena in which gender trauma is reenacted (E. Ziv, 2020).

The formulation implies that it is indeed possible to adhere to a flexible and rich Oedipal model, one that celebrates the diversity and multiplicity of human experience, as long as one remains loyal to the complete Oedipal model and views the repression of the negative complex as the product

---

experiences and psychopathologies in adulthood, insisting instead on the individual's infinite creative potential. Different versions of this trend can be found, among others, in Kohut, Bion, interpersonal psychoanalysis and relational psychoanalysis.

2 The most radical versions of these claims were put forward by Deleuze and Guattari, as part of the French philosophical tradition. According to them, the Oedipalization of Western culture exacts a high price: the enervation of the social passions by individualizing them and channeling them into the nuclear family, and the reduction of the human identificatory potential to a homogenizing Oedipal identification, which leads to the reproduction of hierarchies and the erection of partitions between the self and the other, between different social groups, and between the human and the non-human (Deleuze & Guattari, 1984, 1988).

3 Furthering Effi Ziv's argument (2020), I would emphasize that a heterosexual relationship is not necessarily heteronormative. Heterosexuality can exist between a man and woman of flexible gender, in a contractual arrangement that is not based on split functions.

of oppressive societal forces and not as a developmental ideal; as long as one's understanding of the Oedipal situation appreciates the variety of existing drives, rather than restricting it to genital ones; as long as one insists on distinguishing between the sexual object and the sexual aim. A clinical application of this model would strive toward renewed contact with parts of the self that were split off by the gendering process, and to the reunion with repressed identifications and desires – in every person, whatever their sexual orientation or gender identification.

Another undisputed critical claim concerns the fact that Oedipal theory privileges the nuclear family, a structure that was reflective of the social reality in which the theory emerged. The family configuration in which two married heterosexual parents raise shared biological children together under a single roof currently reflects less than half of the families in the Western world, yet it is a model which nonetheless continues to enjoy hegemonic status as a cultural ideal.

Despite this, it is difficult to imagine a psychoanalytic approach that does not rely on some version or another of the Oedipal model, since, due to its flexibility and continuous transformations over time, it serves as a key to understanding many of the psychological challenges confronting every human being: the internalization of the significant objects in a person's life through the interplay of desire and identification; acceptance of the reality principle and the social law; recognition of human finality and lack and the relinquishing of an omnipotent or omniscient position; acceptance of the differences between infantile sexuality and mature sexuality; coming to terms with the inevitable experiences of exclusion and inferiority; the transition from dyadic to triangular relations; the murder of parental authority and the ordering of intergenerational relations, and more. These challenges, according to many versions of the psychoanalytic theory, led to the development of crucial psychological capacities, including the construction of an autonomous identity and a sense of separateness; the consolidation ot gender and sexual identity; the development of thinking and creative capacities; introspection and empathy; the ability to sustain intimacy within a couple relationship; and even the ability to tolerate and contain psychological pain.

This inexhaustive overview of aspects of the Oedipal model illustrates clearly that Oedipal theory cannot be forfeited without pulling out the carpet from beneath any approach that can be defined as "psychoanalytic." "We can only disrupt Oedipal theory's hegemonic reach," claimed Jade

McGleughlin, a contemporary queer psychoanalyst, "when alternative narratives disrupt the shared symbolic register. When we expand and supplant traditional theorizing in our social unconscious, we are freer to imagine new ways of living and loving" (McGleughlin, 2021, 329).

Throughout this book, I have sought to challenge some of the foundational premises of the Oedipal model and thus "expand and supplant traditional theorizing," as McGleughlin advocates (ibid.). First, I showed that heterosexual couplehood is not a necessary condition for creating an Oedipal foundation for the child. Recognition of the difference between the sexes, which is achieved by the child independently of their parents' sex, might be used by children raised in a heterosexual family as a conveniently available ground for splitting between the parental figures. However, any parent-couple creates the potential ground of differences upon which the Oedipal splitting can rest, be these personality differences, differences in parental functioning, or in the quality of the relationship with the child. Secondly, I showed that the split between desire and identification is not an inherent and inevitable outcome of the Oedipal dynamic but is rather a by-product of the elementary split between the sexes, which characterizes the heteronormative family. As will be recalled, during the Oedipal phase, most of the children chose as love objects the parent who was their early primary caregiver, in other words, for them desire and identification are complementary aspects of attachment. In addition, instead of the unifying Oedipal narrative, I exposed the existence of diverse narratives, including Oedipal ones (the full-blown, Platonic, and alternating Oedipal configurations) and non-Oedipal ones (the anti-competitive and multiple configurations). In so doing, I also indicated the possibility of a primal scene phantasy in which more than two parental figures take part, depending on both the concrete and psychological circumstances in which the child develops (designated as the "multiple configuration"). Finally, I challenged the basic premise of the dominant kinship ideology, which privileges the place of the biological parent within the child's inner world, and showed that the child's curiosity about his or her origins, as well as the phantasies about the birth others who participated in their conception do not substitute for the Oedipal dynamic that the child enacts with his or her two parents, but rather coexists with it.

Now, based on the insights collected in this book, I will attempt to formulate several recommendations for the beneficial application of the Oedipal model in work with same-sex families, and new families more generally.

The position I lay out seeks to profit from the richness of Oedipal theory while paying careful attention to the different ways in which it is embodied in diverse family circumstances.

References

Corbett, K. (2002). The mystery of homosexuality. In M. Dimen & V. Goldner (Eds.), *Gender in psychoanalytic space: Between clinic and culture*. Other Press.

Deleuze, G., & Guattari, F. (1984). *Anti-Oedipus: Capitalism and schizophrenia*. Athlone.

Deleuze, G., & Guattari, F. (1988). *A thousand Plateaus: Capitalism and schizophrenia*. Athlone.

Freud, S. (1905). Three essays on the theory of sexuality. In *The standard edition of the complete psychological works of Sigmund Freud 7* (pp. 123–246). Hogarth Press.

Friedman, L. (2013). *In the footsteps of psychoanalysis: A postmodern gendered criticism of Freud*. Bar-Ilan University Press.

Grotjahn, M. (1951). 'Historical notes: A letter from Freud.': *The American Journal of Psychiatry*, April, 1951, 107, No. 10, pp. 786 and 787. *International Journal of Psychoanalysis, 32*, 331.

Harris, A. (2002). Gender as contradiction. In M. Dimen & V. Goldner (Eds.), *Gender in psychoanalytic space: Between clinic and culture* (pp. 91–115). Other Press.

McGleughlin, J. (2021). Rethinking Oedipus or not. *Psychoanalytic Dialogues, 31*(3), 329–339.

Van Haute, P., & Geyskens, T. (2012). *A non-Oedipal psychoanalysis? A clinical anthropology of hysteria in the work of Freud and Lacan*. University Press.

Ziv, E. (2020). Insets [Hebrew]. *Mafte'akh, 15*, 13–33.

Chapter eleven

How to work with same-sex families?

Bringing a child into the world involves four central stages: planning, conception, pregnancy and birth, and childrearing. A set of heteronormative premises continues to supply ready-made answers about the role of the man and women in each and every stage, and to assume a correspondence between the four stages, despite the fact that in contemporary life, each of these stages is open to diversity.[1]

The term conception has two meanings: the first denotes becoming pregnant and the second refers to the abstract formation of an idea. In the current moment, each of these meanings may represent a different basis for parenting: is the parent the one who played an active role in physical conception or perhaps the person who conceived of the child in their minds – as an idea?

The variety of possibilities requires careful therapeutic inquiry into each of the four stages, so as to understand the unique circumstances into which each individual child was born: was conception spontaneous, or was it preceded by a planning stage, or even by a long period of anticipation and striving? Was the child – as an idea, or as a wish that aims to materialize in reality – conceived in the mind of a single parent, in the minds of two parents, or more? Who carried the pregnancy – a heterosexual woman? A lesbian? A transexual man? A surrogate who neither planned nor was designated to function as a mother? What feelings did the pregnancy arouse in the parents who conceived of the child in their imaginations? Who cared for the infant when it first came into the world? If there was more than one caregiving figure, what was the division of labor between them? Did this division persist over time, or did it change? And if so, in what way?

---

1 I am grateful to Yael Khenin for formulating this insight.

DOI: 10.4324/9781032663333-16

The book's chapters illustrate that the unique family circumstances in each of these stages, and the transitions from one to the next, occasion particular intrapsychic and interpersonal conflicts, which need to be learned and apprehended.

Part I of this book examined Oedipal and non-Oedipal formations among children raised in same-sex families. The findings presented showed that contra the predictions of Oedipal theory, in its classical version, most of the children constructed an Oedipal configuration relating to two parents of the same sex. The casting of the parents into the role of object of desire versus the role of Oedipal rival did not correspond to the complementary gender role division of the couple, but was based rather on the quality of the relationship between each parent and the child. Thus, a parent who served as primary caregiver or who was more emotionally available during the first years of the child's life usually established their position as the child's primary attachment figure and was later chosen, in most cases, as an Oedipal love object.

Simultaneously, I showed that contemporary theories that place the transition from dyadic to triangular relations at the center of Oedipal development – rather than issues of sex, gender, and sexuality – are missing part of the picture. Despite the assumption that children experience erotic attraction toward parents of both sexes – an assumption deriving from Freud's complete Oedipal model – it needs to be taken into account that an Oedipal attraction toward a parent of the same-sex clashes with the societal taboo on homosexuality. The prohibition imposed on the desire of a child toward a parent of the same sex enlists defensive strategies on the part of both the parent and the child, defenses that ultimately shape the organization of the relations in the child's psyche.

Considering that the taboo on male homosexuality is more severe than the taboo on lesbian relations, Oedipal relations between fathers and sons are more susceptible to emotional complications. Thus, erotic feelings that any parent inevitably experiences when engaged in the bodily care of their child (Laplanche, 1987) may induce in a gay father particularly powerful feelings of guilt, confusion, and dread. He is liable to interpret expressions of intimacy between himself and his son as acts of seduction that may "sow the seeds" of homosexual desire in the child. As a result, the father may exhibit a pattern of avoidance or denial that conveys to his son an unconscious message that romantic or erotic relations between the father and son are not just out of bounds in reality, but are also prohibited in phantasy, in play – where indeed they are necessary in order to establish an Oedipal dynamic. This pattern, as Butler (1995) suggested, characterizes the relations between the father and the son in heteronormative culture in any case; however, when both parents are men, this means that there is no object available to the child which is a-priori exempted from this potential emotional complication. The role of therapeutic space, therefore, is to help the gay father work through feelings related to the internalization of homophobic messages, and especially early Oedipal experiences in his relations with his own father, experiences that have at times been tainted with shame and dread (Maurer, 2007). In this way, therapy can help promote the legitimacy of erotic feelings that arise in relations with the child, and to assuage the father's feelings of guilt and anxiety in such a way as to allow him to establish a playful erotic space that affirms his son's developing sexuality.

The book's second part focused on questions concerning the relationship between biology and kinship. I showed that unlike the expectations flowing from the heteronormative kinship discourse, biological affiliation has no impact on the child's attachment processes or on his or her preference patterns. Nonetheless, the research materials illustrated that the meanings that parents attribute to biological affiliation do impact family relations in myriad ways, including the child's Oedipal patterns.

Let us consider again the four stages outlined previously. When planning to have a child, lesbian mothers may construct an egalitarian vision of parenting, but this vision is soon derailed by the unavoidable asymmetry that comes into relief in the following stages: during conception and pregnancy, only one of the women is involved, and in most instances, these experiences prime her to fulfill the role of the child's primary caregiver during the child's infancy, whereas the social mother may find herself struggling to establish her place. By way of contrast, among gay fathers the asymmetry is usually a factor only during the conception phase, and therefore issues of competitiveness, envy, and concern over the quality of the relationship with the child tend to manifest less intensely. At the same time, however, many gay fathers choose to conceal the genetic affiliation of their child. This may paradoxically amplify the importance of genetic affiliation, and even plant in the child's minds an "unthought known" (Bollas, 1987) – impressions of experiences that are incapable of verbal expression, making it difficult for them to form a coherent narrative about their origins.

The role of the therapeutic space, in these contexts, is to encourage discourse between the parents about the issues relating to the structural biological asymmetry within their family, in order to help the couple recognize the sensitivities and tensions resulting from this factor. Such a discourse is capable of bringing to the surface parapraxes and enactments on the biological parent's part, deriving from a possible sense of ownership over the child; it can also help the social parent recognize instances where they interpret conflicts that are both inevitable and vital for the child's development through the prism of their own anxieties about their parental status. Another therapeutic issue relates to possible tensions and crises with the extended family, revolving around the question of the child's biological affiliation. It is my hope that the findings presented in Part II of the book will help strengthen and recuperate the status of the social parent.

Part III was dedicated to the place that the birth others occupy in the child's inner world as well as in their parents' psyche. The findings reveal a disturbing discrepancy between, on the one hand, the degree to which the child is curious about the way he or she came into the world and invested in phantasy about the birth other, and, on the other hand, the degree to which these issues are articulated directly in interaction with his or her parents. Some of the parents I interviewed were aware of this gap and understood it as the child's attempt to protect them. Parents, for their part, tended to enlist defensive strategies based on the need to affirm and reinforce the boundaries of their nuclear family. A defensive response on the parents' part to children's phantasies about the birth other not only stifles the possibility of sharing such issues with them, but may also invest these infantile phantasies with anxiety and guilt, sometimes to the point that the child is unable to work through these issues in thinking, phantasy, and play. Such responses are rooted in an incorrect understanding of infantile phantasies as a threat of losing the child's love, or as proof of a disastrous lack that causes suffering and anguish in the child. In fact, however, the existence of such phantasies in the child's mind is merely evidence of the child's secure attachment to her or his parents and of normal psychological development.

The task of psychic integration placed on the parent in regard to the representation of the birth other is far from being a simple one. It requires recognition of the fact that a broad spectrum of feelings – including gratitude, admiration, romantic thrill, sexual threat, envy, hostility, and anxiety about the possibility that the birth other will desire the child for themselves or steal the child's love – relate to a single object. If that were not enough, this object is a stranger whose very anonymity provokes anxiety. Facilitating this crucial and complex integration task is the responsibility of any psychotherapeutic intervention with individuals and families who have chosen to use gamete-assisted conception. But as we shall see presently, this can only be undertaken from a position that respects the inherent difficulty of this psychological task.

Like many parents who were assisted by gamete donation, Sandra described her fears and quandaries about discussing the topic with her daughter. These fears led her and her partner Efrat to seek psychological counseling in order to consolidate a coherent narrative about sperm donation, one that they could share with their daughter. As will be recalled, Sandra's challenges in her attempt to consolidate an integrative birth other imago were so excessive that they bred a continual uncanny experience – for a long time Sandra felt persecuted by the figure of the donor – as conjured in her imagination – and by his imagined offspring (see the subsection titled "The birth other as uncanny," in Chapter Nine). During our conversation, Sandra recalled those counseling sessions with a sense of gratitude, but the repeated contradictions in her statements revealed that they had not helped her achieve an integrated representation of the birth other. The sessions may have even intensified the confusion surrounding his figure, as the following statements suggest:

> I think that some of the good things that happened to me there, during those two sessions, was that I understood that it wasn't just technical, it's not technical. I think there is a person in the background. Okay, so he has no feelings for us, we don't know him, but there's a person. We don't know him, but he helped us, and there's a third side, he's here. He's not in our life, he isn't really. In my imagination, there isn't some person there, it's not a family triangle. But he helped us create it, so it's not technical, it's not genetic material. Maybe it is genetic material, but there is someone there, there's a person behind this operation. I guess so, I don't know.

The confusion in Sandra's speech seems to be precipitated by her efforts to align herself with the professional guidance she was given: to avoid reducing the birth other to genetic material, to make space for the "third" participant in the creation of her children, and to feel gratitude toward him. But she does so without sufficient integration of the negative feelings that his figure arouses in her: the sense of alienation and ignorance as to his identity, anxieties surrounding his connection to the child and his

How to work with same-sex families? 271

representation as a potential kidnapper, as well as the inherent difficulty of making space for a "third" within the parental couple structure, a difficulty rooted in the primal scene phantasy. Sandra's words offer an opportunity to think about the dangers entailed in hasty therapeutic interventions that, while grounded in analytic theory, are delivered to the patient in a clichéd and tacked-on manner that fails to take into consideration the patient's emotional situation or current capacities. This is what Freud (1910) called "wild analysis."

False integration based on the gratification of the therapist may result in a situation where, as in Sandra's case, the negative feelings – for which no legitimate place has been found in the context of reverie about the birth other – find an outlet through projective identification and thus return to assail her in her encounter with external reality. "I told you about my sister," Sandra continued her conversation with me.

> I sit with her and help her choose sperm. Do you think I want to choose sperm with her? Not at all. I've gone through this already. It feels awful, it makes me feel awful, all this going over the traits. It makes me feel bad. It takes me back to places I don't want to go back to.

One may speculate that her children's future investigations about their origins, so crucial for their development, will oblige her to revisit the very places she wants to avoid, and may induce similar feelings of aversion like those she experienced when helping her sister choose a sperm donor.

Ehrensaft (2000, 2007) argued that, within the politics of family life, no construction or concept exists yet that treats the sperm donor as a whole object that is not a parent. This is the reason why the donor is often reduced to a part-object – to semen, or "sperm," as Sandra referred to him. Alternatively, he may be represented in a split way that denies the emotional ambivalence toward him: at one pole, we may encounter expressions about "the generous man who helped us have a child," typical of same-sex couples or heterosexual couples who were assisted by gamete donation; at the other pole, we may witness the fabricated illusion of a whole object as a parent figure or a sexual partner, where no such object exists – a response typical mostly of single parents.

How then can one help families construct a representation of the birth other as a whole object, or more precisely, as an emotionally integrative object, without collapsing toward either of these two poles – erasure or

272 Afterword

reduction to genetic material on one end, or fabrication of a parent figure on the other?

Terms such as "surrogate mother" or "biological father" appear frequently in contemporary psychoanalytic literature to describe the female or male birth others, respectively. Even Corbett (2009), who critiqued psychoanalytic treatments that accorded heterosexual coitus the status of reality testing in regard to sexual reproduction, assigned the very same status in his coinage of the term "donor dad," proposing it for the everyday language use of lesbian mothers.

It should be noted that the participants in the research documented in this book preferred, without exception, to identify the birth others as a "donor" or "surrogate," and furthermore, many of them reported their continual frustration at the way their social environment uses of the terms "father" or "mother" to describe the birth others. For example, at the conclusion of the interview, I asked Amos and Daniel whether there were any other issues drawn from their experience that were important for them to comment on, and they replied:

Daniel: "Lots of times, people, when they ask about the egg donor, they ask about the mother. They say 'mother.' There's something galling about that. As if people still have difficulty relating to us as a unit that doesn't have a mother."

Amos: "People just don't get it. Suddenly they say, 'surrogate mom,' or 'donor mom.' There are some terms like that that simply are '*not*,' they have nothing to do with reality."

If we assume that family discourse has been stifled due to parental anxiety about the intrusion of a third factor into the primal scene, or about a potential kidnapper of the child's love, and in the case of gay fathers, also because of the emotional strains associated with their transgression of socially sanctioned gender imperatives, then to employ a term that ascribes parental custody to this potential intruder will only serve to exacerbate the anxiety, invite resistance, and make the parent's integration work much harder. Instead, terms such as "sperm donor," "egg donor," or "surrogate," which validate the family structure and help construct and reinforce its boundaries, will enhance the sense of security and protection that are necessary for the parents to be able to engage in psychological introspection, and subsequently for the children's ability to do so.

The need to continuously protect oneself from heteronormative expectations that undermine the perception of kinship on which the family unit is based came up repeatedly in connection with the status of the social parent. The sense of a double bind was typically expressed, as I have demonstrated, in the social mothers' impossible choice between giving in and over-compensating, or, in the case of social fathers, between concealment or confession.

While I deem that sensitivity and respect toward the kinship system that the patients have established is a necessary condition for creating a therapeutic alliance, my suggestion to avoid designations such as "father" or "mother" to refer to the birth others is not motivated by political correctness. This book has attempted to take the readers on a journey to acquaint them with the conscious and unconscious emotional nuances of the families' members, in order to forge insights that faithfully reflect the reality of same-sex families, in all their complexity. My goal has been to lay out the different parts of the picture side by side, to show that the phantasies about the birth other reside within the child's psyche, alongside established Oedipal relations with both parents. Moreover, the greater the investment of the child's libido in the Oedipal dynamic with her or his actual parents, the greater is their need to construct a "family romance," that is, the need for an identificatory phantasmatic relationship with a figure external to the family system. The birth other is then positioned in phantasy not as the potential partner of the biological parent, but as a family alternative to the parent couple.

Understanding the child's preoccupation with the birth other in terms of the family romance phantasy, rather than in Oedipal terms, will help affirm the family structure and fortify its boundaries, thus reducing the sense of threat that the child's curiosity arouses. Parents can then navigate more flexibly toward a position that accepts the child's psychic investigations and releases her or him from the possible complications of guilt and anxiety.

Following Winnicott, what is being proposed here is a therapeutic stance centered on the recognition that one will never pose the question "Did you conceive of this or was it presented to you from without?" (Winnicott, 1971, p. 12). In other words, one must not ask whether the birth other is a phantasmatic creation or an actual parental figure. "The important point is that no decision on this point is expected. The question is not to be formulated" (p. 12.).

References

Bollas, C. (1987). *The shadow of the object: Psychoanalysis of the unthought known*. Columbia University Press.

Butler, J. (1995). Melancholy gender – refused identification. *Psychoanalytic Dialogues*, *5*, 165–180.

Corbett, K. (2009). Nontraditional family reverie: Masculinity unfolds. In *Boyhoods: Rethinking masculinities*. Yale University Press.

Ehrensaft, D. (2000). Alternatives to the stork: Fatherhood Fantasies in donor insemination families. *Studies in Gender and Sexuality*, *1*(4), 371–397.

Ehrensaft, D. (2007). The stork didn't bring me, I came from a dish: Psychological experiences of children conceived through assisted reproductive technology. *Journal of Infant, Child, and Adolescent Psychotherapy*, *6*(2), 124–140.

Freud, S. (1910). "Wild" psycho-analysis. In *The standard edition of the complete psychological works of Sigmund Freud 11: Five lectures on psycho-analysis, Leonardo da Vinci and Other Works* (pp. 219–228). Hogarth Press.

Laplanche, J. (1987). *New foundations for psychoanalysis*. Blackwell.

Maurer, O. (2007, July). Can anyone love me at all: Some thoughts on the fate of homosexual love. *Paper presented at the annual conference of the international association for relational psychoanalysis and psychotherapy in Athens*. Greece.

Winnicott, D. W. (1971). Transitional objects and transitional phenomena. In *Playing and reality* (pp. 1–25). Tavistock Publications; Basic Books.

Coda

The Kids Are All Right: A psychoanalytic reading in Lisa Cholodenko's film

Lisa Cholodenko's film, *The Kids Are All Right* (USA, 2010), depicts a moment of crisis in the lives of a lesbian couple and their adolescent children, when the sperm donor appears as an interloper in the life of the nuclear family. The plot development follows a familiar cinematic formula, where a stranger disturbs the peace of a photogenic and relatable all-American family, bringing to the surface conflicts whose intensity had been blunted by the convenience of bourgeois suburban existence. In this instance, however, the stranger is none other than the sperm donor who helped bring the children into the world.

According to the film's plot, the donor's intrusion into the family unit is made possible because of the mothers' past choice of an open donation, which permits their children to initiate contact with the donor when they reach the age of 18. The screenplay was written by Cholodenko, with Stuart Blumberg as co-writer, at a time when she herself was about to have a child with her partner, Wendy Melvoin, with the assistance of a sperm donation (Khanna, 2006). Consequently, the script's overt themes are informed by the phantasies and anxieties that would be familiar to a same-sex parent deliberating whether to choose an open or closed donation, rather than being a depiction of the trajectory of events in the case of an open donation. A psychoanalytic reading of the film suggests that the drama be seen as a reflection of underlying dynamics that are always at play, even when an actual meeting with the donor is out of the question, either because of the children's young age or because the parent chose a closed anonymous donation from the outset. I propose viewing the film's plot as an enactment or dreamwork, in which all the conflicts about the place of the birth other in the family's life are given expression. The following is an attempt to analyze the portrayal of these conflicts as well as other central issues that have been elaborated throughout this book.

DOI: 10.4324/9781032663333-17

As mentioned, the film depicts a family consisting of a lesbian couple and their two adolescent children. The mothers share an intimate and loving relationship, albeit not devoid of tensions: Nic (Annette Benning) is a workaholic physician with judgmental tendencies and a strong need for control, who relieves stress by consuming wine in excess; Jules (Julianne Moore) is a suburban stay-at-home mom, adept housekeeper, and home cook who spends quality time with her children, but struggles to fulfill her professional aspirations and often feels criticized and belittled by Nic. Joni (Mia Wasikowska) is a straight-A student suffering from romantic inhibitions. She is about to turn 18 and will soon be departing for college. Laser (Josh Hutcherson), her 15-year-old brother, is an athlete, an average student, whose homoerotic involvement with his best friend, allows him to test parental boundaries, and explore his own identity and sexuality: together they race around on skateboards, experiment with drugs, and watch a pornographic video they discover in his mothers' bedroom.

As Joni's 18th birthday approaches, Laser prevails on her to exercise her right to make contact with the sperm donor. Fifteen-year-old Laser is incapable of suppressing his curiosity and waiting three more years to reach the right age. Joni is reluctant, fearful especially of hurting her mothers, but finally gives in to his entreaties. The differences between Joni and Laser's attitudes correspond to the patterns seen in the children presented in this book: as will be recalled, children whose biological sex differed from that of their parents tended to exhibit a fiercer curiosity about the birth other and were more immersed in phantasies about them. As a boy, Laser's sex is not only different from that of his mothers, but also than that of his sister: in other words, he experiences gender solitariness. Like seven-year-old Tom, whose curiosity about male figures is so obvious, that, "You can suddenly see him standing at the playground and staring at an interaction between a father and a son," (as Mommy Vicky reported), Laser is presented at the opening of the film starring enviously at an interaction between his best friend and his father. In that scene, the father asserts his authority over his son, wielding his physical strength to set boundaries, unlike the use of "touchy-feely" discussions that Laser is familiar with in his interactions with his mothers. Laser's relationship with his friend corresponds to the twinship phantasies presented by seven-year-old Tom, a phantasy centered on the need to share intimacy based on similarity. It can therefore be assumed that an increased preoccupation with the figure of the birth other reflects a developmental need to identify with an adult figure of the same sex as part of forming one's own gender identity. As underscored throughout the book, the need is not for an actual figure to play an active role in the child's life, but rather for permission to explore and identify with such a figure in phantasy.

After Joni decides to respond to Laser's need and reach out to the donor, she secretly searches for contact information about the agency that facilitated the sperm donation. Here the film intercuts shots from a somewhat failed sex scene between the mothers, and from a parallel scene where Joni is searching for documents in the adjacent room. This montage of the two scenes appears to emphasize the twin aspects of the primal scene phantasy: recognition of the parents' sexuality as well as the child's curiosity about their origins. Among children born through assistive gamete donation, these two aspects are unreconcilable.

In a revisiting of the Oedipus myth, Quinodoz (1999), a contemporary psychoanalyst, identified the element of the family romance embedded in it. Oedipus has two "sets" of parents: the progenitors who are presented as a sexual and murderous couple who abandon him, and his adoptive parents, who are presented as sexually infertile but as devoted and nurturing parents. This splitting, according to Quinodoz, enables the child to avoid the conflict that arises when faced with the parents' different parts, and it performs a central defensive role vis-à-vis Oedipal anxieties and the sense of loneliness bred by recognition of the parents' couplehood. In accordance with this split, the mothers' sexuality in the film is presented as barren – not just in the sense that is not procreative, but also because of its dearth of genuine passion. The sexuality of the two mothers is negatively juxtaposed with that of the sperm donor, Paul (Mark Ruffalo), portrayed in sex scenes brimming with passion and including nudity (Halberstam, 2010). These contrasting representations may be interpreted as reflecting a defensive split between the child's relations with their parent figures and the "family romance" that the child constructs regarding the birth other. Sometimes, the child's inner world will reflect an inverse state of affairs, where recognizing the parents' libidinal sexuality results in the male birth other being represented as a kind of incorporeal "Holy Ghost," or the female birth other as a kind of symbiotic safe haven.

To avoid offending their mothers, the two siblings arrange to meet with Paul, the sperm donor, unbeknownst to their mothers. This choice reflects the need that most of the children in the study expressed: to spare their parents the knowledge about their preoccupation with the birth other, fearing that will be experienced by the parent as an act of ingratitude or loss of the child's love.

When the mothers learn about the meeting between the children and the donor, Jules suggests that, now that they've met, the children can move on. This response resonates with the approach of many of the parents I met: they would describe some occasion on which the child had asked a question about the family's difference, or about how they came into the world, claiming that the child accepted the answer that was given her or him and moved on. Sandra and Efrat recounted: "When Ruth was two, I was diapering her when suddenly she asked, 'Where's my Daddy?' Something like that. So we explained it to her. I was prepared, I had a prepared narrative, I told it to her. And that's it!" The notion that "that's it" – that a one-off response is enough to put the topic to rest – is more reflective of a parental wish than that of the child's emotional reality, according to the material gathered from my encounters with the children. The topic requires, rather, an ongoing process of working through, to enable psychic integration and grief-work, and it is likely to come up again in different guises at every developmental crossroad, in accordance with emergent emotional needs. This need for repeated exploration of the birth other is also reflected in the somewhat unexpected desire that Joni articulated in the preceding scene to see the donor again.

In an intimate conversation Nic and Jules share their ambivalence about their children's curiosity, on the one hand acknowledging the children's need, but also feeling dejected about it, worrying that their own status and centrality as parents is threatened.

As noted earlier, Oxenhandler (2001) suggests that the difficulties stemming from the child's increasing separateness, and recognition of the fact that she or he will eventually leave home, exacerbate parents' guilt about inevitable parental failures. These feelings are projected onto a malevolent "other" who is liable to kidnap the child or their love. Ehrensaft (2007) adds that, for parents who created their children with the assistance of gamete donation, the representation of this conniving kidnapper merges with the representation of the birth other. In the film, we see how the anticipated separation from Joni, who is about to leave for college, arouses self-doubts in the mothers in regard to their own parental status, and these are translated into the fear that Paul, the sperm donor, will steal away from them the little time they have left with the daughter, as well as her love.

Concerned that opposing the children might only increase their interest in Paul, the mothers choose another tack: they open their home to him, hoping to "kill him with kindness." Thus, in the course of a family meal to which he has been invited, Nic tries to devalue Paul in various ways. One of the ways she does this is by the tried-and-tested tactic of reducing him to a part object by describing the process of choosing a donor as searching for "sperm." While Nic and Jules consciously deploy any weapon at their disposal in order to nip in the bud the new-found connection between their children and Paul, most parents are not aware of the way in which reducing the birth other to a part object, objectifying them, or devaluing them in the context of family discourse, is damaging to the bond that is being wrought between their children and the birth others in phantasy and may even over-burden this phantasmatic relationships with guilt and anxiety.

From this point onward the film's plot develops in the direction of what might be called an apocalyptic scenario, or realization of the parents' most threatening phantasies about the birth other. Paul embodies in the most lit-eral way a representation of the conniving kidnapper: he spends time with the children privately, attempts to mentor them, or behaves like a parent figure. The children, for their part, long for his closeness, idolize him, and, inspired by him, rebel against their mothers' parental authority. In other words, they use his figure as an avenue for constructing their separateness and asserting an autonomous identity in a manner that coincides with the role of the family romance phantasy. If this were not enough, Jules cheats on Nic and has an affair with Paul. In other words, Paul embodies not only the figure of the kidnapper but also of the intruder into the primal scene.

Nic, who is identified with the "father" role, through her portrayal as "butch," as the sole breadwinner, and as having a more authoritative parent-ing style, feels that Paul has not only stolen her partner but also her place as head of the family. However, after the affair between Paul and Jules comes to light – a moment involving a crisis of trust and intense pain for all the family members – it quickly becomes clear that the family's loyalties belong primarily with each other, that the bonds among them are powerful and profound and irreplaceable. Paul is no more than a supporting actor in the family's story: his role, it will soon become apparent, is that of a catalyst who brings to the surface unexpressed conflicts and provides an opportunity to work through them, together and separately, in the inter-ests of growth (Halberstam, 2010). The film ends with a sense that all the characters have benefited from the crisis, and that the family, as a single unit, emerges strengthened, despite some difficult residues.

One of the most interesting issues in the film is the gap between the mothers' choice of an open donation that allows the children to contact the donor when they grow up, and their hurtful and threatened emotional response to the children's actualization of this possibility. A real discrepancy is revealed between the mothers' professed agenda and their actual ability to contain the emotional repercussions of their choice. A similar discrepancy could be seen among many of the parents I interviewed, in various contexts. Most pronouncedly it was evidenced in my conversation with Moran and Shir – one of the few couples that, like the mothers in the film, had chosen an open donation that would allow their children to contact the donor when they turned 18. Moran and Shir spontaneously mentioned the film *The Kids Are All Right* in their interview, as the realization of an apocalyptic scenario: "*The Kids Are All Right* had just come out – the one with the open donor," Shir said.

> Which is like, really shocking. And it's like, depicted there in an extremely harsh light. Not a positive experience in any way. But despite this we said, "We're giving the children the possibility of choosing if it's something they're curious about."

As the interview went on, I asked them whether they had ever thought about the moment of encounter between their sons, Adam and Eden, and the sperm donor. The dialogue that ensued between the two mothers could easily have been part of the film script that they had just described as horrific:

Me:	"Do you ever think about a moment like that: a moment of . . ."
Moran:	"Yes."
Me:	"Of a meeting?"
Moran:	"Yes."
Shir.	"Not a meeting. He is obligated to respond once."
Moran:	"He can. A meeting is an option too, Shir."
Shir:	"I don't know if he'll agree. He's only obligated to answer either an email or phone call."
Moran:	"He seems a cool guy. I think he'll agree."
Shir:	"What do you mean a cool guy, Moran? You forget . . ."
Moran:	"He'll agree."

Shir:	"He said, 'I'm for any donating and I hope it will have value for science, and I understand that people are curious. I have no desire to take on a mentoring role or anything that is emotionally meaningful, but the curiosity I get.' Doesn't sound cool at all."
Moran:	"What doesn't he sound like?"
Shir:	"He didn't sound like he was cool."
Moran:	"Didn't sound cool? Like, I wouldn't want to have him as a friend, but I felt he sounded like a cool guy."
Me:	[to Shir] "So as far as you are concerned, you'd prefer him just to answer one call and that's it?"
Shir:	"No. If Adam or Eden are curious, fine. But that's their thing. It's not mine. It won't threaten me. Like, it doesn't threaten me. No, it doesn't threaten me."

Shir repeated four times that she wasn't threatened by the possibility of a meeting between the donor and her children, as if trying to convince herself of the fact. At the same time, she trusted the donor to set a boundary to her children's potential curiosity, while painting a negative image of him. I could virtually imagine her internal chaos and loss of control in some future moment when her children and partner choose to regard the sperm donor – now a concrete person – as someone cool whose company they seek out, in precise correspondence with the plot of the movie that she described as "shocking."

But, as noted, the film's plot need not be realized concretely in the lived reality of families. The future is "presented," that is, embedded in the present, and can be sensed in Shir and Moran's dialogue, just as the film's main conflicts can be recognized in families that chose a closed anonymous donation.

The issue of the children's genetic affiliation is only subtly alluded to in the film. Joni is Nic's biological daughter. Like Nic, she is a perfectionist, an honors student who says that she "works hard" for her achievements, and an obedient daughter. Her identification with Nic is apparent, although it is also the source of tension as she attempts to form an independent identity. Laser is Jules' biological child. Like her, he is indecisive, inquisitive, and searching for his identity. In one of the scenes, Jules takes offense when Nic expresses concern that Laser is wasting his potential. She accuses Nic of intimating that, in respect of his lack of focus and direction, Laser takes after Jules, his biological mother. In families in which each of the parents creates a biological offspring, there was a similar emphasis not only on competitive comparisons between the children but also on the affiliation of each child to their biological parent and his or her family of origin. This sense of affiliation is underscored when the identity of the gamete donor is unknown, and perhaps even denied by the parents. Each of the children is then regarded as a genetic clone of their biological parent.

In one scene at the beginning of the film, depicting a family dinner, the framing of the shots emphasizes the lines of biological affiliation: Laser sits next to Jules, his birth mother, whereas Joni sits across from them. Arriving late from work, Nic takes her place at the head of the table, as befits the head of the family, her partner Jules sitting on one side, and her biological daughter Joni, on the other. At the dinner that takes place in Paul's home, each child sits next to their biological mother, but this time Paul is seated at the head of the table, with the two biological children sitting to his sides.

In one of the film's final scenes, Jules delivers a speech to the rest of the family, expressing contrition to those hurt by her affair with Paul. She faces the three others, who are seated side by side on the sofa – Nic at the center with the two children at either side. Laser, who in the first meal scene had ignored Nic's entry upon returning from work, this time extends a supportive hand – an intimation that although genetic affiliation may in some ways define the array of identifications within the family, ultimately, Nic is no less of a mother to Laser, and at a moment of vulnerability he identifies with her and stands by her side.

Jack Halberstam, one of the most prominent spokespeople of contemporary Queer theory, offered a critical reading of the film, his central argument being that the two mothers in the film have been merged into a single maternal unit. This unification of the two mothers, despite their distinct personality differences, into a joint parental unit, is performed throughout the film by their children, who call them "moms." No less so, this merger stems from the mother's characterization as exhibiting only minor gender differences (Nic is a soft butch, and Jules is slightly femme), and as having a sexual relationship devoid of passion. In this state of affairs, it is not out of the question that the "phallic" father will defeat Nic by offering Jules genuine passion, and the children an escape from the stifling situation of surfeit maternality (Halberstam, 2010).

In Oedipal terms, under conditions in which two mothers merge into a joint maternal function, and the passion between them does not generate sufficient tension, the triangular space is likely to collapse into a dyad

(Heineman, 2004). The tendency to merge parental figures into a single unit, it will be recalled, was typical of children who were classified as exhibiting an anti-competitive, non-Oedipal configuration. Another characteristic of such children was their preoccupation with protecting their parents from potential feelings of jealousy. In the film, this pattern characterizes 18-year-old Joni in several ways: she does not exhibit any preference at all for either mother; when one is attacked by the other, she rushes to her defense, and she suppresses her curiosity about the sperm donor for many years in order not to offend them. Like the children classified as exhibiting the anti-competitive configuration, who avoided "playing house" or experimenting with infantile romantic feelings, Joni avoids age-appropriate romantic or sexual experimentation. These inhibitions are emphasized through the introduction of an antagonist: her libidinous close friend. The event that triggers Joni's entry into the romantic sphere is her acquaintance with Paul, the charismatic sperm donor, who provides her, according to the film, with the first opportunity to experience an Oedipal romance. The painful discovery that Jules is having an affair with Paul is presented as the shattering of an illusion in regard to her mother's asexual nature, and as her first experience of rivalry with her mother: over the gift of sexual relations that Paul has given the mother. It is this Oedipal event that propels her for the first time to enter into a situation of romantic rivalry and to claim for herself the love of a boy she had desired, secretly, up until that point.

Unlike Joni, her brother Laser exhibits an Oedipal preoccupation, albeit a minor one, as well as curiosity about the romantic and sexual relations between the moms: he expresses a subtle preference for his birth mother Jules, and ignores Nic's presence; he rummages through the mother's bedroom and finds a vibrator and porn video and watches it with his best friend. In one scene, he approaches to say goodbye to his mothers who are cuddled together in front of the TV; when the two wave to him and ask for a hug, Laser snaps defiantly at Jules, urging her to hug Nic instead, or, in other words, to seek physical comfort from her romantic and sexual partner. This statement, mingling embarrassment and resentment, exposes the distinction in Laser's psyche between his mothers. He does not perceive them as a single entity. His curiosity is apparent, not only in relation to parental sexuality: he is also curious about father figures in his near environment, and his intense curiosity about the sperm donor is what initially drives the plot.

Joni's inhibition in the development of Oedipal dynamics cannot be explained merely by the parents' failure to create a triangular space, since her brother Laser has still managed to establish an Oedipal configuration of relations involving his two mothers. One factor impeding the establishment of an Oedipal dynamic between Joni and her mothers seems to stem from the taboo on homosexual relations. From among the participants in the research presented in this book, the non-Oedipal anti-competitive configuration was typical of sons to gay fathers, rather than of daughters to lesbian mothers. The latter tended to organize their relations in a Platonic or alternating Oedipal configurations.

Nonetheless, it should be stressed that, even if we regard Paul as the product of the children and the mothers' unconscious phantasy rather than as an actual human interloper in the family's life, still the Oedipal event presented in the film is a kind of distortion that can be explained as a product of the heteronormative set of expectations. As this book demonstrates throughout, most of the children construct an Oedipal configuration in relation to their two parents; the evidence for this is abundant both in the open interactions and in their phantasy life. When phantasies appear in relation to the birth other, they take the form of a family romance: the birth other is positioned as a substitute parent for the actual parents, and her or his status as such helps the child maintain emotional equilibrium in the face of the Oedipal upheavals they experience. Evidence of an Oedipal phantasy or structure in which the child attributes to one of his or her parents a romantic or sexual relation with the birth other did not appear in the material of any of the children I met. I argue that the reason for this is that the aspects related to the child's origins are, in the case of donor children, distinct from the aspects related to the parental sexual union and its emotional impacts. For this reason, and unlike the predictions suggested by popular cultural representations such as the film *The Kids Are All Right* or by psychoanalytic ideas that might stem from the concept of the primal scene, Oedipal development does not require parent figures of two different sexes.

The film's final shot presents the two mothers in a car traveling home after driving Joni to college. Jules is at the wheel, and Nic is beside her in a scene suggesting closeness and reconciliation. They look at each other and hold hands meaningfully. This scene echoes the final scene of Ridley Scott's 1991 film *Thelma and Louise*, where Thelma says: "Let's keep going . . . Go" (Sturken, 2000, p. 62). Like Thelma and Louise, Nic and Jules choose to continue their shared journey and to take leave of the patriarchal world, represented by Paul, the sperm donor, but while Thelma and Louise's car gallops into the Grand Canyon, Nic and Jules' car cruises with teenage son Laser sitting in the back seat, heading back home, back to the comfort of suburban life.

References

Ehrensaft, D. (2007). The stork didn't bring me, I came from a dish: Psychological experiences of children conceived through assisted reproductive technology. *Journal of Infant, Child, and Adolescent Psychotherapy, 6*(2), 124–140.

Halberstam, J. (2010). Jack Halberstam: The kids aren't alright! *Bullybloggers* [online blog]. Retrieved July 15, 2010, from https://bullybloggers.wordpress.com/2010/07/15/the-kids-arent-alright/

Heineman, T. V. (2004). A boy and two mothers: New variations on an old theme or a new story of triangulation? Beginning thoughts on psychosexual development of children in non-traditional families. *Psychoanalytic Psychology, 21*(1), 99–115.

Khanna, A. (2006). Dark and personal. In J. Mistry & A. Schuhmann (Eds.), *Gaze regimes: Film and feminisms in Africa* (pp. 161–167). Wits University Press.

Oxenhandler, N. (2001). *The eros of parenthood: Explorations in light and dark.* St. Martin's Press.

Quinodoz, D. (1999). The Oedipus complex revisited: Oedipus abandoned, Oedipus adopted. *International Journal of Psychoanalysis, 80*(1), 15–30.

Sturken, M. (2000). *Thelma & Louise.* Bloomsbury Publishing.

Appendix A

Children's family drawings

1 "The princess's family" – Abigail's family drawing.
2 "A princess who found a kangaroo and they ended up being a family" – Anna's first family drawing.
3 "The queen of the cats with a baby in her tummy" – Anna's second family drawing.
4 "A queen and two hedgehogs" – Libby's family drawing.
5 "Mommy Inbal holding a royal family of birds" – Nina's family drawing, first part.
6 "Nina, the birthday girl, embraced by Mommy Tali" – Nina's family drawing, second part.
7 "Amusement park" – Eithan's family drawing.
8 "The family goes on a trip" – Ella's family drawing.
9 "Two basketball teams" – Lior's family drawing.
10 "A family flying to a far-away country – Ariel's first family drawing.
11 "Two girls going to a demonstration" – Ariel's second family drawing.
12 "A family in which everybody's holding a parrot" – Omer's family drawing.
13 "An African family that saw a monkey" – Tom's Family drawing.
14 "I am showing the egg" – Nadav's family drawing.

Appendix B

List of cards

Card 1: "Parental coitus." The image was designed to elicit contents related to the primal scene.

Card 2: "Two lionesses and a cub." The image was designed to elicit contents related to the Oedipal situation in same-sex families.

Card 3: "A family hug." The image was designed to elicit contents related to the Oedipal situation and to stimulate issues of jealousy, exclusion, and triangular space.

Card 4:[1] "The Bedroom." This card was borrowed from the Children's Apperception Test (Card #5, CAT-A). The image was designed to elicit contents related to the primal scene, including experiences of exclusion and jealousy vis-à-vis the parental exclusive relationship.

Card 5: "Tug-of-war." This card was also borrowed from the Children's Apperception Test (Card #2, CAT-A). The image was designed to elicit contents related to Oedipal rivalry, and to evoke representations of coalitions inside the family unit, exclusion, jealousy and guilt over them.

Card 6: "An infant being held." The image was designed to elicit contents related to primary parental holding. It is deliberately vague to allow the child to identify the holding hands as belonging to a father or a mother figure, or as belonging to two parental figures of any sex jointly holding the baby.

Card 7: "A woman with blurred features." This image was designed for children of gay fathers. It was meant to elicit feelings of curiosity and mystery regarding their egg donor, surrogate, and mother figures generally.

---

1 All cards were illustrated by Inbar Heller Algazi, except for Cards 4 & 5, which were selected from the CAT-A © CPS Publishing LLC, All Rights Reserved.

Card 8: "Silhouette of a man." This image was designed for children of lesbian mothers. It was meant to elicit feelings of curiosity and mystery regarding their sperm donor and father figures generally.

Card 9: "A man carrying suitcases." This image was designed for children of lesbian mothers. It was meant to elicit feelings of curiosity and mystery regarding their sperm donor or father figures generally, and to examine whether the children have abandonment phantasies.

Card 10: "A chick hatching from an egg." The image was designed to elicit contents related to womb phantasies, birth phantasies, and representations concerning with development toward separateness.

Card 11: "A boy in a suitcase." This image was designed for boys. It was meant to elicit contents related to womb phantasies, birth phantasies, and the question of origins.

Card 12: "A hen sitting on eggs." The image was designed to elicit contents related to womb phantasies, birth phantasies, and the question of origins, as well as the issue of the difference between the sexes.

Card 13: "Polar bears." The image was designed to elicit contents related to a symbiotic parent-baby relationship. It is deliberately vague to allow the child to ascribe any gender to the characters.

Card 14: "A girl in a suitcase." This image was designed for girls. It was meant to elicit contents related to womb phantasies, birth phantasies, and the question of origins.

Card 15: "A vague female figure carrying a suitcase." This image was designed for children of gay fathers. It was meant to elicit feelings of curiosity and mystery regarding their egg donor, surrogate, and mother figures generally, and to examine whether the children bear abandonment phantasies.

Index

abject 163, 164

adoption xx, xxi, xxvi, xxix, 14, 15, 17, 18, 20, 21, 109, 126, 169, 176, 202, 203, 210, 212, 213, 226, 277

Althusser, Louis 6, 173, 176

anxiety: as to child's sexual orientation 79, 89, 98, 100; and discrimination 90, 91, 137, 240; and eroticism in father-son relationships 83–87, 99, 100; and gamete donation, anonymous 157, 186, 189, 198, 214, 219–222, 241, 243, 247; and gamete donation, known donor 16, 238; manifestations in children's drawing 59, 62, 63; as to hurting the parent 45, 157, 186, 205, 208, 214; as to losing the child's love (*see* birth other, as conniving kidnapper); and the social parent's status 92, 109, 110, 126, 127, 133, 137, 143, 146, 147; and triangular relations 11, 59, 78, 186

Aron, Lewis xvii, xxiv, 2, 9, 85, 101

assisted reproduction technologies xxix, 20, 108, 255

attachment xix, xxiii, 4, 5, 16, 18, 45, 48, 79, 81, 110–113, 115, 124, 130, 132, 133, 143, 147, 175, 190, 193, 236, 240, 254, 264, 267–269; *see also* genetics, and attachment

Benjamin, Jessica 3, 77, 120, 248

Berman, Emanuel 10, 272

biological father *see* father, genetic father

biological sex 3, 5, 13, 14, 24, 44, 46–49, 55, 56, 78–81, 98–101, 198–200, 207, 208, 218, 267, 276

Bion, Wilfred 11, 157, 219–221, 244, 262

Birenbaum-Carmeli, Daphna xxix, 108, 175, 176

birth other xix, 6, 15, 182, 241; (the) child's idealized representation 54, 187, 196–199, 206, 222, 240 (*see also* Phantasies, merger with an idealized parental figure); and child's longings and curiosity 23, 24, 54, 184, 186–195, 211–214, 218–222, 241, 254, 269, 276, 278; and child's Oedipal structure xix, 6, 49, 182–184, 208–211, 222, 273, 284; as conniving kidnapper 16, 213, 214, 238–242, 248, 254, 269, 278; defensive strategies in relation to 241, 249, 253, 269 (objectification 242, 244; reduction to material 241, 242, 270, 279; voyeurism 243, 244); egg donor (*see* gamete donation, egg donation); and gender identification 199, 206–208, 212, 213, 276; merging the egg donor and surrogate into a single mother figure 188, 210; as parent's alter-ego 234, 235; and primal scene 226–233,

235, 236, 279; sperm donor (*see* gamete donation, sperm donation); surrogate (*see* surrogacy)
bisexuality xx, 2, 48, 73, 262
Bollas, Christopher 146, 156, 177, 219, 234, 268
bonding 15, 96, 110, 113, 114, 123, 136, 147, 148, 161, 176, 234, 240, 241
breastfeeding 94, 96, 109, 111, 116, 119–126, 135, 138, 143, 192
Britton, Ronald 6, 11, 42, 48, 49, 60, 75–78, 80, 102, 107, 211, 220, 235
Butler, Judith 3–5, 10, 79, 167, 268

castration xviii, 5–10, 12, 59, 81, 94; *see also* penis envy
Chodorow, Nancy 2–4, 9, 77, 112
Cholodenko, Lisa xv, xvi, 275
compulsory heterosexuality 118
concealment: and the child's genetic affiliation 25, 116, 149, 150–152, 156, 273; vs. confession 149, 151, 152, 273; and gamete donation 21, 22, 24
conversion therapy 2, 261, 262
Corbett, Ken xvi, xvii, xx, xxiv, 12, 15, 25, 45, 84, 85, 157, 177, 183, 187, 209, 211, 222, 235, 253, 255, 261, 272
couvade syndrome 138, 250
curiosity: and the birth other (*see* birth other, and child's longings and curiosity); curiosity level and the child's and parents' biological sex 23, 71, 193, 195, 199, 202, 204, 207, 253, 276, 283; and inhibition 11, 45, 70, 76, 78, 153, 198, 219–222, 244, 276, 283

Davies, Judy 5, 48, 79, 84
debt to the mother 94, 95, 97, 164, 239
discrimination 17, 25, 139, 161, 238, 246

dreams 91, 92, 163, 228, 229, 239–241
dyadic relations 5, 7, 48–52, 76–78, 87, 101, 120, 263, 267; *see also* symbiosis

egg donation *see* gamete donation, egg donation
ego psychology 2, 261
Ehrensaft, Dianne 15, 16, 45, 157, 182, 187, 209, 213, 226, 238, 240, 241, 244, 248, 253–256, 271, 278
enactment 43, 235, 269, 275
enigmatic messages 46, 86, 87, 132, 133, 156, 219, 267
envy 11, 13, 20, 43, 47, 121, 122, 128, 138, 217, 241, 268, 269; *see also* penis envy; womb envy
exclusion xix, 4, 6, 11, 14, 43, 45, 47, 54, 57, 75–78, 100, 121, 125, 133, 136–138, 181, 182, 190, 201, 209, 212, 222, 263
extended family xxix, 153, 159–165, 172, 175, 269

familism xxvi, xxvii
family drawings *see* projective tests, Kinetic Family Drawing
the family reverie xix, 157, 253–255
(the) family romance 12–16, 44, 45, 187, 189, 204, 209–215, 222, 240, 241, 273, 277, 279; and claustrophobic phantasies 215, 216; and its relations to the parents' conniving kidnapper phantasy 240, 241; and its relations with the Oedipus complex 12, 14, 45, 189, 209–211, 222, 273, 277, 284; and longing for the long lost parental figure 15, 187, 189, 210–213, 241; and rivalry between a feminine and a masculine parental figures 209, 213–219
father: father figures 190–193, 196, 202–204, 206, 208, 217, 218, 222,

244, 254, 276, 283; gay fathers xv, xxi, xxv, xxvi, 4, 18–20, 24, 46, 88–90, 92, 96–98, 112, 143, 149, 150, 176, 188, 198, 216, 219, 267; genetic father 6, 20, 24, 90–92, 113, 116, 147, 148, 152, 154, 170, 183, 189; heterosexual fathers 4, 19, 20, 48, 81, 83, 87, 88, 93, 121, 126, 136, 138, 268; social father 20, 90, 91, 114, 115, 143, 146–152, 156, 162

feminism iv, xvii, 3, 9, 94, 118, 122, 142

femme 46, 229, 282

Femme-Butch 46, 279, 282

Ferenczi, Sendor 48

Fliess, Whilhelm 1, 10, 12

Freud, Sigmund xxiv, 1, 2, 7–14, 44, 45, 77, 79, 94, 101, 133, 183, 189, 192, 193, 209, 210, 217, 219, 228–230, 239, 240, 244, 247, 248, 252, 261, 262, 271

gamete donation xviii, xxi, 16, 22, 108; egg donation xxix, 18, 20, 24, 50, 169, 187–189, 226, 234, 236, 238, 239, 241, 272; open vs. anonymous donation 24, 208; and the primal scene (*see* (the) primal scene); sperm donation 18, 23, 24, 140, 195, 197, 207, 226–231, 233–236, 239, 241–245, 247–254, 270, 271, 275–281, 283, 285; *see also* anxiety, gamete donation, anonymous/ known donor; concealment, and gamete donation

GAYBY-boom xxiv, xxvi, xxix, 16, 168, 227

gender: as binary system 6, 9, 19, 46, 77, 89, 98, 165, 208, 262, 266; and castration 8–10, 81, 239; gender dysphoria xv; gender Identity 8, 89, 121, 129, 162, 199, 207, 277; gender interpellation (*see*

interpellation); gender signifier 227, 241; and identification xviii, 1–4, 6, 8, 10, 23, 44, 46, 54, 75, 79, 93–95, 98, 127, 136–138, 162, 164, 190, 199, 202, 207, 262–264 (*see also* birth other, and gender identification)

gender solitary 44, 62, 199–208, 212, 276

genetics: and attachment 110–113; genealogical heritage 15, 23, 209, 250, 255; genetic asymmetry xix, 19–21, 116, 154, 168, 175, 176, 181, 269; genetic father (*see* father, genetic father); genetic kinship discourse (*see* kinship, genetic kinship discourse); genetic mother (*see* mother, birth mother); genetic resemblance 113–166 (*see also* play, spotting resemblance); genetic siblings 155, 166, 169, 170, 242, 244, 249, 251, 255, 277

genitor and genetrix 49, 168, 181, 208

Green, Andre 101

guilt 15, 16, 59, 65, 70, 84, 89, 92, 94, 95, 98–100, 114, 116, 120–123, 128, 157, 187, 204, 206, 208, 213, 215, 222, 238–241, 254, 255, 267–269, 273, 278, 279, 287

Halberstam, Jack 277, 279, 282

Haraway, Donna 167, 246

Hayden, Corrine 169, 227, 228

Heineman, Tony 49, 65, 70, 77, 110, 111, 283

heteronormativity i, xvi–xix, xxv, xxviii, xxix, 17, 19, 26, 44, 46, 79, 81, 82, 86, 115, 118, 159, 168, 169, 171, 172, 181–186, 201, 214, 227, 228, 230, 232, 242, 262, 264, 266, 268, 273, 284; heteronormative expectations xvi, xviii, xix, xxv, xxviii, xxix, 26, 44, 46, 79, 86, 159, 168, 169, 171, 172, 186, 230, 266, 268, 273, 284;

Index

heteronormative families xvii, xxiii, 17, 81, 115, 118, 262, 264, 268; heteronormative representations 79, 86, 184–186, 228, 230
heterosexual fathers *see* father, heterosexual fathers
heterosexual mothers *see* mother, heterosexual mothers
heterosexual parents xv, xvi, 4, 16–18, 20–26, 44, 46, 47, 77, 80, 81, 87, 90, 119, 121, 126, 150, 157, 184, 226, 232, 233, 255, 262–264, 271
homonationality xxviii, xxix, 168
homonormativity *see* homonationality
(the) homosexual closet xxv, 16, 89, 98, 145–157
Horney, Karen 9, 94
humor 63, 228, 230, 231

identification *see* gender, and identification; birth other, and gender identification
identity xxvii, 2, 8, 9, 15, 17, 22, 23, 24, 44, 79, 85, 89, 115, 121, 129, 234, 235, 245, 256, 262, 263, 276, 277, 279; *see also* gender, gender identity
inhibition *see* curiosity, and inhibition; (the) primal scene, and inhibition
internalized homophobia 81–87, 93, 97, 98, 268
interpellation 6, 9, 173, 176
in vitro fertilization (IVF) 108

jealousy 1, 2, 11, 20, 47, 48, 50, 54, 57, 65, 76, 109, 119, 120, 122–126, 133, 136, 137, 142, 143, 148, 181, 182, 188, 190, 200, 201, 209, 212, 217, 283, 287
Jentsch, Ernst 246, 247

The Kids Are All Right, Movie xv, 275–285
kinship 107, 124, 166, 248; genetic kinship discourse xix, xxvii, xxix, 71, 107, 108, 110, 112, 113, 132,

154, 159, 162, 165–169, 171, 175, 181, 182, 264, 268, 273; kinship discursive clash 168, 181, 209, 210, 222, 229, 230–232, 242, 249; performative kinship discourse 166–174, 176, 177, 273
Klein, Melanie iv, xxiv, 5, 6, 9, 11, 49, 75, 183, 204, 208, 211, 215, 217, 219, 239
Koestler, Arthur 230
Kosofsky-Sedgwick, Eve 149–152

Lacan, Jacques 48, 60
(the) law in Israel xxvi, 20, 80, 83, 170, 207, 219
lesbian mothers *see* mother, lesbian mothers
Levi-Hazan, Yael xvi, 26, 81, 82
logical fallacy xxiii, 145, 154, 231–233, 242

Maurer, Offer 87, 88
McDougall, Joyce 4, 48, 79, 81
melancholic identification 4, 79
mother: birth mother 20, 24, 46, 49, 56, 57, 59, 63, 91, 92, 97, 110–112, 114, 118–129, 133, 136–143, 149, 159, 161, 171, 182, 208, 227, 281, 282; heterosexual mothers xxi, 119, 121, 226, 227 (*see also* heterosexual parents); lesbian mothers xv, xxi, xxii, xxiv–xxvi, xxix, 16, 18–20, 23–25, 46, 56, 61, 64, 65, 78, 80, 85, 86, 89, 98, 99–101, 110–112, 116, 118, 119, 121–126, 134, 140, 142, 143, 149, 150, 162, 170, 185, 195, 198, 218, 219, 227, 232, 239, 244, 268, 272, 275, 276; mother figure 44, 45, 52, 53, 92, 98, 164, 187–189, 207, 208, 211–215, 217, 218; social mother xxvi, 19, 20, 57, 92, 109–112, 114, 118–121, 124, 126, 129, 130, 133, 136–140, 142, 143, 147, 159, 161, 162, 190, 208, 227, 228, 268, 273

narrative seeds 22, 157, 254
negative Oedipus complex *see* Oedipus complex, negative Oedipus complex
non-Oedipal configurations 48, 65, 70, 75, 77, 80, 100, 101, 264, 267, 283, 284; anti-competitive configuration 48, 65–70, 78, 87, 100, 264, 283, 284; multiple configuration 48, 70–73, 91, 100, 264; *see also* Oedipal configurations
Nordqvist, Petra 113, 167

object: partial object 119, 197, 198, 215, 228, 237, 238, 243, 271, 279; whole object 183, 215, 228, 237, 238, 241, 271
Oedipal configurations 47, 65, 80, 99, 100, 112, 264, 284; alternating Oedipal configuration 47, 61–65, 80, 99, 100, 264, 284; full-blown Oedipal configuration 47, 49–56, 65, 76, 78, 80, 81, 98, 99, 112, 208, 211, 264; Platonic Oedipal configuration 47, 56–61, 65, 80, 87, 99, 100, 112, 203, 264, 284; *see also* non-Oedipal configurations
Oedipus complex xxiii, 1–7, 11, 12, 76, 81, 101, 183, 222; negative Oedipus complex 2, 4, 5, 11, 48, 79, 262, 267; Oedipal illusion 76, 78; Oedipalization 91, 170, 262; Oedipal model xvi–xx, 2–4, 49, 79, 91, 94, 166, 169, 183, 261–265, 267; Oedipal Object choice xix, xxiii, 39, 47, 78, 111, 112, 114, 115, 130, 140, 165, 175, 183, 187, 194, 203, 208, 267, 283; Oedipal rivalry 4, 14, 45–48, 55, 60, 69, 75–79, 84, 128, 177, 195, 208, 210, 267, 283 (*see also* (the) family romance, and rivalry between a feminine and a masculine parental figures); (The) Oedipal situation 5–7, 11, 12, 54, 75, 76, 107, 189, 207,
263; Oedipal stage xviii, xx, 8, 49, 83, 87, 112, 140, 190; Oedipal structure xix, 3, 7, 49, 65, 76–78, 101, 183, 184, 189, 208, 284
Ofer, Marganit 6, 45, 49, 183, 187, 195, 208, 253
Ogden, Thomas 6, 92, 217, 220
Oxenhandler, Noelle 15, 16, 240, 278

Palgi-Hecker, Anat 5, 9, 94, 95
parental coitus *see* (the) primal scene
parental role division xix, 19, 46, 100, 107, 111, 112, 126, 134, 142, 143, 244, 266, 267; breadwinner and caregiver 111, 112, 279; Egalitarian role division 11, 46, 110, 118, 121, 125, 126, 147, 268
parental separation or breakup xvii, xxvii, 169, 175, 176, 219
parenting partnership xvii, xx, xxi, xxv, xxvi, 115, 170, 201
penis envy 8, 9, 94, 166, 239; *see also* castration
performativity 3, 4, 48, 60, 94, 118, 166–168, 171, 173, 174, 181
Phallus 54, 94, 166, 192, 213, 217, 282
Phantasies xxiii, 5, 6; castration phantasy (*see* castration); and children's drawings 50, 187, 205, 206; and claustrophobia 215, 216; cloning (*see* parthenogenic phantasies); (the) family romance phantasy (*see* (the) family romance); incubation in the womb 12, 50, 52, 187, 211, 212, 216; merger with an idealized parental figure 187, 196–199, 206, 208, 213, 233, 235; parthenogenic (self-fertilization) phantasy 140, 151, 228, 242, 243, 282; primal phantasies 7, 8; (the) primal scene phantasy (*see* (the) primal scene); seduction phantasy (*see* Oedipus complex)

play: and exploration of the mother's body 210, 211; playful space, collapse of 16, 45, 100, 220–222, 270; playful space xxiv, 63, 69, 84, 212, 255, 268; playing house 54, 69, 70, 72, 185, 283; rough-and-tumble play 85, 86; seed planting 195; spotting resemblance 67, 113–115, 153–156, 159

(the) primal scene xix, 7, 8, 10–12, 181–183, 279; the children's inner-Representations 54, 55, 195, 211; combined parental figure 11; and the multiple configuration 72–73, 264; parental sexual union vs. conception phantasies 182, 183, 211, 222, 226–233, 271, 272, 277, 284; the Parent's inner-Representations 108, 136, 226–233, 235, 242, 279; and the sadistic view of coitus 10, 11, 218, 219, 222

projective identification 216, 235, 236, 250, 262, 271

projective tests xxiii, xxiv, 147; apperception task xxiii, xxiv, 41, 52, 54–56, 69, 72, 185, 188, 189, 194, 196, 202–204, 206, 211–218, 220, 221; CAT-A (Children Apperception Test - Animals) xxiii, 56, 69; Kinetic Family Drawing (KFD) xxiii, 39, 50–54, 57–59, 61, 62, 131, 141, 172, 174, 175, 187, 190, 191, 193, 200, 201, 205

pronatalism xxvi, xxix

queer theory xxix, 3, 9, 81, 107, 264, 282

reality principle 57, 263

research xv, xvi, xx, xx–xxiv, 3, 4, 14, 16–27, 46, 121, 150, 157, 167, 207, 208, 222, 238

reverie 157, 271

Rich, Adrienne xvi, 3, 9, 118

rivalry *see* Oedipus complex, Oedipal rivalry

Riviere, Joan 94, 239

Schneider, David 166, 167

sexual difference 5, 6, 75, 107, 118, 126, 193, 264

sexual identity (Orientation) xxvii, 5, 17, 25, 46, 78, 79, 89, 108, 151, 152, 155, 244, 263; *see also* anxiety, as to child's sexual orientation

single-parenting xx, xxvi, 23, 182, 199, 226, 244, 266

Slavin, Jonathan 88

social constructions xvi, 7, 9, 219

social father *see* father, social father

social mother *see* mother, social mother

sperm donation *see* gamete donation, sperm donation

Steiner, John 6, 42, 76

stepmother archetype 128

surrogacy xviii, xxi, xxv, xxvi, 17, 18, 20, 21, 24, 25, 50, 66, 72, 73, 89–91, 155, 169, 176, 187–189, 201, 211, 216, 226, 239, 240, 266, 272

symbiosis 119, 123, 124, 128, 133, 138, 187, 189, 210, 215, 277

taboo: incest taboo 4, 84, 107, 231; taboo on homosexuality 4, 80–82, 84, 89, 98, 99, 107, 267, 284

Thelma and Louise, movie 284

triangular relations xxii, 49, 52, 60, 77, 212, 263, 267, 282

triangular space 6, 54, 75–77, 80, 283

twins 50, 71, 73, 111, 116, 120, 129, 145, 150, 162, 170, 171, 200, 210, 215, 236, 254

twinship 202

uncanny (Unheimlich) 58, 245–253, 270
unthought known 146, 156, 177, 219,
    220, 234, 268

wellbeing xv, 17, 18, 22, 25, 70, 79,
    199, 208
Weston, Kath xxvii, 46, 167, 227, 228,
    241

Winnicott, Donald 10, 48, 63, 95, 219,
    273
womb envy 9, 94–97, 164,
    239

Ziv, Amal xxvi–xxix, 20, 46, 107, 118,
    150, 152, 166
Ziv, Effi 262

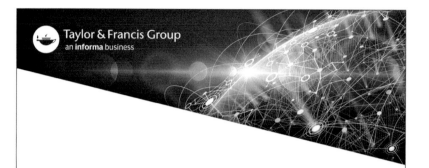